Stories and
Old Manchester

CONTAINING ALL THAT APPEALS TO THE HEART
AND THE IMAGINATION IN THE MANCHESTER OF
MANY YESTERDAYS

BY FRANK HIRD

Selected and Edited By

PRINTWISE PUBLICATIONS LIMITED
1991

© Published 1991 by PRINTWISE PUBLICATIONS LTD.
47 Bradshaw Road, Tottington, BURY, LANCS, BL8 3PW.

Warehouse and Orders —
40-42 Willan Industrial Estate, Vere Street,
(off Eccles New Road), SALFORD,
M5 2GR.
061-745 9168

'Stories and Tales of Old Manchester' have been selected from *'Lancashire Stories'*
2 vols. Published about 1911, written by Frank Hird.

This compilation and edition
© PRINTWISE PUBLICATIONS LTD.

Prints and text chosen, researched and edited by

 _liff Hayes

ISBN No. 1 872226 22 4

Printed & bound by Manchester Free Press,
Paragon Mill, Jersey Street, Manchester M4 6FP.
Tel: 061-236 8822.

Front cover illustration: Market Street, Manchester. J. Harwood 1840.

Foreword

I first set foot in Manchester one spring afternoon in 1954. I had applied for a job on the Manchester Guardian and I stood outside the old building in Cross Street plucking up courage to venture where C.P. Scott had once reigned.

I entered by the side door but the commissionaire's box was empty so I paused, wondering where to go. An old gentleman, laden with books and papers, had followed me in.

I told him I had come to see the Editor, Mr Wadsworth.

This way, he said.

I followed him up the stairs, chattering cheerfully about this and that, and he led me into a book-lined office.

Sit down, he said. And I realised that this indeed was A.P. Wadsworth, editor, scholar, and historian.

He asked me about my home town, Newcastle upon Tyne, and I spoke eagerly about its activities and its antiquity.

Then he told me about Manchester. Manchester then, Manchester in the previous century, in the 18th, the 17th, the Middle Ages. I was enthralled.

Then he offered me a job. And from that day to this I have been fascinated by Manchester, its past as well as its present.

I welcome this volume because the stories in it enrich our enjoyment of a city which has always been true to itself.

Brian Redhead.

ACKNOWLEDGEMENTS

I must thank Tony Gibb, one of life's gentlemen, for the original introduction to this and many other Old Manchester books. I would like to also thank another "real gentleman of the book trade", Frank Morley for all his help and support over the years I have been publishing books.

DEDICATION

Matthew Wallace Worrall, my late father-in-law, whose pride in Manchester and Salford and whose love of Manchester and its history rubbed off on me. Matt's stories of the docks and everyday life awoke in me a love of Manchester's past.

Introduction

Since I started publishing I promised myself to bring back to life at least one book per year that would help students of Manchester history and people interested in Manchester's past. This I have kept to, as you can see from the list of our other publications on page 168.

Liverpool Daily Post and Echo

But all the time I have been looking for something different, something lighter; a book of stories, not dry, factual histories but tales — a real gossipy book. I spent over a year looking and roped in many friends in the secondhand and library trade. Then Tony Gibb, the owner of that fascinating bookshop on Charlotte Street, Manchester handed me a large, 2 volume, 900 page book called "Lancashire Stories" by Frank Hird.

"This is really worth reprinting," he said. "It seems to be what you're looking for." I went away and was delighted with the book. Written around 1910, it was a real collection of stories, with facts and theories — the local radio of the day.

Having costed out a reprint of the 2 volumes, even in paperback it would have cost £10 to print, so it was reluctantly put on a shelf and left in abeyance, although I still found myself dipping into it on many occasions, as I found it fascinating.

I then decided to try again and approach the project with the same plan as with "Lancashire 150 Years Ago" and split the county into three. I took the book again, and for weeks was up at the crack of dawn and every weekend, and read and re-read the 900 pages. Each Saturday morning I would listen to early morning radio while I edited and made notes to check out some of the facts.

So may I present the Manchester section, edited and cut just a little, with added drawings and sketches but still — I hope — in the Frank Hird style. I wish that I knew more about this man I have come to admire through these 3 books but all enquiries have drawn a blank, except that he lived in South Liverpool and is thought to have been a 'stringer' (a freelance writer) for quite a few newspapers.

But I am very grateful that he wrote the original book, and I hope that you agree that between us we have produced an interesting and informative book.

liff Hayes

P.S. Please remember that they were written in approximately 1910, so if it refers to 40 years ago, it refers to 1870. If the story states 100 years ago then it means 1810 etc...

Hunt's Bank and Chetham's School

Contents

Original Foreword

FROM whatever point of view it may be approached—topographical, archæological, commercial or romantic — no county possesses so varied a history as Lancashire.

Lancashire has had many historians, such as Whitaker, Baines, Harland and Whatton. There is a literature, dealing with the county from every aspect, which fills many pages in the British Museum catalogue. But, although the greatest pains in research have been taken to ensure historical accuracy, *Lancashire Stories* does not claim to be a history. It may be described as the result of a consideration of the history of the county entirely from the human point of view; and, that there should be variety and constant change of interest, no order of dates has been followed. Human nature is the same to-day as it was in the days of the Normans; the story has been the one object of the writer, not the period.

It has been suggested that a bibliography should be printed with this work, but in a publication destined for the general reader, rather than for the historian and archæologist, such a list would be out of place. The authorities are given in the text wherever it has been deemed essential to the interest and value of the story.

Ready and most courteous help has been extended to me by the Lancashire libraries in the search for material and for illustrations to these stories. All the books, old prints, etc., in their possession were freely placed at my disposal, permission at the same time being given for photographs to be taken of anything germane to my purpose. My warm thanks are therefore due for this valuable assistance to Mr. A. E. Sutton, of the Manchester Reference Library; Mr. George T. Shaw, of the Liverpool Reference Library; Mr. R. J. Gordon, of the Rochdale Public Library; Mr. Charles Madeley, of the Warrington Public Library; Mr. Charles Leigh, of Owens College Library, Manchester; Mr. J. N. Dowbiggin, of the Public Library, Storey Institute, Lancaster, and to the Harris Free Library, Preston and Mr. James Brockbank, of the *Manchester Courier*, and Mr. J. L. Edmondson, of the Manchester *Daily Mail*, for their valuable suggestions.

My acknowledgments are specially due to the London Library and its assistants.

FRANK HIRD.

The Skull House

SEVEN miles from Manchester the woods and gardens of Wardley Hall form an oasis in a world of coal-mines and factories. The beautiful old house, which was built in the reign of Edward VI., has been rescued from the neglect and decay into which it had fallen by Colonel Hart-Davis, the chief agent of the Earl of Ellesmere, and although its surroundings have entirely changed, and rural scenery has been replaced by the dirt and smoke of a widespread industry, Wardley Hall to-day bears much the same appearance, except that its stones are mellowed by age, as when it was first built by Thurstan Tyldesley, whose family had owned the property since the reign of Edward II. The house, black and white, and half-timbered, is built round a quad-rangle which, with its quaint gables, pro-jecting eaves, carved oak beams and mullioned windows, is a perfect specimen of Tudor architecture. A wide moat surrounds the Hall on three sides, the portion on the fourth side, which formerly was crossed by a drawbridge leading to the entrance gate, having only recently been filled up.

The interest of Wardley Hall, however, does not lie in its perfect restoration, but rather in the presence of a human skull which, having for more than two centuries been preserved by successive occupiers of the house, has given it the name of " The Skull House." Mystery and legend sur-round this skull, which to-day is kept in a niche high up in the wall of the great hall. The niche is really a square hole cut right through the thick wall, opening on one side upon the hall and on the other side upon the staircase, where it is on the level of the eye. Each side of the hole is covered with glass, and there are also oak doors which can be drawn across, so that the skull can be completely screened from sight.

Thurstan Tyldesley, a few years after he had built his stately manor-house sold it to a London family, who in turn disposed of it to Roger Downes, the head of an ancient Cheshire family, who, settling at Wardley, was succeeded there by his son Francis, a zealous and devout Roman Catholic. He died in 1648. His brother John, who followed him in the ownership of Wardley, had married the daughter of Sir Cecil Trafford, a stout old Puritan, and the story goes that Sir Cecil, whilst endeavouring to convince the brothers of the error of their religious views, which at that period brought every kind of persecution and social disability upon their holders, was himself converted from Puritanism to Roman Catholicism by the elder brother Francis. The scene of this historic argument—the deep recess in the great hall in which the fireplace stands—is still pointed out at Wardley.

John Downes did not long survive his brother, and his wife dying shortly afterwards, their two children, Roger and Penelope, were left without any guardians. According to the then existing law the two children were brought up as Protestants. For many generations the skull at Wardley was believed to be that of Roger Downes. This was the story : —

When Roger Downes grew to manhood he became one of the most profligate members of Charles II.'s merry and licentious court. During a drunken orgy he swore he would kill the first man he met, and rushing " hot from the stews," drawing his sword as he staggered along, he met a poor tailor whom he ran through with his weapon and killed upon the spot. This wanton and brutal murder brought Roger Downes to justice, but his interest at court soon procured him a free pardon, and he immediately began to pursue his usual reckless course. " In the lusty vigour of a drunken debauch," says Roby, " passing over London Bridge, he encountered another brawl, wherein, having run at the watchman with his rapier, one blow of the bill which they carried severed his head from his trunk. The latter was cast over the parapet into the Thames, and the head was carefully packed up in a box and sent to his sister at Wardley Hall." Another account says that Roger Downes met his death at Epsom Wells in 1676, being killed there by a watchman in a drunken brawl; whilst a third account says, " while in London, in a drunken frolic, he vowed to his companions that he would kill the first man he met ; then sallying forth, he ran his sword through a poor tailor. Soon after this, being in a riot, a watchman made a stroke at him with his bill, which severed his head from his body. The head was enclosed in a box, and sent to his sister, who lived at Wardley Hall."

Such was the foundation upon which the legends of " The Skull House " were built.

Nothing is known of the history of the skull during the next seventy years, and it was only discovered at Wardley during the Jacobite Rebellion of 1745. The Jacobite army under the Young Pretender was encamped in a field near the Hall, which is still called " Rebel Field." Wardley was then occupied by a farmer called Moreton, who held it on a life lease from Lady Penelope Cholmondeley, the grand-daughter of Roger Downes's sister, Penelope, who had married the Earl of Rivers. It was Lady Penelope Cholmondeley who sold Wardley to Francis, Duke of Bridgwater, the ancestor of the present owner, the Earl of Ellesmere. " As the Jacobites marched along Wardley

Lane," says Colonel Hart-Davis, "on their return to the North, a detachment visited the Hall to demand carts and horses for transport purposes. They threatened to fire the buildings unless their demands were complied with, so that in spite of moat and arised drawbridge, the farmer order to make room for the looms, and as the work of demolition was proceeding a box or chest fell out of the ruins. Thinking it to be a treasure chest, he ordered the bystanders to stand back, and himself broke off the lid with a pick-axe. The box was found to contain a skull

THE SKULL SEEN FROM THE STAIRCASE

had to yield. His son Matthew was sent with the carts and horses. But the Duke of Cumberland coming up with the Jacobites, young Moreton, to save his life, abandoned his property, and made his way home. The loss so impoverished the family that they determined to take up hand-loom weaving to retrieve their fortunes.

"Moreton commenced to pull down a somewhat ruinous part of the building in furnished with a goodly set of teeth, and having on it a good deal of auburn hair. A maidservant of the Moretons, knowing nothing about the skull, being sent to clean the room in which it was kept, mistook it for the head of an animal and threw it into the moat. The same night there was a furious storm, and Matthew Moreton, the younger, being a superstitious man, and having ascertained that the skull had been thrown into the moat, ascribed the storm to the indignity to which it had been subjected. He therefore at once caused the water to be run off, recovered the skull, and restored it to its place."

From this time forward the skull was declared to have magical powers. It was declared that if it was moved from its resting-place, strange sounds were heard at night, and the dwellers at the Hall had no rest or peace until it was replaced. On one occasion, legend says, an attempt was made to bury it, but instantly a violent storm of thunder and lightning broke out and the skull was found back in its niche. Mr. Fletcher Moss in his *Pilgrimages to Old Homes*, written quite recently, says: "If anything were done to it, or it was not treated with proper respect, such commotions arose about the house that no one dared live in it. Windows were blown in, cattle pined in the stall, and the things were bewitched. . . There is plenty of testimony to the ill-luck that has happened when the skull has been disturbed; and this has not come from the superstitious only, but from shrewd observant men of business whose word is as their bond."

A Manchester antiquary called Thomas Barritt visited Wardley Hall towards the close of the eighteenth century, and has left a curious account of his experience of the skull.

"There is at Wardley," he says, "a human skull, which, time out of mind, hath had a superstitious veneration paid to it (by the occupiers of the Hall), not permitting it to be removed from its situation, which is on the topmost step of a staircase. There is a tradition that, if removed, or ill-used, some uncommon noise or disturbance always follows, to the terror of the whole house; yet I cannot persuade myself this is always the case. But some three years ago, I and three of my acquaintance went to view

this surprising piece of household furniture, and found it as above-mentioned, and bleached white with the weather that beats in upon it from a four-square window in the hall, which the tenants never permit to be glazed or filled up, thus to oblige the skull, which, they say, is unruly and is disturbed at the hole not being always open. However, one of us, who was last in company with the skull, removed it from its place into a dark part of the room, and there left it, and returned home; but the night but one following, such a storm arose about the house, of wind and lightning, as tore down some trees, and unthatched outhousing. We hearing of this, my father went over in a few days after to see his mother, who lived near the Hall, and was witness to the wreck the storm had made. Yet all this might have happened had the skull never been removed; but withal it keeps alive the credibility of the tradition (or the credulity of its believers)."

Barritt heard the story of Roger Downes's death and the despatch of his head to Wardley from old people in the neighbourhood, which shows how firmly the tradition had taken root. For tradition pure and simple are all the stories of Roger Downes. It is true that he was a "wild blade," and a "rake-hell," and that he died at an early age after a short career of roystering and extravagance at the court of Charles II.; but when the family vault of the Downeses in Wigan Church was opened, some years previously to the visit to Wardley recorded above, the young man's coffin was discovered, and in it was a complete skeleton, the head of which had never been severed from the body. The upper part of the skull had been sawn off a little above the eyes, by a surgeon, probably by order of his relatives, who might reasonably wish to know the disease of which he had died in London. The assertions made by many writers that the skull not only resented being touched or moved, but would not permit the square aperture in the wall to be glazed without creating a disturbance, was disproved by the late Mr. Harland, who on a visit to Wardley Hall found that " a locked door concealed at once the square aperture and its fearful tenant." There were two keys to this door, one of which was kept by the tenant of the Hall, and the other by the late Countess of Ellesmere (wife of Francis, first Earl of Ellesmere), who frequently brought visitors from Worsley Hall, and unlocking the door showed them the skull within. Mr. Harland says he paid another visit to Wardley in 1861, and again held the old skull in his hands. " The bone of the lower jaw had become detached, but there is no sign of violence about the skull itself. If the tradition as to the violent death of its owner be correct, that result has been effected without any fracture of the bone." There is no record of violent storms following the handling of the skull by Lady Ellesmere and Mr. Harland.

It has now been proved beyond all doubt that the skull so carefully preserved at Wardley Hall is that of Edward Barlow, a friend and kinsman of Francis Downes. He was a Roman Catholic priest, known in religion as Father Ambrose, and for many years conducted the forbidden services of his Church in the secret chapels at Wardley Hall, and also at Morleys Hall. In 1641 he was arrested, tried at Lancaster, and condemned to death because he was a priest of the Roman Catholic faith, his sentence being to be " hanged, dismembered, disembowelled, quartered and boiled in tar," the judges who tried him having had instructions from the Puritan Parliament to see that the extreme penalty of the law was executed upon any priest convicted at Lancaster, " for a terror to the Catholics who were numerous in that county." After this barbarous execution Father Ambrose's head was impaled on a spike, and stuck upon the tower of the Collegiate Church at Manchester, whence it is believed to have been rescued by Francis Downes, and taken to Wardley Hall, where for a hundred years it lay hidden in the box in which the faithful friend had placed it. One of the strongest proofs that the Wardley skull is that of Father Ambrose is that he had light chestnut hair, and that when the skull was discovered, and for many years afterwards, hair of this colour was still adhering to it.

THE DUTIES OF
SPECIAL CONSTABLES IN 1817

DURING the winter of 1817 such was the state of lawlessness in Flixton and the neighbourhood that special constables were enrolled, and to these the following letter was addressed by a magistrate of the township :—

" To the Special Constables of Flixton, Urmston, Stretford, and Barton-upon-Irwell.

" Gentlemen,

" The learned Chairman at the last Quarter Sessions held at Manchester, thought it a matter of importance to call the attention of the Grand Jury to the great number of Burglaries lately committed in these several townships, and I entertain no doubt but his representation made a strong impression upon the minds of such of you who might happen to be present. Taking into consideration the necessity of our attending to this alarming object, I have thought it my duty as a Magistrate to call you, Gentlemen, before me immediately upon being sworn into office, in order to state to you, what I conceive to be the Law of the Land, with respect to your duties as Special Constables, and to exhort you to become diligent in the exercise of these duties; because it undoubtedly must be a circumstance highly afflicting to us all, that since the commencement of the last winter, no less than ten dwelling-houses, situate within these townships, have been daringly broken into and robbed, at the dead hour of the night, by the worst description of thieves, and the peaceable families thus dreadfully alarmed : from many of these houses the robbers carried off considerable booty, and are yet, for any thing we know to the contrary, still abroad, and have hitherto escaped that punishment which the Laws have directed to be inflicted upon such horrible offenders. Should it hereafter happen that crimes so atrocious in their nature be again practised amongst us, it will become your imperative duty to be watchful, and always on the alert to assemble instantly at the place of robbery ; to follow the robbers freshly and enter with them pell-mell into their hiding-places ; and I can therefore truly say, that the appointment of a large number of Special Constables, for the support of the Civil Power and the preservation of peace and good order, is of great utility, when regularly enforced and continued.

" I am sorry to observe, that villainies are committed in these towns, to an extent of mischief and danger not generally apprehended. House-breakers, common thieves and receivers of stolen goods, all carry on their trade of plunder, in a connected system ; and multitudes of men are regularly trained amongst us in the practice of fraud and robbery.

" The plain and obvious inference from all this, is the necessity of frequent and general nightly patrols, properly conducted, with a regular entry of all their proceedings in a book ; and of an active and vigilant inspection of public-houses. In short, of the utmost exertion of prudence and fortitude in the exercise of the powers with which you are invested, and in the discharge of the duties you are called upon to perform.

" Penal Law is a system of charity to prevent crimes ; not of malice to destroy offenders.

" I am, Gentlemen,
" With much respect,
" Your Friend and Servant,
" R. Wright.
" Flixton, December 1817."

Manchester Race Courses

THE Manchester Race Meeting was first established in 1730 on Kersal Moor, which was, therefore, one of the oldest racecourses in the kingdom. The meeting met with determined opposition from John Byrom, the Lancashire poet, and from Edmund Chetham and Mrs. Ann Chetham, Byrom issuing a pamphlet in which he condemned horse-racing and all such sports because of their immoral tendencies. But the majority of the gentry round Manchester supported the races, and they were held every September until 1745, when Prince Charles Edward and his Highlanders marched into the town. There were no races that year, and through the influence and agitation of Byrom and his supporters fifteen years passed before they were held again, but on October 1, 1760, the meetings were resumed and have gone on uninterruptedly ever since. The prizes of the meeting were restricted to one for each day, and were made to yield plenty of running, being thoroughly well earned by multiplied tests of three or four miles each. An official printer of the race lists, Mr. Joseph Harrop, was appointed in 1765. In 1766 there was no race on the middle day for "want of horses"; blank days also occurred on other occasions. The meeting was extended to four days in 1767, a silver cup being added for hunters, but after a three years' trial the extra day was given up. It had generally been held in August,

September and October, but in 1772 Whitsuntide was fixed for the race week, and in the same year a ladies' stand was erected. That year the racing seems to have been indifferent, for it is recorded that the lack of diversion was compensated by the presence of the fair sex, who "shone forth a pleasing sight to many thousands of spectators, in all the beauty of their sex, in all the gaiety of fashion, and with that delicacy of behaviour which inspires the heart."

During the next ten years the programmes of the races were regularly advertised, but that opposition against them had not been overcome is shown by this manifesto, signed by the borough-reve constable and forty other people, in 1782: "We, the undersigned gentlemen, being of the opinion that it would be for the interest of the town that the races should be discontinued, are determined to subscribe to them no longer." The manifesto had not the slightest effect, and thousands of people flocked to the Kersal Moor course that Whit week as usual. In 1792 the stake was increased to £100, and in 1793 and 1794 there were five days' racing, but only one stake a day was contested, and each race was run in heats; in 1795 two races were run on each day. Writing to the *Sporting Magazine* in 1822, "Nimrod" says: "No course I was ever on is so well kept as Manchester. I have ridden over it amongst a hundred thousand spectators, and nothing can be better than the clear way for the race horses and the good-humour of the people."

For one hundred and two years every Whitsuntide saw the racecourse on Kersal Moor crowded with thousands and thousands of people from Manchester and the large manufacturing district of which it was the centre. In 1847 they crowded to a new course near Castle Irwell, of which Mr. Proctor, in *Our Turf, Stage and Ring*, says: "With the extinction of races on Kersal Moor it seemed probable that the Manchester meetings would suddenly end, and their name be lost by amalgamation with some friendly rival. In this strait it was suggested that Radcliffe Bridge races might be accepted as a substitute; next the good folks of Horwich invited us to their black moor; then Newton did its best to please us by fixing its races to our time—the Wednesday, Thursday and Friday of Whit week. At the eleventh hour, however, when all these claims had been mooted, and when White Moss had been rejected, a site was secured near Castle Irwell." The site was on some flat ground forming a delta of the Irwell between Broughton suspension bridge and Pendleton, and belonged to Mr. Fitzgerald, who lived at Castle Irwell. "Apart from association," Mr. Proctor continues, "I never had much fancy for the new course at the foot of the old moor. Being in a dead level, there is no convenient hill within its circle of ropes and chains whence the heads of the crowd may be overlooked. One of the pleasantest features of our new course is the river Irwell, winding round three sides of the arena. The river is also the source of occasional merriment. As the approaches to the race ground are jealously guarded by toll-men, it follows that many urchins, penniless tramps, and artisans out of employ are usually excluded. Of these unfortunates, some turn listlessly homewards, while others, more persevering, gather in groups along the banks of the stream, and select a place for fording. The youngsters then strip and fasten their huddled apparel upon their heads; the men turn up their trousers, slinging their shoes and stockings over their shoulders; thus prepared, they enter the water, some crossing with comparative ease, but others, on dropping a cap or swimming a stocking, or sinking deeper than they expected, lose heart and return, to the infinite amusement of those on the winning side. After the river, the suspension bridge that spans it is the chief point of interest. Several times have I curiously examined the mechanism of this structure since 1831, in which year it betrayed forty or fifty marching soldiers, treating them to a plunge bath in the stream beneath, when they least expected or desired such a visitation. Though several of these involuntary bathers were severely injured, no one was drowned or killed. The first race on the new course (May 1847) for the Wilton Stakes ended in a dead heat, which was considered a favourable omen. On account of the Art Treasures Exhibition there were four days' races in 1857. During the race for the 'Exhibition Stakes' a serious accident occurred. Josephine, one of the competing horses, fell at the back of the course, through catching her leg against the rails, and her boy-rider, Johnson, fell under her. In the races of 1861 a wild, unmanageable horse, named North Lancashire, ran on the rails and threw his rider, Motley, who received a fracture of the right leg. While galloping riderless along the course, the horse knocked down a boy, inflicting a severe concussion of the brain."

The Manchester Race Meeting was afterwards transferred to a piece of ground adjoining Trafford Park, but this course is now No. 9 Dock of the Ship Canal. Manchester Racecourse to-day is in a loop of the Irwell, on the outskirts of Salford.

THREEDYWHEEL IN DROYLSDEN

A CURIOUS custom was introduced into the Wakes at Droylsden in 1814, from Woodhouses, near Failsworth, where it had been in vogue for over thirty years. The ceremony began at Greenside. Two men on horseback, one John, the son of Robert Hulme of Greenside, grotesquely dressed as a man, the other James, son of Aaron Etchells of Edge Lane, dressed equally grotesquely as a woman, rode slowly through the street, keeping up a dialogue in very halting verse, and spinning flax in the old manner, on spinning wheels placed before them on the saddle. This was called "Threedywheel," which meant "Thread the Wheel." At intervals the pair broke off their dialogue to gather contributions from the spectators, who joined in the chorus.

He.

It's Dreighlsdin wakes, un' wey're comin' to teawn,
To tell yo o' somethin' o' greet reneawn;
Un' if this owd jade ull lem'mi begin,
Aw'l show yo heaw hard un heaw fast aw con spin.
Chorus. So it's threedywheel, threedywheel, dan, don, dill, doe.

She.

Theaw brags o' thisel'; but aw dunno' think it's true,
For aw will uphowd the, thi faurts arn't a few;
For when theaw hast done, un' spun very hard,
O' this aw'm weel sure, thi work is ill marr'd.
Chorus. So it's threedywheel, &c.

He.

Theaw saucy owd jade, theaw'dst best howd thi tung,
Or else aw'st be thumpin' the ere it be lung;
Un iv'ot aw do, theaw'rt sure for to rue,
For aw con ha' monny o' one as good as you.
Chorus. So it's threedywheel, &c.

She.

What is it to me whoe yo con have?
Aw shanno' be lung ere aw'm laid i' my grave;
Un' when 'ot aw'm deod, un' have done what aw con,
Yo may foind one ot'll spin os hard os aw've done.
Chorus. So it's threedywheel, &c.

He.

Com, com, mi dear woife, aw'll not ha' the rue,
Un' this aw will tell yo, un' aw'll tell yo true,
Neaw iv yo'll forgie me for what aw have said,
Aw'll do my endavur to pleos yo instead.
Chorus. So it's threedywheel, &c.

She.

Aw'm glad for to yeor 'ot yo win me forgive,
Un' aw will do by yo os lung os I live;
So let us unite, un' live free fro' o' sin,
Un' then us shall have nowt to think at but spin.
Chorus. So it's threedywheel, &c.

Both.

So neaw let's conclude, and here undeth eawr song,
Aw hope it os pleost this numerous throng;
But iv it os mist, yo needn't to fear,
We'll do eawr endavor to pleos yo next year.
Chorus. So it's threedywheel, threedywheel, dan, don, dill, doe.

The song was sung to a rather plaintive tune. The words were taken from an old man who, in his younger days, had often taken the part of the woman. He related that on one occasion the man taking the part of the husband got so tipsy that he fell off his horse in the yard of Cinderland Hall, and a substitute had to be found and hastily instructed. The spinning-wheel, which they bore in front of them, was turned vigorously during the singing of the chorus. It is a very old dialogue, for portions of other verses, which are incomplete, clearly point to hemp or flax-spinning at an early period. Says one—

"The two that aw' spin is five shilling a peawnd,
Un' that yo mun kneaw by mi wheel going reawnd.
Chorus. So it's threedywheel, &c."

The wife boasts to the husband in another fragmentary verse—

"Aw con o'er sing thee, by th' mass."

To which he replies—

"Aw con o'er-spin thee, by th' mass."

Another piece of abuse was—

"Theaw cankert owd besom, aw cann endure
Ony lunger a temper loike thoine is, aw' sure."

The idea of the dialogue was evident to represent a man and wife quarrellin over the domestic manufacture of line yarn.

"LIFTING" AT EASTER

THIS curious custom, which was supposed to represent the Resurrection of our Saviour, was not universal in Lancashire, but was confined to Manchester, Liverpool, Bolton, Whalley, Warrington, and to several rural districts. On Easter Monday the women "lifted" the men. Several women would seize upon a man in the street, and taking him by the arms and legs raise him in a horizontal position three times in the air. On Easter Tuesday the men "lifted" the women. Towards the end of the eighteenth century the practice was prohibited by the magistrates in Manchester, but it still continued in the lower quarters of the town. "On Easter Monday, between Radcliffe and Bolton," says the author of the *Pictorial History of Lancashire*, " we saw a number of females surround a male, whom they mastered and fairly lifted aloft in the air. It was a merry scene. What humour in the faces of these Lancashire witches! What a hearty laugh! What gratification in their eyes! The next day would bring reprisals : the girls would then be the party to be subjected to this rude treatment."

That the custom did not have its origin in Lancashire, and that formerly it was general throughout the country and amongst all classes, is shown by this entry in the household accounts of King Edward I., in 1225. "To the Ladies of the Queen's Chamber, 15th May, seven ladies and damsels of the Queen, because they took" (*i. e.* "lifted") "the King in his bed, on the morrow of Easter, and made him pay fine for the peace of the King, which he made of his gift by the hand of Hugh de Cerr (or Kerr) Esqre., to the lady of Weston, £14." From this it would seem that the "lifted" paid a fine. The custom was also known as "heaving."

"NOTHING NEW UNDER THE SUN"

THERE is nothing new under the sun. "Looping the loop," when it was introduced at Exhibitions and places of amusement some few years ago, was regarded as a brilliant and patronized this form of amusement in those days, and it may perhaps be deduced from the fact that as only the prices of admission and of reserved seats are given, the public were not

NOW EXHIBITING NEXT DOOR TO THE MECHANICS INSTITUTION

COOPER STREET, MANCHESTER

GRAND CENTRIFUGAL RAILWAY.

With two Circles 80 Feet in circumference. Never before exhibited

ADMITTANCE 2:   RESERVED SEATS 4:

daringly new invention. But, as will be seen from the illustration, they "looped the loop" in Manchester seventy years ago, only then they called it the "Grand Centrifugal Railway." According to this old print ladies do not seem to have allowed to make the whirling trip, but that it paid its twopences and fourpences to see the startling spectacle of other people spinning round two circles, eighty feet in circumference, on their heads.

"A GOOD story of an 'Owdham' man," says Mr. Newbigging, "is the following: At one of the Old Trafford County Cricket matches we heard a conversation that took place between two 'Owdhammers.' A pickpocket plying his avocation had been caught in the act of taking a purse, and quite a commotion was created in that corner of the field, as the thief was collared by a detective and hauled away to the police-station. Says the Oldham man to his friend who was seated next him—

"'Sharp as thoose chaps are, they'd have a job to ta' my brass. Aw'll tell thi what aw do, Jack, when aw comes to a place o' this sooart; aw sticks mi brass reet down at th' bottom o' mi treawsers pocket, and then aw puts abeut hauf a pint o' nuts at top on 't; it tae's some scrawpin out, aw can tell thi' when tha does that!'"

A Famous Museum

ONE of the most noted collectors in the eighteenth century was Sir Ashton Lever of Alkrington, near Manchester, and the Museum which he formed was for many years one of the sights of Lancashire. When it was removed to London it became one of the great attractions of the Metropolis.

Sir Ashton, who was born in 1729, was educated at the Manchester Grammar School and afterwards at Oxford. From his earliest years he had a passion for horsemanship, archery, and all field sports, and especially for collecting objects of every variety. At first he collected live birds, and in such numbers that his aviary at Alkrington became the best in the kingdom ; but when he was about thirty he purchased several hogsheads of foreign shells at Dunkirk, and so greatly was his interest excited that for some time afterwards he devoted himself entirely to collecting shells and fossils. This interest was displaced by one for stuffed birds, of which he collected an enormous quantity, and gradually, instead of specializing, he collected all kinds of natural objects together with savage costumes and weapons. By the time Sir Ashton Lever had reached his forty-fourth year his collection had grown to such dimensions that it was visited by people from all parts of Lancashire. Some of the curious objects which he collected are detailed in an article written upon the Museum in the *Gentleman's Magazine* for May, 1773, by a person who had seen it, and though many specimens of natural history are mentioned, the collection had evidently not then attained its full size. There were "upwards of one thousand three hundred glass cases containing curious objects placed in three rooms, besides four sides of rooms shelved from top to bottom with glass doors before them." Amongst these objects was, "A head of His present Majesty" (George III.) "cut in cannel coal, said to be a striking likeness, indeed the workmanship is inimitable. Also a drawing in Indian ink of a head of a late Duke of Bridgewater, valued at one hundred guineas ; a few pictures of birds in straw, very natural, by Miss Gregg ; a basket of flowers cut in paper, a most masterly performance, the flowers are justly represented ; not the least dot of the apices of the stamens was wanting, or the least fault in the proportion ; every part perfect, and it may be truly observed that it was new to me every time I went to see it and gave me great delight. This curious basket of flowers was executed by Mrs. Groves. There are a great number of antique dresses and parts of dresses of our own and other nations—near two hundred spears and warlike instruments, ancient and modern ; but as I am no friend to fighting, of these I took no further notice, or else I might have mentioned a tomahawk, a scalping knife and many more such desperate instruments of destruction, invented no doubt by the devil himself."

In the year following the appearance of this quaint notice, Sir Ashton was persuaded to remove his Museum to London. He took Leicester House, in Leicester Square, a magnificent mansion belonging to the Sidneys, Earls of Leicester, and which had been occupied by Frederick Prince of Wales, the father of George III., whose dull and unhappy childhood had been spent in the house. Sixteen rooms and various passages and staircases were filled with Sir Ashton's curiosities, and giving it the title of "The Holophusicon" he threw open the doors to the public, advertising that the Museum was to be seen each day from ten to four, "admittance five-and-threepence each person."

For eleven years Sir Ashton's Museum was one of the sights of London, occupying precisely the same position that Madame Tussaud's Waxworks and the Zoological Gardens do to-day, and each year he steadily added to it, until, in the opinion of travellers such as Sir William Hamilton (the husband of Nelson's enchantress) and Baron Dimsdale, it had not its equal in Europe. Sir William said that in different journeys to and from Naples, where he was ambassador, he had seen every public and private museum in Holland, France, Germany, Italy and Sicily, and he thought Sir Ashton Lever's collection was in every respect the finest. Baron Dimsdale said that he had seen the cabinets of curiosities at Moscow and St. Petersburgh, and also those at Paris and Dresden, which were esteemed very curious and valuable, but that they were not, altogether, to be compared with Sir Ashton Lever's Museum.

The following verses written by so young a child are as great a "curiosity" as anything Sir Ashton could have had in his Museum—

VERSES ADDRESSED TO SIR ASHTON LEVER, BY A LITTLE BOY OF TEN YEARS OLD, ON BEING FAVOURED WITH A SIGHT OF HIS MUSEUM.

If I had Virgil's judgment, Homer's fire,
And could with equal rapture strike the lyre,
Could drink as largely of the Muses' spring,
Then would I all Sir Ashton's merits sing.

Look here, look there, above, beneath, around,
There great Apollo consecrates the ground.
Here stands a tiger mighty in his strength,
There crocodiles extend their scaly length;

Subtile, voracious to devour their food,
Savage they look, and seem to pant for blood.
Here shells and fish, and finny dolphins seen,
Display their various colours blue and green.

View there an urn which Roman ashes bore,
And habits once that foreign nations wore.
Birds and wild beasts from Afric's burning sand,
And curious fossils ranged in order stand.

Now turn your eyes from them, and quick survey,
Spars, diamonds, crystals, dart a golden ray;
View apes in different attitudes appear,
With horns of bucks and goats and chamois deer.

Next various kinds of monsters meet the eye;
Dreadful they seem, grim-looking as they lie.
What man is he that does not view with awe
The river-horse that gives the Tigris law?

Dauntless he looks, and eager to engage,
Lashes his sides, and burns with steady rage.
View where the elephant's broad bulk appears,
And o'er his head his hollow trunk appears:

He seems to roar, impatient for the fight,
And stands collected in his utmost might.
Some I have sung, much more my muse
    could name,
A nobler muse requires Sir Ashton's fame.

In his zeal for collecting Sir Ashton seriously impaired his fortune, and in consequence was compelled to dispose of his Museum. It was felt that the collection

THE LEVERIAN MUSEUM

I've gained my end, if you can, Sir, receive
This feeble present, which I freely give.
Your well-unknown worth, to distant nations
    told,
Amongst the sons of fame shall be enrolled.
             T. P. KENNINGTON.
November 6, 1778.

should be secured to the country because of its educational value, and it was therefore valued by a Parliamentary Committee at no less a sum than £53,000. Sir Ashton offered it to the British Museum at a much less sum than the valuation, but the Trustees declined to buy it. This was in 1783, and during the next two years many unavailing attempts were made either to dispose of it, or to come to some arrangement with the Government by which it could be taken over by the country. Finally, in 1785, the House of Commons passed a special Act of Parliament to enable Sir Ashton to sell the Museum by a lottery of 36,000 tickets at a guinea each.

The following advertisement appeared in the newspapers: "Sir Ashton Lever's Lottery Tickets are now on sale at Leicester House every day, Sundays excepted, from nine in the morning till six in the evening at One Guinea each; and as each ticket will admit four persons, either together or separately to view the Museum, no one will hereafter be admitted but by the lottery tickets, excepting those who have already annual admission.

"This collection is allowed to be infinitely superior to any of the kind in Europe. The very large sum expended in making it is the cause of its being thus to be disposed of, and not through deficiency of the daily receipts, as is generally imagined, which have annually increased, the average amount for the last three years being £1833 1s. per annum. The hours of admission are from Eleven till Four.

"Good fires in all the galleries."

Unfortunately for Sir Ashton only 8000 of the 36,000 lottery tickets were sold, so 8000 guineas was all he received for the many thousands of pounds he had expended. The purchaser of the winning ticket was a Mr. Parkinson, who, for one guinea, thus obtained a collection which had been valued at £53,000. This gentleman erected a building on the south side of the Thames, near Blackfriars Bridge, called the "Rotunda," which consisted of seventeen large rooms, occupying nearly 1000 square yards. "In these rooms were assembled the rarest productions in the animal, vegetable, and mineral kingdoms with inimitable works of art, and the various dresses, manufactures, implements of war, etc., of the Indian nations in North and South America, Otaheite, Botany Bay and other foreign ports, collected by the late Captain Cook and other navigators."

For a time the Leverian Museum still attracted the wonder and interest both of Londoners and visitors to the Metropolis, but gradually it fell into neglect, and in 1806 was put up for public auction. The sale began on the 5th of May and continued to the 18th July, occupying sixty-five days. The lots numbered 7,879, the catalogue of which filled 410 pages.

Sir Ashton was spared the pain of seeing the dispersal of his Museum by the auction. He had retired to Alkrington Hall, practically ruined by his indulgence of his taste for collecting curiosities, and died very suddenly at the Bull's Head Inn in Manchester in 1788. Sir Ashton had been High Sheriff for Lancashire in 1771 and was knighted in 1778 in recognition of his services to the public. The ticket of admission to this famous Museum is reproduced in the heading of this story.

Sir Ashton Lever was probably one of the most accomplished naturalists of his time, but there was always a strong vein of eccentricity in his character which, as he grew older, became more and more marked. Fanny Burney (afterwards Mme. d'Arblay), the authoress of *Evelina*, has left a vivid picture in her diary of Sir Ashton's oddities in this description of a visit she paid in December, 1782, to the famous Museum in Leicester Square—

"I went this morning with my dear father to Sir John Ashton Lever's, where we could not but be entertained. Sir Ashton came and talked to us a good while. He may be an admirable naturalist, but I think if in other matters you leave the *ist* out, you will not much wrong him. He looks fully sixty years old, yet he had dressed not only two young men but himself, in a green jacket, a round hat, with green feathers, a bundle of arrows under one arm, and a bow in the other, and thus accoutred as a forester he pranced about; while the younger fools, who were in the same garb, kept running to and fro in the garden carefully contriving to shoot at some mark, just as any of the company appeared at any of the windows. After such a specimen of his actions, you will excuse me if I give none of his conversation."

EASTER SPORTS AT THE MAN= CHESTER FREE GRAMMAR SCHOOL

THE following account of the sports which were held at Easter at the Manchester Free Grammar School in the early part of the nineteenth century was sent to a local paper, about the year 1860, probably by an "old boy."

"On Easter Monday the senior scholars had a treat and various festivities. On the morning of that day masters and scholars assembled in the school-room, with a band of music, banners, etc. One essential thing was a target, in a square frame, to which were suspended one or more pairs of silver buckles, constituting the chief archery prize, the second being a good dunghill cock. These were the only prizes, and they were duly contested for by the scholars, the whole being probably devised in the old times with a view to keep the youth of Manchester in the practice of the old English archery, which, on the invention of gunpowder and firearms, fell rapidly into desuetude. The gay procession thus provided, the scholars, bearing their bows and arrows, set out from the Grammar School, headed by some reverend gentlemen of the Collegiate Church, by the masters of the school, the churchwardens, etc., the band playing some popular airs of the day, and took its route by Long Millgate to Hunt's Bank, and along the Walkers' (*i. e.* Fullers') Croft, to some gardens, where it was then the custom for artizans on Sunday morning to buy 'a penny posy.' Here the targets were set up, and the 'artillery practice,' as it was the fashion to call archery, commenced. At its close the prizes were awarded, and the procession returned in the same order, along Hunt's Bank, the Apple Market, Fennell Street, Hanging Ditch, and Old Millgate, to the Bull's Head, in the Market Place— in those days a very celebrated house— where the junior boys were treated with frumenty—wheat stewed, and then boiled in milk, with raisins, currants, and spices, till it forms a thick, porridge-like mass, exceedingly palatable to young folk. The masters and assistants and the senior scholars partook of roast beef, plum pudding, etc. The abolition of this Easter Monday custom, said to have been by Dr. Smith, was by no means relished by the Grammar School boys."

COCK-FIGHTING

COCK-FIGHTING was one of the most popular sports—if so barbarous a practice can be called a sport—in Lancashire during the eighteenth century. A cockpit might be found in almost every town, but Manchester and Liverpool were the chief centres. The cruel pastime was carried out under carefully-drawn-up regulations. The following " RULES FOR MATCHING AND FIGHTING OF COCKS, which have been in practice ever since the reign of King Charles II," are set out in the " Manchester Racing Calendar " from 1760 to 1800.

1. To begin the same by fighting the lighter pair of cocks which fall in the match first, proceeding upwards towards the end that every lighter pair might fight earlier than those that are heavier.

2. In matching, with relation to the battles, it is a rule always in London that, after the cocks of the main are weighed, the match-bills are compared.

3. That every pair of dead or equal weight are separated, and fight against others ; provided it appears that the main can be enlarged thereto.

A famous cock-fight, or " cock-match," as it was called, was fought on April 15, 1761, and upon the three following days. Twenty-eight battles were fought, Mr. Dickonson's birds being declared the winners. The following year there was a " match of twenty-five battles," and again Mr. Dickonson was the winner. It is almost incredible that women should have witnessed this cruel sport, once classed amongst the national sports of England ; but this apparently was the case in 1772, when the " ladies' stand "

on the racecourse at Kersal Moor was erected. At the close of the races there was a cock-match " between the gentlemen of Yorkshire and the gentlemen of Lancashire," when the birds of the latter were defeated.

At Liverpool the cockpit was in Cockspur Street, and in 1790 took place an encounter that was talked of for years afterwards, " the great main of cocks between Thomas Townley Parker, Esquire, of Cuerden, and John Clifton, Esquire, of Lytham, to be fought on Easter Monday, April 5, and the three following days, at the new cockpit in Cockspur Street—to show forty-one cocks each. Ten guineas each battle, and two hundred guineas the main." Large sums of money were lost and gained by betting on the combatants, and at Eccles there used to be a tradition that the tithes of the town itself were once staked upon the issue of one of these encounters. The fight took place at Westminster in the reign of Henry VIII. Sir John Anderton of Lydiate produced the first duck-wing cock that had ever been brought into the cockpit, with this challenge—

" There's a jewel of England !
For a hundred in hand,
And a hundred in land,
I'll fight him 'gainst any cock in England ! "

The Duke of Suffolk, to whom the tithes of Eccles had been granted by Henry VIII., took up the challenge, wagering the gift of his royal master on the success of his bird. Sir John Anderton's duck-wing cock gained the day, and its owner the tithes of Eccles. The story is believed to be a fabrication, but tradition is stronger than truth, and to this day, in Lancashire, duck-winged cocks are called " Anderton Jewels."

"THE HUMOURS OF SMITHY DOOR MARKET"

SMITHY DOOR was one of the oldest streets in Manchester, and was the scene of a Saturday market which a well-known writer, Thomas Wilson, thus described in the early years of the nineteenth century, under the above title.

" **G**OOD laws! what a medley of groups
  On Saturday haunts Smithy Door!
  What squalling and bawling and shouts;
What wise, simple, gentle, and poor!
And is it not truly and funny,
  The devil a thing you can name,
But here you may have it for money,
  Provisions, apparel—the same.

The merchants all aiming at brass,
  Give out what they have for to sell;
And people invite as they pass,
  On terms for ' a bargain ' some tell.

'Twould puzzle a counsellor's pate,
  A parson's or judge's wise nob,
The various things for to state;
  'Twould be such a difficult job.

There's *Moshes*, with pictures he stands,
  And jewels presents to your view,
Fine tooth-pickers, glasses and fans;
  But always take care of a Jew;
There's pincushions, needles, and pins;
  Of patchworkers, laws! what a tribe!
Brushes, brooms, baskets and tins,
  Cow-heels and sheep-trotters beside.

There's Eccles-cake merchants a-many;
  Here's ' hot-pies ' and ' good Cheshire cheese';
There's matches eight bunches a penny;
  And snuff to make old women sneeze.
There's bacon, and butter and eggs,
  And pills that will give you relief;
Then, just turning round on your legs,
  There's plenty of mutton and beef.

There's plenty (of) ale to be sold,
The toper does very well know;
And if that the weather proves cold,
There's gin, rum and brandy also.
The sharper is on the alert;
I'd have you take care of your cash,
Or out of your pocket he'll jert (jerk)
The revits; then off in a flash.

There's potatoes, salads and greens;
Big turnips, red cabbage and peas,
There's onions and parsnips and beans,
And 'posies' as gay as you please.
Abundance of fruit you will find;
Turkeys, ducks, pigeons and geese;
Numerous birds of each kind,
And *guinea*-pigs, *shilling* a-piece.

There's an animal painter resides,
Who will picture your dog or your cat,
Pigs, horses, or each thing besides,
From an elephant down to a rat.
Silk winders and reelers are flocking
To purchase their stock of bean traps,
Shoe-ribbon, and dashing white stockings,
Brass brooches and ninepenny caps.

Next *Catchpenny*[1] opens his gates;
Some wonderful horrors in book,
Or murder so dreadful relates,
And tells it with pitiful look.
Your ears are then stunn'd with the noise
Of crockery ware at each step;
'Ony proice,' this fellow cries;
That—'Ladies, aw'll sell 'um yo che'p.'

'Two a penny, paste blacking-balls,' there;
And cotton-balls, black, red, and blues;
You may rig yourself out, if you're bare
With coats, waist-coats, hats, stockings,
and shoes.
You'll see the grave Sheffielder there,
With razors, rings, scissors and knives;
Combs for the fine lasses' hair;
And currant loaf cut into shives.

So now, in conclusion, good folks,
I'll give you my wishes for health;
May everyone relish their jokes,
And trade give you plenty of wealth.
May Smithy Door Market prevail;
Your pockets be well lined with cash;
Fill all your bumpers with ale;
And banish all sorrow with wash."

[1] See " Cocks and Catchpennies."

"UP AND DOWN" FIGHTING

A MOST brutal method of settling quarrels in Bolton and its neighbourhood was the " up and down " fight. The " up and down " meant that both men had the right to kick—" punching and purring," as it is called—on every part of the body, and in all possible situations, and also to squeeze the throat. At races and fairs contests of this kind were witnessed by crowds of people, who took sides, and saw no more inhumanity in the disgusting spectacle of two men kicking one another and tearing at each other's throats than if it had been an ordinary boxing match. Seeing that the men either wore clogs or heavy wooden-soled shoes, both of which were covered with iron plates and studded with large nails, the death of one of the combatants was no unusual occurrence, and so numerous did the cases become that the judges revived the practically obsolete punishment of branding in the hand those who were convicted of manslaughter by kicking. Branding in the hand was abolished in 1822 in the reign of George IV. The severest possible punishments were meted out to those who indulged in " up and down " fighting, a practice which was described as being " a disgrace to any civilized country." But in less than sixty years a great change came about, for in 1831 " up and down " fighting with " purring" was less frequent amongst the forty thousand inhabitants of Bolton than it had been amongst the fifteen thousand in 1773.

THE DUKE'S DAUGHTER AND THE MANCHESTER APOTHECARY

HOW Lady Barbara Fitzroy, the daughter of the Duke of Cleveland, and a granddaughter of Charles II., came to live in the house of a Manchester apothecary is shrouded in mystery. Her father was the son of Charles II. and the notorious Barbara Villiers, Lady Castlemaine, whom the "Merry Monarch" created Duchess of Cleveland. He was named Charles after the King, and when his mother died in 1709, he succeeded her as first Duke of Cleveland. Lady Barbara was one of the three daughters by her father's second marriage, but how she came to be disowned by her mother, as set out in the curious inscription on her gravestone in the choir of the Collegiate Church, is unknown.

There are two brass plates upon the stone. The upper one bears the arms of Charles II. with the bar sinister and this inscription:—

"Lady Barbara Fitzroy
Eldest daughter of the
Most Noble Charles
Duke of Cleveland and Southampton
Died January 4th 1734."

Upon the lower plate are the arms of the Dawson family, and the following inscription:—

"Here are deposited the remains
of William Dawson, Esq, who died
On the 17th of August 1780,
And in the 60th year of his age.
He desired to be buried with the above
Named Lady, not only to testify his
Gratitude to the memory of a kind
Benefactress, altho' he never
Reaped any of those advantages from
Her Bounty to his Family, which
she intended;
But because his Fate was similar to her's
For she was disowned by her mother,
And he was disinherited by his father."

This William Dawson was an apothecary, and the father of the luckless "Jemmy" Dawson who was executed in London for his share in the 1745 Rebellion, and whose sad story has been preserved in the ballad "Jemmy Dawson."

"My Lady Barbara Fitzroy that lived with Mrs. Dawson, and Mrs. Mort were both buried this week," wrote a friend to John Byrom. "My Lady has made Mr. Dawson her heir, if he can but come at the money," Mr. Dawson did not "come at the money" as he caused to be recorded upon the gravestone, forty-six years after Lady Barbara's death.

The father who disinherited him was an eccentric person, and was buried by his own express direction in a "cuffed shirt and cravat, a night-cap of brown fur, a striped morning gown (orange and white), deep crimson-coloured silk waistcoat and breeches, white silk stockings and red morocco slippers. In his bosom was placed a folded piece of white paper, which enclosed two locks of hair cut from the heads of two boys for whom Mr. Dawson had a great regard. They were the sons of a gentleman named Cooper, who was his steward and with whom Mr. Dawson lived. To this person he left his estate."

Several years before his death the elder Dawson engaged an engraver to inscribe the plate he proposed to have placed over his remains, and this he kept in his room until his death.

What a story lies hidden here! A king's granddaughter, either driven from her home or leaving it of her own accord, and seeking refuge in the family of a Manchester apothecary! Why did she come to Manchester? How did she make acquaintance with the Dawsons? Those are questions to which no answers can be found. Nor do we know why her host and entertainer was disinherited by his father.

Lady Barbara died a few months before her father, and it is therefore not improbable that she had no fortune to bequeath to Mr. Dawson.

OLDHAM'S FIRST MEMBER OF PARLIAMENT

A LTHOUGH William Cobbett was not a Lancashire man he was intimately connected with those stirring times which preceded and followed the passing of the first Reform Bill, and became a prominent figure in the political life of the county. He also was the first Member returned to Parliament for Oldham.

Before he took to politics Cobbett had a varied and surprising career. His father was a poor Surrey cottager, and the future Member of Parliament spent his early years in the fields. But he had much force of character and educated himself so effectually that he was able to take the post of copying clerk to an attorney in London. Wearying of desk-work, Cobbett enlisted in a line regiment, and no sooner was he in the Army than he began to study English literature. He speedily gained promotion, and for eight years served with his regiment in Nova Scotia. When he left the Army, in 1791, he got into trouble with the authorities for writing a pamphlet called *The Soldier's Friend*, which supported an agitation then being made for the increase of soldiers' pay, and in order to avoid the possible consequences he went to St. Omer in France, where he learnt French. Thence he migrated to Philadelphia, where he taught English to French refugees, published various newspapers, kept a bookshop, and wrote numerous pamphlets on American politics. Wherever he was, Cobbett could not keep out of politics, and as he took the Loyalist side in America, after eight years' residence he found it wiser to return to London, where he was warmly received by the Government.

After the failure of a newspaper and of a bookshop he started *Cobbett's Weekly Political Register*, which continued until his death, more than thirty-three years afterwards. At first the Government gave the *Register* every support, but after a prosecution for libel, because of some plain-speaking articles on Ireland, which ended in his conviction Cobbett began to think he was on the wrong side in politics. He had already been leaning towards Reform, and this prosecution for free speech and criticism sent him openly into the arms of what was then the popular party. The *Register* in consequence became one of the most valuable advocates in the cause of Parliamentary Reform, and Cobbett naturally became anathema to the Government and all anti-reformers. An article on military flogging brought another prosecution by the Government, and he was fined one thousand pounds and condemned to prison for two years. This was in 1810.

When he came out of prison Cobbett found himself financially ruined. He threw himself without reserve into the cause for Reform, and by reducing his *Register* to twopence gained an enormous circulation amongst the labouring classes. But in 1817, having reason to fear another Government prosecution, he went to America, where he kept a farm and continued his pamphlets. He returned to England two years later, and such was his reputation as a firebrand and ultra-Radical that, when, shortly afterwards, he accepted an invitation to a public dinner at the Union Rooms in George Leigh Street, Manchester, the authorities absolutely forbade his entry into the town. But Manchester was destined to see a good deal of Mr. Cobbett and his canary-coloured waistcoat, as well as to benefit by the reforms he agitated, when, after the lapse of nearly two hundred years, the right was given to the town to be

29

represented in Parliament. She had had no member since the time of Cromwell, when Richard Radcliffe of Pool Fold had followed Major-General Worsley of Platt. This first election in 1832 was a great day in the history of Manchester, and William Cobbett was one of the five candidates! The nomination took place on the 12th (afterwards Lord Sydenham), Mr. Samuel Jones Loyd (afterwards Lord Overstone), Mr. John Thomas Hope, and Mr. William Cobbett, the latter entering the ground in procession, heralded by a band of music. Whigs, Tories and Radicals—as thus represented at the nomination—were equally alert, equally hopeful, and wild

WILLIAM COBBETT

December in St. Ann's Square, and is thus described by an eye-witness, Mr. Richard Wright Procter, in his *Memorials of Old Manchester*—

"The novel field of candidates consisted of five, the various party colours displayed representing Mr. Mark Philips, the Right Honourable Charles Powlett Thomson with the joy of their new franchise. Many shops were closed, and numerous banners waving aloft gave the town a holiday appearance. St. Ann's Square was crowded to suffocation, not omitting its dotted roofs and gay balconies. We arrived early, and luckily, as we thought, secured a central position near the hustings. As the time approached for business the multitude gathering behind and around became uneasy, swaying backward and forward like an agitated sea. Repeatedly were we forced amongst the guarding constables, triple-lined, and as rudely forced back again.

"The candidates (save Mr. Thomson, an absentee), supported by the proposers, the seconders and most prominent partisans, being all duly arranged in their several compartments, silence was proclaimed and the writ was read out. The Borough Reeve (Mr. Benjamin Braidley) then advanced to the front of the hustings, being received with general cheers. He warmly congratulated the people on the possession of their new privilege, hoping they would exercise the trust in such a discreet manner as to form a precedent for future elections. Reminding them that fair play is proverbially a jewel —an Englishman's boast—he besought them to listen patiently to each speaker in turn, and then, separating the true from the seeming, the kernels from the shells, decide in favour of the best men. A hearty clapping of hands marked the general approval of sentiments so admirable, and the returning officer resumed his place. We soon gleaned by the remarks of the people about us that it was in the present instance an easy matter to pick the good from the bad, as upon one side were ranged, they said, rosy angels, and on the other their blue antipodes. It was still easier, they affirmed, to follow the excellent advice of the Borough Reeve, for to support the cherubim and crush the imps of darkness with his utmost ability was the self-evident duty of every true man. No sooner did a gentleman step forward to propose a red candidate than the nature of the blues and greens became manifest. They hooted and howled till not an angelic word could be heard. They could not,

however, prevent their rivals from drowning the discord with prolonged cheers, especially as some friend upon the hustings was kind enough to wave his hat when a point fell from the speaker, or when an extra effort was needed to maintain the preponderance of noise upon the speaker's side. . . . When the blues, in turn, essayed to speak, the reds repaid them in the same clamorous coin, and with such vigorous interest to boot that their eloquence was speedily reduced to dumb show and shorthand. The uproar reached its climax during the address of the stranger candidate, Mr. Hope, who was persistently refused a hearing. Yet as often and earnestly as the crowd hooted the Tory the ladies waved for the gentleman, nearly all the favour from the balconies and windows being bestowed upon Mr. Hope, who was young and prepossessing. If Venus in the good time coming be allowed to elect the Member of Parliament it will be useless to oppose Adonis.

"Ultimately the show of hands—the bootless privilege of the cottagers—was carefully taken by Mr. Braidley, and declared to be favourable to the reds and greens. But the losers ridiculed the decision in ironical terms, while denouncing the returning officer's lack of vision. Any one might see, as was petulantly averred, that the majority of hands and hats, kerchiefs, and ribbons favoured the other side. With a few soothing words from the Borough Reeve, thanking the people for their peaceful attention to the important business of the day, and acknowledging with a smile their flattering opinion of his decision, the proceedings ended."

Cobbett came out at the bottom of the poll with 1305 votes, Mark Philips at the top with 2923. Only 9688 votes were polled, a curious comparison with Manchester elections of to-day; and the expenses of the whole election were only £729 2s. 6d.

Defeated at Manchester, Cobbett turned his attention to Oldham, which had likewise received the privilege of sending a Member to Parliament under the Reform Bill. There he was successful, but his entry into Parliament was too late, he being then seventy years of age. He represented Oldham until his death three years later.

Cobbett's ideas of history and politics were crude, and he injured his reputation by an overweening self-esteem and virulent language, both in his writings and public speeches. But his ardent sympathy for the welfare of the poor, and his insistence upon schemes for their betterment, won him the affection and esteem of the working classes, and were the chief factors that led to his return for Oldham.

Mr. Procter thus describes an impression he had of Cobbett before the Manchester nomination day : " The first was William Cobbett in his perennial canary-coloured waistcoat, and with his customary fair, Saxon, county-squire appearance. He was delivering, prior to the nomination day in question, an election address at Mr. Jager's hayloft, near the corner of St. George's Road and Miller's Lane. The number of street listeners was moderately, not excessively, large. On that occasion our eyes must have been busier than our ears, for, while still retaining a vivid recollection of the orator's features and apparel, every syllable of his earnest oration has been forgotten."

Cobbett appears to have had a strong liking for Lancashire, for out of the four parliamentary seats he contested, three of them were in the County Palatine. The third seat was that of Preston, in 1826.

DIDSBURY WAKES

THE Didsbury Wakes in 1825 were thus announced in the *Stockport Advertiser* of the 5th of August that year.

" DIDSBURY WAKES will be celebrated on August 8, 9 and 10. A long bill of fare of the diversions to be enjoyed at this most delightful village has been established. The enjoyments consist chiefly of ass-races for purses of gold; prison-bar playing, and grinning through collars, for ale; bag-racing, for hats; foot-racing, for sums of money; maiden plates for ladies under twenty years of age, for gown pieces, shawls, etc. ; treacle-

loaf eating, for various rewards, smoking-matches, apple-dumpling eating ; wheel-barrow racing, the best heats ; bell-racing and balls each evening. The humours of Didsbury Festival are always well regulated ; the display of youths of both sexes, vieing with each other in dress and fashion, as well as cheerful and blooming faces, is not exceeded by any similar event, and the gaieties of each day are succeeded by the evening parties, fantastically tripping through the innocent recreation of country dances, reels, etc., to as favourite tunes, at the 'Cock' and 'Ring o' Bells' inns."

GORTON TOWN

This song was written and composed in 1865 by John Beswick, well known as "Parish Jack," a singer and fiddler who was in great request at "stirs" and merry-makings. He was also a member of the Gorton choir. It was printed as a broad-side, and was very popular because of its representation of the state of trade and politics after the Civil War in America.

" GOSH, dang it, lads, we're coming
    again,
    Though many a mile I've been;
A Gorton lad I'm born and bred,
    And lots of sights I've seen.

But when I did come back again,
    I nearly fell in fits,
For times and folks so alter'd look'd,
    I thought I'd lost me wits.

I turn'd me north, I turn'd me south,
    I turn'd me east and west,
And every thing so alter'd look'd,
    And some were none for th' best.

They'm even alter'd Goose Green pump,
    They'm turn'd it upside down;
And th' well they'm choked with paving-
    stones,
    Since I left Gorton town.

When I left home some years ago,
    Th' old folks had lots of trade;
Some right good jobs came tumbling in,
    And every one well paid.

We'd good roast beef and pudding,
    And ale some decent swigs;
Egad ! they liv'd like fighting-cocks,
    And got as fat as pigs.

But now, egad ! there's none such things;
    Poor folk have empty tripes;
There's no roast beef to stuff their hides,
    Its Poor Law soup and swipes.

An honest working man's no chance;
    Grim want does on him frown;
I ne'er thought things would come to this,
    When I left Gorton town.

In days gone by our fine young men
    Ne'er told such dismal tales;
They'd ne'er a man transplanted then
    As far as New South Wales.

We'd honest men in Parliament
    Both Tories, Rads and Whigs;
They were never known poor folk to rob,
    But now they're turned to prigs.

Our manufac'rers worked full time,
    Their mills were seldom stopt;
No general turn-outs were there then,
    Their wages never dropt.

These Corn-law folks and Chartist lads,
    Might talk till all were brown,
Without being sent to treading-mills
    When I left Gorton town.

In days gone by I never thought
    Such days could come as these,
When lads were all as gay as larks,
    And wenches bright as bees.

Right merrily they jogg'd to th' fairs
    In clogs and light shalloon,
And every one could sport a face
    Just like a harvest moon.

But now the clogs and light shalloons,
    Each one has thrown aside,
And lasses now are faded moons;
    They're grown too proud to stride.

The foolish frumps sport mutton pumps,
    And yet, their pride to crown,
They've bustles tied behind 'em
    Half as large as Gorton town.

But dang it, lads; aw'st ne'er forget,
    When first I came i' th' town,
A pretty wench came up to me,
    And says, ' Where art thou bound ? '

But putting all these jokes aside,
    We hope these times will mend;
There'll come a day yet when the rich
    Will prove the poor man's friend.

When work and honest poverty
    Will meet with due regard;
And plotting knaves and creeping slaves
    Will get their just reward.

It's soon or late, as sure as fate,
    Such things will come to pass;
And when we all get lots of work
    We'll soon get lots of brass.

With right good trade, and fairly paid,
    I dare bet thou a crown,
There'll not be such a place i' th' world
    As merry Gorton town."

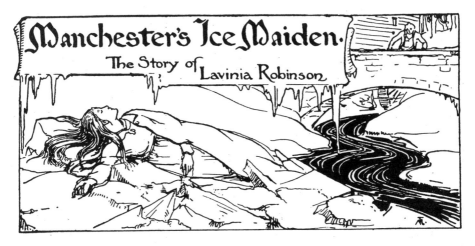

Manchester's Ice Maiden.
The Story of Lavinia Robinson

D URING the winter of 1813, Manchester and its neighbourhood were thrilled by a mystery attaching to the disappearance of a young school-teacher called Lavinia Robinson, who left her home in Bridge Street one evening in December with her lover, a young surgeon, to whom she was to be shortly married, and never returned.

Lavinia Robinson was the daughter of a wire-worker, but, having been educated at the Moravian boarding school at Fairfield, she was in every respect superior to girls of her station. At the age of twelve she lost her mother. When she was seventeen her father died, leaving six daughters and three sons, who all continued to live in a house in Bridge Street, where Lavinia started a small school which for four years she conducted with considerable success. In the same street there lived a young doctor, and from being neighbours, he and Lavinia became engaged, the wedding being fixed for January 1814.

It was the coldest winter in the memory of those living; the country was buried beneath stupendously heavy falls of snow, and the frost continued, in one unbroken spell, for thirteen weeks from the middle of December. Rivers were frozen over and amongst them the Irwell, a circum-stance which added an uncanny mystery to the girl's disappearance.

On the morning of December 17, Lavinia's sister found that she had not returned on the previous evening, and that her bed had not been slept in. The family immediately instituted inquiries but without any effect, except the discovery that a tragic scene had taken place between their sister and her lover. It appears that Lavinia had excited the interest of another young man, whose attentions she had refused. Hearing of her approaching marriage, and rendered desperate, this young man forced himself upon her and made a final appeal to her feelings, but with no success. Lavinia only loved the surgeon. The latter, however, was a witness of the close of this painful interview, and wholly misconstruing the parting words of the rejected swain, brought an entirely unfounded charge against his future wife.

In vain Lavinia pleaded her innocence. The surgeon would not listen, and left the house, Lavinia following him as far as the bridge near the New Bailey. Here, the quarrel reached its height, sharp words were exchanged, and according to the evidence of a passer-by, Lavinia was struck and fell. But it is more probable that while she was endeavouring to

embrace the surgeon he pushed her away, and this caused her to fall, for, rising to her feet she put her arms round his neck, begging him to believe her "truthful words." But, unhappily, the surgeon was convinced of her guilt. Lavinia then bade him a last farewell.

In his statement to the police the lover said that he left Lavinia near the prison, and went home, thinking that she would make the best of her way to Bridge Street. This the unhappy girl appears to have done, for a note was found on the parlour table, in which she solemnly declared her innocence and her determination not to live under her lover's suspicion. Her distracted sisters thought of the river, but on the night of Lavinia's disappearance a partial thaw had been followed by intense frost and the Irwell was frozen from bank to bank.

A month later they issued the following advertisement, offering thirty guineas for her recovery, "living or otherwise":—
"She was of middle size, and good figure; of a fair complexion with long light-brown hair; she had on a fawn-coloured twilled stuff dress; a pink and yellow shot figured silk handkerchief on her neck; a brown cloth mantle; a black beaver cottage bonnet; and her linen is marked L. R."

The reward of thirty guineas was afterwards increased to one hundred guineas by the town authorities.

As the ice-bound days passed on and no word or sign came from the unhappy girl, a conviction gradually became general that the frozen Irwell held the secret. A large number of men, some of whom were paid by the authorities, but the larger number of whom gave their services voluntarily, were set to work to break up the ice in the river. On February 7, nearly eight weeks after her disappearance, their efforts were rewarded, for, that morning, a Mr. Goodier being near his mill at Mode Wheel, some three miles away from Manchester, saw the body of the unhappy Lavinia, "reclining on a sandbank, environed by masses of ice, and with icicles gemming her hair in the place of orange blossoms." The body had been preserved from all decay by the icy coldness of the water.

Word of the discovery being sent to Manchester, the police and some of Lavinia's friends were quickly upon the spot, and the body having been formally identified, it was removed in a hearse to her home in Bridge Street. Public feeling ran very high, and it was confidently anticipated that the poor girl's lover would be subjected to a strict examination at the inquest. After being cautioned by the Coroner he handed in his evidence in writing, but it was not required, as the jury after long deliberation returned an open verdict to the effect that the unhappy Lavinia had been found drowned, but that there was no evidence to show how she came into the river.

This was tantamount to a decision that there was nothing to incriminate the lover, who, to do him justice, frankly admitted that the evidence, and especially the medical evidence, completely satisfied him that his cruel suspicions had been unfounded. He spoke with the bitterest sorrow of having thus wrongfully accused his unhappy sweetheart. But, although he was considered guiltless by the coroner's jury, the people of Manchester held a contrary opinion, which they expressed in so forcible a manner—breaking his windows, and throwing stones at him in the street—that after a while he was forced to leave the town. What became of him is not known. There was an account of his death by suicide in a Shrewsbury paper during the same year, but eight years later it was stated that he was "wandering the earth, a modern Cain."

Lavinia was buried the day after the discovery, on February 8, 1814, and so widespread was the interest in her fate and its surrounding tragedy, that thousands of people attended the funeral. A public subscription was raised to assist her family in the heavy expenses they had incurred in connection with her loss. On a gravestone in St. John's Churchyard, Byrom Street, under the names of her father and mother, these lines were inscribed :—

" Also LAVINIA their daughter, who departed this life 17th of December, 1813, aged 20 years.

More lasting than in lines of art
   Thy spotless character's imprest ;
Thy worth engraved on every heart,
   Thy loss bewail'd in every breast."

ARCHERY AT CHEETHAM HILL

CHEETHAM HILL was famed, not only locally, but all over Lancashire, for the skill of its inhabitants in archery. Even so late as eighty years ago this old English sport was keenly followed there. The butts were at Broughton ; the archers keeping their bows and arrows at the Griffin Inn, which was their meeting-place and hostelry. And near the Griffin was " Pilkington's Bow and Arrow Shop," an establishment which had a reputation for making all the necessary weapons and targets, far beyond the confines of the county.

Amongst many well-known archers, born and bred at Cheetham Hill, James Rawson was the most famous. In his prime he was said to be the best archer in the whole country. He was born in 1715, and lived to be eighty. By trade Rawson was a handloom weaver, and lived in a small cottage nearly opposite the Griffin. Many were the stories related of his feats with the bow and arrow. One of these was to shoot an arrow from a considerable distance into the very centre of the bull's-eye, then with a second arrow split the first in two, and then with a third arrow to split the second. Archery champions from far and near came to contest the honours won by Rawson, but he was invariably the conqueror. It is said that on one such occasion, both the Cheetham Hill champion and his opponent placed arrow after arrow in the bull's-eye, until Rawson, being the last to shoot, taking careful aim at one of the other man's shafts in the bull's-eye, split it in halves and displaced it with his own, thus winning the match.

Rawson died in 1795. By his epitaph in St. Mark's Churchyard we learn that he kept up his archery until he was sixty. It says—

" His dexterity as an archer was unrivalled.
  From the age of sixteen to sixty he never
  refused a challenge nor ever lost a match.
Grim Death grown jealous of his Art
  His matchless fame did stop,
Relentless aim'd the unerring dart,
  And split the Vital Prop.
This favourite son Apollo eyed
  His virtues to requite,
Convey'd his spirit to reside
  In beams of endless light."

A DETERMINED CRIMINAL

THE fascination that a life of crime exercises over some people is exemplified by the career of Robert Horridge, a notorious Manchester burglar, who, beginning his career in 1862 at the age of thirteen, was finally sent to penal servitude for life in 1887, after having spent seventeen of the intervening twenty-five years in prison. Horridge was the son of respectable and honest parents, his father being a blacksmith and maker of fenders, but the boy himself from his earliest years showed strong signs of criminal propensities. He was apprenticed to his father, and in 1862 made his first acquaintance with prison, being sentenced to six months' imprisonment for stealing money. After his release Horridge returned to work for his father, and for five years seemed to be a reformed character, when it was discovered that he was a receiver of stolen goods on a large scale, and he was sent to prison a second time—for eighteen months. On his release he once more returned to his father, and worked so hard that he managed to save enough money to start in business for himself, taking into partnership an Italian, a steady and industrious man employed by one of the telegraph companies which existed before the telegraphs were bought by the government. This partnership continued until Horridge was very cleverly captured by the police for stealing a watch. It was then discovered that he had corrupted his Italian partner, who shared with him the proceeds of the sale of stolen goods. This time Horridge was sent to prison for seven years' penal servitude with seven years' police supervision, his bad character telling heavily against him.

It was after Horridge's release from prison after serving his first " stretch " that he became a burglar on a grand scale.

He at once started in business, and as he was an extremely good workman, indeed one of the best at his trade, he was very successful, and was soon able to buy a pony and a long cart with low wheels, the shape of which was necessitated by the iron goods he made for the wholesale houses. To all appearance Horridge was leading an honest life : but the police began to grow suspicious. Robberies became more and more frequent, and safes, which had been taken bodily from warehouses or shops, would be found, overturned and emptied of their contents in some lonely spot, with the back or the sides cut out. Shop after shop was broken into, and although the Manchester police had strong reason to suspect Horridge, and the gang which they discovered he had formed, they had no evidence upon which they could arrest him.

At length, one Sunday morning about six o'clock a jeweller's shop at Shudehill was broken into, and as Horridge was seen about half-past six in the vicinity going in the direction of his home and carrying a heavy hammer, it was clear that he had had some hand in this burglary. Very shortly afterwards he was suspected of a burglary in the country, and the county police came to Manchester to arrest him. Knowing they had a desperate man to deal with, the city and county police joined forces, and some twenty or thirty officers surrounded the house in which he was living. A loud knock was given at the door, whereupon Horridge appeared at an upper window, tapped upon the pane and then broke a hole through the laths and plaster of the ceiling and was speedily out on the roof. He hurried over the slates like a cat until he reached Ludgate Hill, a street near by, where, tearing off the slates, he made a hole through the ceiling of a bedroom in

which a number of harvestmen were sleeping.

Down through the hole he dropped amongst the astonished men ; before they could collect themselves Horridge darted down the stairs, but on opening the front door, which was reached by four steps from the street, he found two policemen waiting for him. Without a moment's hesitation he jumped right over their heads, and dropping deftly on his feet ran like a hare and got safely away.

Horridge's strength was equalled by his coolness. On one occasion he and a confederate, who was known as "Long Dick," were seen by a policeman through the shutter of a fancy goods shop, which had a small window in it to permit the police on the beat to look into the interior. Both men were wearing aprons, and whilst one reached parcels down from the shelves, the other carefully examined them. When he saw the policeman Horridge called out, "It's all right, guvnor, we're taking stock." The policeman was completely deceived, and went round to the back of the house to see if all was safe. Horridge here made a mistake. Thinking the policeman had gone round to enter the house in order to arrest them, he rushed into a passage by the side of the shop, knocked the policeman down, and quickly made his escape. "Long Dick" followed him, but was caught by other constables and ultimately received five years' penal servitude. Another attempt was made to secure Horridge in his lodgings, but whilst the police were on the staircase he made his way through the ceiling into the space between the rafters and the roof, and running along dropped into another house, and then made his escape a second time.

Horridge's next exploit showed not only cunning and daring but keen observation. He learned that on Friday night a good deal of money was kept in a mill at Bradford near Manchester, for the payment of Saturday wages. He also noticed that the night watchman left the office each morning at half-past four, going to the boiler house to get up steam, and that on Saturday mornings he locked the office door and took the key with him. Horridge procured a false key for the office door. But his plan on the Saturday morning, when he carried it into execution, was nearly frustrated by the watchman leaving the office rather later than usual. Horridge, with three confederates, drove in his cart to the mill, and when the watchman left the office he at once saw them. Immediately Horridge and one of the men pretended to fight. The others made an elaborate pretence of trying to hold them back. The unsuspecting watchman joined them in their peace-making efforts, and finally the two supposed fighters were reconciled and apparently parted the best of friends, the watchman going on his way to the boiler-house.

On his return to the office he found the door open and that the safe, which contained some six hundred pounds in gold and silver, and weighed over four hundredweights, had been carried bodily away. This daring and cleverly executed robbery caused a great sensation in Manchester. There was no clue of any sort to the thieves, and it says much for the brilliant detective powers of the city police that the perpetrators of the robbery were discovered ; but although the safe itself was found at the bottom of a reservoir at the back of Horridge's workshop, the crime could not be brought home to them because neither the watchman, nor two or three other people, who had seen them near the mill, could identify them.

In 1880 Horridge was "lagged" once more, falling readily into a trap laid for him by the police after he had made one

of his characteristically dashing escapes. A policeman on his rounds found a warehouse door in Redfern Street insecurely fastened. Whilst he was trying it the door suddenly opened and Horridge rushed out. He knocked the policeman down and made off at full speed. The constable was happily uninjured, and quickly rising to his feet, shouted " Stop thief! " with all his strength. One of his comrades heard his shout and rushed directly at Horridge who promptly knocked him down also, as well as a civilian who attempted to stop his passage. With the fleetness of a hare Horridge bounded down the steps that then formed an approach to Victoria Station, and jumping over the parapet went straight into the noisome waters of the Irk. To get into the tunnel running beneath the Grammar School, Walker's Croft and Hunt's Bank was comparatively easy work. He took to the land again in Moreton Street, Strangeways.

A few days later he was at work again as if nothing had happened, but the police were determined to catch him, and Mr. Caminada, who was for so long the noted chief detective inspector of the Manchester police, tells us how they achieved their object by a very simple ruse. An inspector, he says, went to Horridge's smithy, and looking through the window said to him, " Well, Bob, how are you? shall you be busy to-night? " " No," was the reply. Then said the inspector, " I should like to see you at the Prince's Feathers at seven o'clock if it is convenient." Horridge kept the appointment, and was then asked to accompany two police officers to the Detective Office. He was identified as the assailant of the two policemen and the civilian, and received a sentence of seven years' penal servitude.

But he had been in prison only a very short time when he tried to arrange a general escape of the convicts. Only two responded to his signal, and these, when called upon to surrender by the guard, threw up their hands. Horridge was wounded three times by the shots of the guards before he gave up running. He was liberated in April 1887.

Seven months later he was standing his trial for robbery and attempted murder. Whilst robbing a shop in Rochdale Road he was surprised by the policemen on the beat. Saying he would not be taken alive, Horridge unbolted the back door, and finding himself face to face with a constable fired a revolver straight at his head, happily only wounding him in the neck. Before the man could recover from the shock Horridge was in full flight. Another policeman tried to stop him and received a bullet in the chest for his pains. Mr. Caminada traced Horridge to Liverpool by following his wife, and there, whilst he and his fellow detectives were disguised, they came upon their man in the street. Seizing him by the arms, Mr. Caminada and one of his colleagues began to drag him to the nearest police station. Horridge made the most desperate efforts to free himself and to get at his hip pocket, all the time protesting that he had no arms. Mr. Caminada very wisely struck him on the head with the butt of a revolver, otherwise both he and his companion might have lost their lives, for Horridge was a man of great strength, and when he was searched a fully loaded six-chambered revolver was found in his trousers pocket. The outcome of this robbery and the shooting of the two policemen was that Horridge was sent to penal servitude for life, and, as Mr. Caminada says, " the public had the pleasure of knowing that the career of one of the most accomplished and desperate thieves that ever lived in Manchester was brought to an end."

ECCLES CHURCH

IT will come as a surprise to all the lovers of Eccles cakes—whose name is legion far beyond the borders of Lancashire—that no town or village of Eccles really exists. There is a parish of Eccles, but the place itself, which for centuries has passed by that name, is really Barton-upon-Irwell. In the beginning of things Eccles was a district, so called from the Latin word *Ecclesia*, meaning church. Tradition fixes the foundation of the church, that gave the name to the scattered dwellings which gradually sprang up in its immediate vicinity, as A.D. 1111; but this date is purely conjectural. However, we know that it was in existence in the year 1192, for there is a deed which shows that the lady of the manor, Edith de Barton and Robert de Gresley gave a moiety of the church of Eccles, with two closes of land and two pastures, to Geoffrey de Byron, the clerk or parson. This Lady Edith married a Yorkshire knight, and her grandson sold the advowson of Eccles to John de Lacy, Constable of Chester and Baron of Halton, who was killed before the walls of Tyre in Syria in the Crusade led by King Richard Cœur de Lion. This John de Lacy [1] gave the advowson of Eccles to the abbot and monks of Stanlaw, who, at a later date exchanged their dreary monastery on the marshy banks of the Mersey for a more pleasant and fertile site on the banks of the Calder at Whalley. Thus the abbots of Whalley became rectors of Eccles, and, in order to store the tithes of corn they received from the parish, they built granges and tithe-barns. One of these was at Monton, which is believed to be a corruption of Monkstown; another was on the site of an old house near the church, which is still called Monk's Hall. During some four hundred years the advowson of Eccles belonged to the Abbey of Whalley, and when the last abbot was hanged by Henry VIII., in 1537, it passed, together with all the other property of the abbey, into the possession of the Crown. Monk's Hall was sold, and in the latter part of the reign of Queen Elizabeth was owned by Ellis Hey. His son, of the same name, was so staunch a Royalist that in order to avoid the forfeiture of Monk's Hall and his estate, he was obliged to compound with the Parliament by paying three hundred and ninety pounds.

Amongst the many monuments in the ancient church is one which, in the light of later history, possesses an especial romance. The effigy of a knight in full armour lies recumbent upon an altar tomb, with his wife in Elizabethan dress beside him. Round the edge of the tomb runs a Latin inscription, of which this is the translation—

"Here lie the bodies of Richard Brearton de Tatton and Worsley Esqre, and of Dorothy, his wife, daughter of Richard Eggerton de Ridley, knight: and Richard, their son; which Richard died 17th December 1598, and the said Dorothy died 4th April 1639. And the said Richard, their son, who was an infant, died in 1575. And the said Dorothy caused this Monument to be made in 1600."

This inscription actually tells us the beginning of the Egerton family, more particularly that phrase: "And the said Richard their son, who was an infant, died in 1575." This was the only child of Richard Brereton of Worsley and his wife Dorothy, and when he died twenty-three years later he left all his property

[1] The story of John de Lacy's two sons is told in "The Leper's Inheritance."

to the "said Dorothy's" half-brother, Thomas Egerton (the illegitimate son of her father Sir Richard Egerton), who became Lord High Chancellor of England. From Thomas Egerton descended in a direct line the Dukes of Bridgewater.[1] It is not unreasonable to presume that but for the death of the infant Richard Brereton, in 1575, Lancashire would not possess the industrial history which is one of her glories to-day. Had this infant lived to succeed his father, Francis Egerton, the third and last Duke of Bridgewater, would have had no Lancashire property upon which to make his famous canal; and to the Bridgewater Canal Lancashire owed her first step towards her supremacy in the worlds of industry and manufacture. So, it is not an exaggeration to say that the prosperity and the livelihood of millions may be traced to those Latin words on the Brereton tomb in Eccles Church: "And the said Richard, their son, who was an infant, died in 1575." The passing of that little life set gigantic forces in motion two hundred years later.

A curious and somewhat unseemly custom used to be observed at weddings in Eccles Church, of which the following account was written early in the nineteenth century—

"The following ancient custom formerly existed at Eccles Parish Church. When a marriage took place at the Church, on the parties leaving the church, the schoolmaster sent a boy or two to demand a small sum of money from the new-married couple. If they refused to give anything, he then sent more of his boys to insist upon something being given, or, if they still refused, to take the bride's

garter. The custom having become very obnoxious, the churchwardens abolished it about the beginning of the present century, and in lieu of it directed fourpence for every marriage to be paid to the schoolmaster of Eccles and double dues in Lent. These sums be now received."

The marriage fees to the schoolmaster were, however, abolished at a later date.

By the old custom of letting leases for lives, and not upon terms of years, the holders of glebe-lands at Eccles were sorely put upon. They held their land upon the life of the vicar, which meant that upon the death of the incumbent a new lease had to be made out on the life of his successor; and each new lease entailed the payment of a fee. Amongst the papers belonging to Eccles Church is a petition from the tenant of a small holding on the glebe, George Bridge by name, to the "well-disposed people" in the neighbourhood, which clearly shows the evil and injustice of the system. In the space of five years three vicars of Eccles died, and the unfortunate Bridge had been obliged to pay the fine for the renewal of his lease for each life. His petition bears the signatures of the then curate and churchwardens of Eccles, as well as those of many clergymen in the neighbourhood.

In common with many other places during the eighteenth century, Eccles suffered from the appointment of non-resident vicars. One of these was Thomas Vaughan, who already had a living near Lichfield, where he lived. His only concern with his living at Eccles seems to have been more financial than spiritual. The parish clerk acted as his agent, and there is something ghoulish in a letter from this vicar, written during a bad epidemic at Eccles: "I suppose the sur-

[1] The story is told in "The Duke of Bridgewater."

41

plice fees rise very highly this sickly time. Take care they do not cheat me nor the country. I must depend on you as my agent."

This fee-seeking gentleman was succeeded by another non-resident vicar, Benjamin Nicholls, who was so ardent a politician that he had no time to spare for his spiritual duties. But he, like his predecessor, had a keen eye to business, for, not satisfied with the revenues of the

gregation, in fiery and most un-Christian words, that they should go and hunt out Barlow, "that noted Popish priest." This proposition, made in a sacred building—and on the day of a most solemn Festival, the Day of Peace—met with an eager response, and the congregation, "being about four hundred in number, armed with clubs and swords, followed the parson marching in front to the house where Barlow, having finished Mass, was making an exhortation to his people,

MONK'S HALL, ECCLES

benefice, he let out the churchyard for grazing, and cut down the trees growing in it, deliberately pocketing the proceeds.

His "behaviour vexed the parishioners," we are told, to such a degree that the churchwardens took legal opinion as to his rights in the matter, but there is no record of the end of the dispute.

An earlier vicar in the time of the first King Charles, one John Jones, a Presbyterian, was noted for his hatred of Roman Catholics. On entering the church on Easter Sunday in ·1641, he heard that Father Barlow, a Roman Catholic priest, was hiding at Morley's Hall, the house of the Tyldesleys. Instead of proceeding with the service he proposed to his con-

about a hundred in number, on the subject of patience. The mob rushed in, crying out: 'Where is Barlow? Where is Barlow? He is the man we want!' And laying hands upon him they secured him, letting the rest go upon giving caution for their appearance. The same day Barlow was carried before a Justice of the Peace, who sent him guarded by sixteen armed men to Lancaster, where he was tried, convicted, and executed September 10th."

In strong contrast to this bigot and the indifferent non-residents was Thomas Blackburne, who was vicar of Eccles from 1818 to 1836. It was to Eccles Vicarage that Huskisson was taken after his fatal

42

injuries at the opening of the Liverpool and Manchester Railway in 1830. The following letter, written to her sister by the mother of the late Dean Stanley, gives a pleasing picture not only of the good vicar and his wife but also of their parishioners—

"There is one person here who interests me very much—Mrs. Tom Blackburne, the vicaress of Eccles, who received poor Mr. Huskisson, and

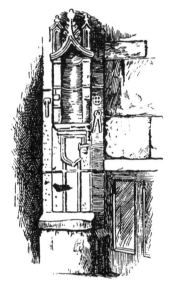

A PILLAR IN ECCLES CHURCH

immortalized herself by her activity, sense, and conduct all through. She made one ashamed of the ease and idleness of one's own life, compared with hers. They have to deal with such a population—twenty-five thousand souls. She has been the ruling spirit evidently, and under her guidance and the help of a sound head and heart, her husband has become the very man for the place with quickness and presence of mind for any emergency ; and she describes the people—all Manches-

ter weavers—as grateful and sensitive, far beyond our agricultural experience. He is in general at home to parishioners from eight to twelve, and from four to six every day, and often fully occupied all the time ; but during the four days Mr. Huskisson was in the house none of them entered the gates. She asked afterwards why it was, and one of them said, ' Eh, we knowed what you were at, and so we did without.'"

The churchyard presents an unusual appearance—as if it were paved with large stones. These are the old gravestones, which many years ago, when the churchyard was enlarged, were laid flat without much regard whether the lettering or the blank side came uppermost. One of these, to the memory of Jane, wife of John Holden ran thus—

Here lies Jone's wife Jane,
As it is very plain ;
And after will come Jone,
As sure as this is a stone."

Another epitaph announced that Dennis Macbride, the son of Dennis and Ann Macbride, "died June thirty-first."

Joseph Andrew who died in 1793, after being sexton of Eccles Church for over thirty years, was given this lugubrious inscription—

" Beneath this stone lie the cold remains
Of those whose hands have by unwearied pains
The graves of thousands made within this yard.
Now theirs are ready, for Death hath no regard
To man or calling, or one should have thought
He would have spared them, but he could not do ;
For in a moment, when at ease and well,
He brought the summons with this awful knell—

' PREPARE TO MEET THY GOD.' "

THE OLD MARKET CROSS AT MANCHESTER

IN the olden days the granting of a charter to hold a market, marked the creation of a village into a town, making the place to which the fathers. It was here that they did all their shopping, tradesmen having booths or stalls; and whilst they bought or sold they heard all the news and gossip of

THE OLD MARKET CROSS, MANCHESTER

privilege had been given a centre for all the surrounding villages and hamlets. Thus the market-place played a very important part in the lives of our fore-the neighbourhood. And, as the market-place was the centre of town life, so the Market Cross was the centre of the market-place. The town beadle, or catchpole, standing on its steps announced the opening of the market by ringing a bell. From the same place he made public announcements, such as the decisions of the magistrates or of the court leet, in the cases of petty crimes, before the offenders were placed in the neighbouring stocks or pillory. In short, all that is now done by printed announcements in local newspapers, or by official bills pasted upon the walls, was then cried out by the parish beadle at various points in the town, but always beginning first at the Market Cross.

Before the days of the Reformation market crosses of wood or stone were erected in every market-place in the country with a double object. One was that the faithful might pray there for the repose of the souls of the dead and the welfare of the living; the other was that the presence of the sacred symbol would prevent any cheating on the part of buyers or sellers in the market-place.

In old Manchester, close by the cross, stood the pillory, the public whipping-post and the stocks. Mounting the steps of the cross the town beadle would describe the offence of some rogue or vagabond, who then, stripped to the waist, would be tied to the whipping-post and receive his punishment. Drunk and disorderly persons were placed in the stocks, where they sat upon a narrow bench, their hands and feet securely fastened through a board in front of them.

The pillory was reserved for more serious offences. Standing upon a small platform with his head and his arms securely fastened in a large board, the baker who was found guilty of selling short weight, the butcher who had attempted to sell bad meat, the ale-house keeper who had "doctored" his beer, and other fraudulent tradesmen, were practically handed over to the resentment of those whom they had victimized. It was a rough-and-ready way of dispensing justice, and the crowd, not content with merely jeering at the unhappy occupant of the pillory, would pelt him with rotten eggs, decaying fish and vegetables; in fact, with anything that came handy provided it was something unpleasant. To pelt a man in the pillory, or some notorious offender in the stocks, added great zest to the amusements of market day.

The market days in old Manchester were on Saturday and Monday. Gradually permanent shops were opened all round the market-place, these being occupied by the better class of tradesmen, who in the old documents are all called merchants. They were drapers, grocers, clothiers and saddlers. At the open stalls the country people sold poultry and vegetables, etc. The butchers and fishmongers also had open stalls. On Saturday the good housewives of Manchester carrying a large basket, or if they were sufficiently well off to keep a servant, having it carried behind them, resorted to the market-place to buy the necessary provisions for the Sabbath. On the following Monday they would once more resort to the market, but this time with a larger basket, for on that day it was essential to lay in provisions for the whole of the week; many of them did not leave their houses between the Monday and the Saturday, except perhaps to go to church. These two days, therefore, were the gala days of the week, when they heard all the news and the gossip of their neighbours, and perhaps enjoyed the spectacle of seeing some baker or grocer who had sold them short weight in their bread, or their " spices," being vigorously pelted in the pillory.

Great care was taken to prevent any adulteration, or the sale of bad food:

thus, there were market "lookers" who carefully examined all the corn, flesh and fish offered for sale. There were "ale founders," "tasters" and "conners," who had the right to enter any of the ale-houses and taste the ale to see that it was or suet was used for the making of bread or cakes.

The conduit which supplied the town with water was also in the market-place, in a small building near the pillory. The water came from a spring near the top of

O yes! O yes! O yes!

SIR OSWALD MOSLEY, Bart. Lord of this Manor of *Manchester*, in His Majesty's Name, strictly charges and commands all manner of Persons not to wear any Swords, Staves, Knives, Falchions, or any other unlawful Weapons but that they, and every of them, be aiding and assisting to the Boroughreeve and Constables, and all other Officers. in suppressing all Routs, Riots, Tumults, and other unlawful Assemblies. during the time in which this Fair hath it's continuance on pain of the Penalties set down by the Statutes in such case made and provided.

God save the King,

Sir Oswald Mosley, Bart. the Stewards, the Boroughreeve and Constables of this most ancient Town and Borough of *Manchester.*

God save the King!

J. Patrick, Printer.

A PRINTED NOTICE CALLED BY THE BELLMAN

ot good quality. One curious law concerning ale-houses was that when a barrel of ale was on tap, a hand had to be placed outside the door. There were also "bread-lookers," whose duty it was to see that the loaves were the required size, quality and price, and that no butter Market-stead Lane, running down that street in a fair-sized stream. Special officers were appointed to see that the conduit was not polluted by people washing the entrails of beasts in the trough in the market-place, and many notices regarding the water-supply of the town were read out by the beadles from the Market Cross. Thus in 1579 there would appear to have been either a shortage of water or an increased use on the part of the inhabitants, for this notice was read out from the Cross——

" No person hereafter shall bring to the conduit any kind of vessel of greater value [*i. e.* capacity] than one woman is able to bear full of water, and but one of every house at one time,

and to have their cale [turn] as hath been accustomed, William Radcliffe, gentleman, only excepted."

The penalty for the breaking of this order was five shillings, a large sum of money in those days. A few years later it was ordered that the conduit should remain unlocked during the summer months from six in the morning until nine at night; and from six in the morning until six at night in the winter.

SUBMISSION.

Whereas, I the undersigned *Patrick M' Ginnis* having committed a most unjustifiable assault upon *James Howarth, Toll Collector,* to *Sir Oswald Mosely, Bart.* when in the discharge of his duty, for which, he has very properly threatened me with a prosecution.

And, whereas, the said *James Howarth,* hath consented to stay all proceedings against me on my making this *Public Submission,* and paying all expences.

Now I do hereby thank the said James Howarth, for his lenity, and do publicly declare my Contrition for the said Offence.

And I authorize the said James Howarth, to Publish this my Submission in such way as he shall think proper. As witness my hand this 5th Day of August, 1829.

HIS

Witness Patrick ✗ *M' Ginnis.*

WITNESS, D. M' GILLVERY.   MARK

Manchester: Printed by M. WITHINGTON, Smithfield Market.

A PRINTED APOLOGY, WHICH IN FORMER DAYS WOULD HAVE BEEN READ BY THE BELLMAN AT THE MARKET CROSS

A GIRL at a tea given by some ladies to the working girls' club of which she was a member, was pressed to take some jam with her bread and butter.

" No, thank yo," she replied. " Aw works wheer they maks it ! "

AN EXPERIMENT THAT FAILED

IT was in 1740 that Peter Boehler, one of the disciples of Count Zinzendorf, the founder of the sect of Moravians, established that faith in England under the title of the Congregation of the United Brethren. Fifteen years later a settlement was made in Lancashire at Dukinfield, but " it soon became apparent that it was not the will of the Lord," says one of their writers, " to carry out there the idea of forming a Moravian village according to the original platform of the Brethren's constitution; but rather to form a gathering-place preparatory to the accomplishment of His purpose elsewhere. The members understood all along they were only in a state of probation." For twenty-nine years, the members of the little sect waited patiently before they could found a permanent settlement, where those who wished to do so could lead a celibate life. In 1784 the foundation-stone of Fairfield was laid, the little community spending six thousand pounds upon its building, although some of the members built their own houses. The chief feature of the settlement was the chapel, and the plan upon which it was made was not unlike those of the garden cities of to-day. Its members lived upon a communal system which was directed by the elders of the Church; and for those who wished to be celibate there was a " Single Brethren's House," and a " Single Sisters' House "; those who lived in these two houses formed a mixed choir for the religious services.

Dr. Aikin, the delightful chronicler of Manchester and its neighbourhood, gives us a clear picture of the appearance of the settlement and the occupations of its inhabitants. " Fairfield," he says, " is a new settlement belonging to the Moravians, near four miles from Manchester and within two fields of the Ashton turnpike road. Though established within these ten years, it has the appearance of a little town. There is a large and commodious Chapel with an excellent organ. The ground plot is laid out with great taste and judgment; it forms a large square. The Chapel, and some large dwelling-houses, well built of brick, form the front. On each side of the Chapel are two deep rows of dwelling-houses; on the back front, behind the chapel, is a row of elegant large houses. These with the chapel form a large square mass of buildings round which is another row of excellent buildings which surrounds the whole, except the front, at a short distance from which is a fine row of kitchen gardens, and, opposite the chapel a large burying-ground, the whole divided and surrounded by quickset hedges. . . . The cotton manufactory forms a principal part of the employment of its inhabitants, including spinning, weaving, etc. Tambour and fine needlework is carried to a great pitch of perfection, and is chiefly sent to London; there are also in the settlement, tailors, shoemakers, bakers, and a sale shop for most articles."

The settlement was self-supporting, but a few years afterwards it was recorded, " As a settlement or Moravian village Fairfield has ceased to exist. The founders were well-intentioned and good results were not wanting, but the idea was neither consistent with human nature nor with human progress. The majority of those who now live in the place do not belong to the Moravian body."

One of the rules of the Moravians was that they should live in communities, the idea being taken from the first settlement of the sect at Hernhut in Saxony on the property of Count Zinzendorf. One of the Moravian Brothers, a carpenter called Christian David, related to the Count the persecutions to which he and his co-religionists were subjected by the Austrian Government, whereupon Zinzendorf offered him a house and some land on his estate, where he and as many of his friends who preferred " liberty of conscience under a foreign sky to religious oppression in their native country," could establish themselves. Three men, two women and five children were the first members of the community of Hernhut, and they were so miserably poor that the Countess Zinzendorf was obliged to give them clothes, and a cow to provide milk for the children. The Count then invited other Moravians to join the community, of which he became the head. By his many pamphlets, and his active proselytising in Northern Europe he attracted considerable attention to the community of Hernhut. On one of his visits to England (1749), through the influence of Archbishop Potter, General Oglethorpe and other influential persons, he succeeded in getting a Bill passed by Parliament permitting the establishment of Moravian colonies in the British possessions in North America. His teaching was a curious blend of Lutheranism and mysticism, but it never took a very firm hold in Lancashire.

TRIPPET

THIS ancient game, which was very popular in East Lancashire some seventy years ago, is still played by colliers in the district. The game is not unlike that of tipcat, which is played at Burnley. A smooth boulder, with a gently sloping side, is chosen by the players, and upon this the " trippet "—a piece of holly-wood about two inches long, and an inch in diameter in the middle, sloping off at either end in a conical shape—is placed, one point overhanging. The player taps the end of the " trippet " with a long, flexible, heavy-headed club, and as it rises he strikes it with all his force. The one who can send the " trippet " the greatest distance in a certain number of strokes, wins the game.

SADDLE=MAKER AND ANTIQUARIAN

THE man who combines the making of saddles and harness with a profound interest in the history of his native city and its surroundings, is not usually met with. But such was Thomas Barritt, a saddler who had his shop on Shudehill. Born in Manchester in 1743, Barritt from his earliest years exhibited the keenest interest in anything appertaining to the antiquities of his native city and its neighbourhood, and made a collection of relics which was dispersed at 'his death in 1820. Such a collection offered for sale to-day would command a very high price. Unfortunately there was not the same interest displayed in the history of their country by Lancashire folk as there is to-day, and many treasures of old Lancastrians were sold for a few shillings, which now would fetch treble the same number of pounds. And many of them, alas! have completely disappeared. Happily the bulk of Barritt's manuscripts became the property of the Chetham Library, and are thus preserved for the use of all those who care to dip now and again into the life of their forefathers. One of Barritt's treasures, however, is not at the Chetham Library. Writing in 1883, Mr. William E. A. Axon says that a manuscript volume, consisting of eighteen leaves of parchment, written by Barritt in close imitation of the illuminated books before the era of printing, was then in the possession of Mr. Eastwood of Manchester. "Each leaf," says Mr. Axon, "treats of a separate subject, and is ornamented by a drawing, sometimes executed in colours. The text is written in characters formed like printed black-letter." In some cases there is writing and inscription on the reverse side of the sheets, which can be read through the cloth or paper with which it is backed. On the back of the first leaf are two verses, and below is written, "Composed for my two boys Valentine and Arthur. Thomas Barritt, 1807." One verse ran—

"The Goose, the Calf, the little Bee,
Are great on Earth I prove to thee,
And rule the great affairs of Man,
Explain this riddle if you can."

This riddle is of a venerable age, the answer being that quills, parchment and wax held the world together for many ages. The second verse, if "Saddle-maker" were substituted for "friar gray," would fitly describe Barritt himself—

"Through old worn books I long have por'd,
And what old people say
I faithfully relate again,
Although a friar gray."

Thomas Barritt did his county a good service in preserving many of her old legends, ballads and traditions.

A MAN called Eccles was very mean, and for that reason, and others, was by no means popular with his old coachman. One day Eccles was expatiating on his own good qualities. "John," he said to the coachman, "John, there are two sorts of Eccleses: there's Eccleses that are angels, and Eccleses that are divils."

"Ay, maister," replied John, "an' the angels ha' been deed for mony a yer!"

ASHTON AND THE SABBATH

S UNDAY observance was rigidly enforced at Ashton-within-Maker-field during the year of the Battle of Waterloo by the inhabitants them- mention the Sabbath, raises the question, were the "day labourers," "every other person under the Degree of a gentleman," and "every person of, or above, the

Ashton within Mackerfield.

MARCH 28th, 1815.

From a Sense of Public Order, and a Regard for the Observance of the Sabbath, the INHABITANTS of ASHTON, at a *Vestry Meeting* assembled, are determined to enforce the following REGULATIONS.

ABSTRACT OF LAWS
AGAINST THE
PROFANATION
OF THE
SABBATH.

NO Person, without reasonable Excuse, shall be absent from some Place of Divine Worship on a Sunday Penalty, *One Shilling*

No Person shall work, or exercise his ordinary Calling, on the Lord's Day Penalty, *Five Shillings*; and for Default, Stocks two Hours.

No Drover, Horse Courser, Waggoner, Butcher, Higgler, or their Servants, shall travel on a Sunday. Penalty, *Twenty Shillings*, and for Default, Stocks two Hours.

No Fruit, Herbs, or Goods of any Kind, shall be carried, or exposed to Sale on a Sunday. Penalty, *Forfeiture of Goods*

No Person shall kill Game on a Sunday. Penalty, from *Ten Pounds* to *Twenty Pounds*, for the first Offence, *Twenty Pounds* to *Thirty Pounds*, for the second Offence; and *Fifty Pounds*, for the third Offence.

No Person shall profanely curse or swear. Penalty, *One Shilling* to a Day Labourer; *Two Shillings* to every other Person under the Degree of a Gentleman, and *Five Shillings* to every Person of, or above, the Degree of a Gentleman. For a second Offence, double, &c.

Every Person convicted of Drunkenness, shall forfeit *Five Shillings* for the Poor, or be set in the Stocks six Hours.

If an Alehouse-keeper be convicted of Drunkenness, he shall forfeit *Five Shillings*, and be deprived of his Licence for three Years.

If any Person, except Travellers, be found tippling in any Alehouse, on the Lord's Day, between the Hours of Ten and Twelve, in the Forenoon, and Three and Five, in the Afternoon, he shall forfeit *Three Shillings and Four-pence*, or be set in the Stocks four Hours. And the Alehouse-keeper, who shall suffer such tippling in his House, shall forfeit *Ten Shillings*, and be deprived of his Licence for three Years.

No Person shall exercise any unlawful Sports, or Play, on Pain of forfeiting *Three Shillings and Four-pence*, or of being set in the Stocks three Hours

If a Constable neglects his Duty, he forfeits FORTY SHILLINGS

RULES AND ORDERS.

ALL Public-Houses are to be cleared from Company, and shut up, when the Chapel Bell tolls, at Half past Nine o'Clock, on Sunday Nights, and, at Half past Ten o'Clock, on all other Nights in the Week

These Regulations shall be printed, and a Copy shall be delivered to each Publican, and shall be pasted up in a conspicuous Place within each Public-House

O LYON PRINTER, MARKET PLACE WIGAN

selves, their sentiments upon the matter, being voiced at a Vestry Meeting. In these days this "Abstract of Laws" would be called tyranny. The rule as to swearing, since it does not specifically Degree of a gentleman" fined upon week-days as well, the one, two or five shillings, and double for a second offence, or upon Sundays only? The thirty-five men who signed the "above Resolutions," in the following year must have been fully occupied with enforcing this one rule alone, for swearing was then a habit common to all classes.

Printed upon the back of these rules for the keeping of the Sabbath is the following—

"Knowing that Social Order produces Social Happiness and that Intemperance and Irregularity make Servants dishonest, Families poor, and Men wicked, we the undersigned, being Inhabitants of Ashton-within-Makerfield, and desirous to establish and preserve moral Order in our Township have made the following resolutions—

"I. As far as we are able, we will set an Example of Sobriety and Regularity in our Conduct.

"II. We will be no Respecters of Persons; but, among all Men we will endeavour to restrain Evil and to encourage Virtue.

"III. In the Discharge of our Duty we will endeavour to unite Firmness and Moderation.

"IV. We will inspect all the Public-houses of our Township every week on Saturday, Sunday, and Monday evenings; and will record the State in which we find them, in a Book, which shall be laid, every Licensing Day, before the Magistrates.

"V. We will divide ourselves into Parties and will attend in Rotation every month.

"VI. In the succession of Parties each person in his District shall give notice to his Successor.

"VII. If any Person neglect his Duty, or be absent without appointing a Deputy, snch person shall forfeit Sixpence, for every such Offence.

"VIII. These Fines shall be distributed by Vote annually for the Relief of the industrious Poor of our Township.

"In the Presence of God, and of each other, we do solemnly promise and engage, faithfully and strictly to observe, as far as we are able the above Resolutions, as witness our Hands and Seals, the first day of September 1816."

Then follow thirty-five names, fifteen of which are those of inhabitants in Ashton-within-Makerfield, the remaining twenty being in Senely Green, Park Lane, and Edge Green.

Rule I. is not without humour. The thirty-five were evidently conscious that they too were human, hence the saving clause " as far as we are able " to their promised " Example of Sobriety and Regularity " in their own conduct.

ECCLES CAKES, WAKES AND GUISINGS

THE origin of Eccles Cakes is lost in the dim mists of time, but it is believed that in the beginning they had a religious significance similar to that of the shewbread placed upon the altar of the Temple by the Hebrews. When the Puritans under the Common- although he was a veritable kill-joy to his unfortunate parishioners, he does not appear to have deprived them of their local cakes, which were already famous. They were sold at most of the wakes and fairs throughout Lancashire and Cheshire.

A fierce controversy has raged, as to

ECCLES CAKE SHOP

wealth forbade dancing upon the village green, the maypole, and all the public festivities of the people, the eating of cakes on special days likewise came under their ban. They believed the custom perpetuated some forgotten religious observance, or at least was merely superstitious. Eccles, as we know, had an uncompromising and militant Puritan parson in the Rev. John Jones, but which was the "original shop" from which Eccles Cakes were first sent out. Two shops lay claim to the distinction. One set forth, "William Procter, late Birch & Co., original Eccles Cake-makers, removed from above." This removal took place somewhere about 1796. The other set forth, "Bradburn's. The Only Old Original Eccles Cake Shop. Never Removed. On the site of these Premises

Eccles Cakes were First Made. Rebuilt 1835," which may be taken as a defiance to the sign of the shop which was "removed from above."

But, wherever the claim may justly lie, both shops maintained the fame of the local dainty, and no wake, gyst-ale (or guisings as they were called) or fair was complete without it.

And Eccles was no less famous for its wakes. They began on the first Sunday in September, and continued during the next three days with every variety of country sports and amusements, not to mention an inordinate amount of eating and drinking. People flocked in hundreds from the surrounding neighbourhood, and this is the description given by a visitor in the year 1835:—

" We found the place encumbered with carriages of all descriptions, and crowded with persons of every age and many conditions in life. The public-houses were full, and in these, according to the Lancashire custom, women sat mingled with the men, performing their full share in smoking and brawling, if not in drinking. Songs, in which the vulgarity of the sentiment was equalled by the harsh dissonance of the voices, were heard on every side. One of these ditties, squeaked by a limping ballad-monger, which I had the curiosity to purchase, was entitled, 'The Humours of Eccles Wakes,' and ran as follows—

' In August last, being holiday time,
And being myself a young man in my prime,
To see Eccles Wakes it was my intent,
So I dressed in my best and away I went.

Chorus (twice).
With Ned and a few men
And Robin the ploughman,
And Sally, and Alley, and Mall.

Each lad took his lass as we passed along,
And when we came there it was a wonderful throng;
There were some crying " Eccles," some " Banbury Cakes,"
For the lasses and lads that attended the wakes.

Chorus.
So Ned treated Sally,
And Bob treated Alley,
And I bought a Banb'ry for Mall.

Yon fine dressy work-folk from Manchester town,
They strutted as if the whole wakes were their own;
Putters-out, warpers, yea, cutters and all,
Dress'd like masters and dames, jeered both me and my Mall.

Chorus.
I ne'er saw their fellows,
They spread their umbrellas
Ere rain from the elements fall.

The Ballart ere long tied the bull to the stake,
The dogs were set at him some pastime to make;
He jostled about, gave a terrible roar,
Tossed the dogs in the air, and the folk tumbled o'er.

Chorus.
Such squeaking and squalling,
Such pulling and hauling,
I ne'er in my life saw before.

Mrs. Race [1] in the dirt spoiled her mousseline gown,
Mrs. Warpingwell had her new petticoat torn;
Their spouses, poor creatures, in quitting the mob
Had their coats torn to spensers, robb'd Stitch of a job.

Chorus.
Rent aprons and shawls,
Which they got in their falls,
Made many poor wenches to sob.

But stop, my good folks, the fun ended not here,
For a Banbury merchant attending the rear,
Crying, " Buy now, or toss," which the bull chanced to spy,
Gave his basket a toss, for he chose not to buy.

---

[1] Race is a term in fustian cutting.

Chorus.

I thought to the wakes,
There were coming with cakes
Confectioners down from the sky.

Next followed the race for a leathern prize;
Tits entered the field amid bustle and
noise;
"Now, Bobbin!" "Now, Short!" "Now
Ball!" was the cry.
But Bobbin beat Short, and Ball pass'd
them both by.

Chorus.

Disputing which won,
Soon to fighting they ran,
And the winner came off with black
eyes.

When racing and fighting were all at an
end,
To an alehouse each went with a sweetheart
or friend;
Some went to Shaw's, other's Phillips's
chose,
But me and my Mall to the "Hare and
Hounds" goes.

Chorus.

With music and cakes
For to keep up the wakes,
Among wenches and fine country
beaux.

There were 'dressy work-folk from Manchester' at the Eccles Wakes on this
occasion, but the majority were from the
neighbouring villages and hamlets, many
of the girls with white frocks, blue stockings and clogs; while the young men
wore, for the most part, velveteen jackets
and scarlet waistcoats, adorned with pearl
buttons and other elegancies to match.
Horse-racing appeared to be a prime
element in the amusements of the day;
and on the course we found a somewhat
superior order of persons on foot and on
horseback, engaged as onlookers, or in
betting on favourite horses. Gambling,
indeed, may be said to be the grand
business of the Eccles Wakes."

An old woman, called Nelly Wood,
who was born in 1792, and lived far
beyond the allotted span, had the clearest
recollection of the Eccles Wakes of her
youth, when she used to run in the races
and won many a sixpence. There used
to be, she said, rough doings, in which
the women fought like "good uns." The
bull-baiting used to take place in a spot
near the present Town Hall, and near
the same place were the stocks. The old
woman remembered having seen men
fixed in them, "their faces black with
passion, and swearing fearfully," whilst
the jeering crowd pelted them with
rotten eggs, mud, and any offal on which
hands could be laid. In those days, she
said, people lived on barley-bread, jan-
nocks and oat-cakes, which accounts for
the Eccles Cakes being considered so
great a luxury.

Eccles had another annual festival
which ran the wakes very close in point
of popularity. This was the gyst-ale or
guising. It generally took place at the
end of the marling season, the men who
took part in it being chiefly those who
had been engaged in marling and manur-
ing the land. A King was chosen and,
gaily dressed, and carrying garlands, the
guisers set forth in a long procession.
At the head a principal garland was
carried, from which hung silver vessels of
every variety, lent by the gentry in the
neighbourhood. Each village strove to
outdo its neighbour in variety of dress and
splendour of the decorated garlands, and
a particularly sharp rivalry arose between
Eccles and Barton, an amusing account
of which is given in a rare pamphlet,
printed in 1778, called "The History of
Eccles and Barton's Contentious Guising
War." The author states that the guising procession at Eccles was originated
by Mr. Charlton, of Monk's Hall, giving
money to some labourers for a "marling
feast," and some neighbours of Barton
township carrying a garland and 3*s.* 6*d.*

in money to the marlpit. This started the spirit of rivalry, and the people of Eccles replied by making a larger garland and a subscription of 4s. 6d. Barton's

Mr. Harland remarks, these were separate amounts, the total amount raised would have been £2,929. But this is scarcely credible, and it is more probable that

REMAINS OF THE OLD CROSS, ECCLES

answer was a subscription of £5. Eccles then raised £15, whereupon Barton produced £37. Then Eccles completely overwhelmed its rival with £347, only to be beaten by Barton's retort of £644. But the victory finally lay with Eccles, which collected £1,881. If, as the £644 of Barton and the £1,881 of Eccles were the total amounts collected in the two places during the struggle for supremacy. The pamphlet gives an account of the Eccles guising on July 14, 1777, when a hundred men and women, with pikes and swords, some dressed as

Robin Hood and Little John, and others as Adam and Eve, "in a single horse-chair, with an orange-tree fixed before them, and oranges growing thereon," proceeded to Barton and various parts of the village of Eccles, with drums beating, trumpets sounding, music playing, and about sixteen couples of morris dancers.

On September 24, Barton made a guising procession of a far superior kind. Two hundred and twenty men and women, with about twenty-one guns, cannon and muskets, which they began to fire as early as five o'clock in the morning, preceded by a bull with bells around his neck, marched through Eccles. This procession had a Queen, who was followed by thirty-four maids of honour; there were several bands of music, twenty couples of morris dancers, banners galore, and a "grand garland drawn by good horses and proper attendance."

In the following month Eccles dealt its crushing blow to Barton. A procession of two hundred and sixteen horsemen and nearly a hundred men on foot, with a Queen who had fifty-six maids of honour, "every one handsomely dressed, and with a watch by her side," could not be bettered, either in numbers or splendour by the humiliated Bartonians. The palm, therefore, lay with Eccles, and the foolish and costly rivalry ceased. In the pamphlet the blame is laid at the door of Barton for having invaded Eccles with guisers: Eccles it says could only defend its own territory; but after reproving both townships for their folly, the author sums up the situation in this philosophical doggerel—

"If Eccles has faults, Barton has the same:
    Wisdom it will be not each other to
    blame."

AN OLD NOTICE OF THEFT

STOLEN,

On Thursday Night or early on Friday Morning, the 18th or 19th September, 1823,

A GREEN-TAIL COW

From a Shop belonging to

Ralph Curwen,

Gun-street, New Cross, Manchester.

Whosoever will give such information as shall lead to the Conviction of the Offender or Offenders, shall be handsomly Rewarded, by applying to the Market Lookers, at the Manor Office, Shudehill New Market, Manchester.

J. Withington, Printer, Manchester.

THE PETERLOO MASSACRE

EARLY in the nineteenth century Manchester took the lead in the agitation for Parliamentary reform which was beginning to spread throughout the country, and one of the most terrible tragedies in the City annals was brought about by the passionate determination of the Manchester workers to change the then existing conditions of Parliamentary representation. On Saturday, July 31, 1819, the Manchester Reformers, wishing to appoint a man called Hunt—known as Orator Hunt—to be "legislatorial attorney for the city," advertised in the *Manchester Observer* that a meeting would take place on August 9th, in the area near St. Peter's Church, and invited their friends and supporters to be present. The magistrates, who had reason to be alarmed owing to the discontent then existing, and the avowedly Republican opinions of some of the bodies sympathising with the Reformers, pronounced this meeting to be illegal, and warned the citizens on their peril to abstain from attending it. The Reformers presented a petition, asking that permission for the meeting might be given, but the magistrates paid no attention to it, whereupon notice was publicly given that the meeting would be held in St. Peter's Field, on Monday, August 16th, with Orator Hunt in the chair.

St. Peter's Field was then a large open space, and the site where sixty thousand people assembled on that August day is now covered by the Free Trade Hall, the Theatre Royal, and Peter Street. The people poured into the city from all the villages and towns round about, and Bamford, in his *History of a Radical*, tells us that by eight o'clock in the morning the whole town of Middleton was on the alert. Even those who would not or could not go to Manchester, he says, came out to see their friends and relations start.

The people, marching five abreast, were headed by twelve young men, two deep, each holding in his hand a bunch of laurel, "as a token of amity and peace." Two silk flags, one blue, the other green, were carried by the Middleton men, bearing these mottoes in gilt letters, "Unity and Strength," "Liberty and Fraternity," "Parliaments Annual," "Suffrage Universal." Between the flags a crimson velvet cap of Liberty was borne upon a pole. The Lees and Saddleworth men had a coal black flag, inscribed with ghastly white letters, "Equal Representation or Death," and above this, "Love," with a heart and two hands joined.

In the middle of St. Peter's Field a rough platform had been made by placing boards across two carts, and around this were placed five banners, two red, two white, and one black. Upon one side of the black banner was a hand holding the scales of justice, with an inscription below, "Taxation without Representation is Unjust and Tyrannical"; on the other side were the words, "Love," "Unite and be Free," "Equal Representation or Death"; and on some of the other banners were, "No Corn Laws," "Let's Die like Men and not be Sold like Slaves."

Meanwhile the greatest anxiety prevailed in Manchester. The shops in Market Street, in Market Place, and elsewhere, were closed, and early in the morning all business was suspended. In the principal streets an immense number of country people were strolling about, but "the more retired parts of the town were silent as death."

The wildest rumours were current, for it was known that a hundred and forty of the Manchester and Salford Yeomanry Cavalry were concealed in Messrs. Pickford's yard, and that the Cheshire Yeomanry and the 1st Dragoon Guards were near the city. In addition to these the magistrates had at their disposal two hundred special constables, and men of the 15th Hussars, the 31st and 88th Foot, and the Horse Artillery. The special constables and the Manchester and Salford Yeomanry were under the direction of the magistrates; the soldiers were under the command of Colonel Guy L'Estrange, of the 31st Regiment.

Such was the general alarm, it being believed that a general attack on property was about to take place, that the magistrates had held continuous meeting since the Saturday morning, listening to petitions and remonstrances against the meeting, and in drawing up a plan of action. After the most anxious discussion it was decided not to prevent the meeting, but to arrest Hunt and the other leaders, "publicly and ignominiously," when the speaking had commenced. The troops were to be held in readiness in case of eventualities. About ten o'clock on the morning of the 16th, three hundred and forty of the 15th Hussars had been marched into the town from their barracks in the suburbs, and stationed in a wide street about a quarter of a mile to the north of St. Peter's Field. The Cheshire Yeomanry were formed up on the left of the same street, whilst the rest of the Hussars and the Artillery were placed between the cavalry barracks and the town. The Manchester and Salford Yeomanry were stationed in a street to the east of the Field. About the same time half the special constables were posted close to the platform in the centre, the other half extending from there in a direct line of communication to a private house on the south side of the Field, to which the magistrates went about eleven o'clock. This house was some three hundred yards from the platform. During the next two hours the Reformers and their friends poured in an unceasing stream into the Field.

An eye-witness, who was clearly not a sympathiser, thus describes Hunt's entry upon the scene: " A few minutes to one o'clock a rolling shout proclaimed the arrival of the great demagogue, and sixty thousand voices shouted welcome to the vain and empty man they delighted to honour. There he was, a handsome, broad-shouldered man, with a restless face. He wore, as usual, his theatrical country squire dress, blue coat and brass buttons, top-boots and impudent white hat, then the badge of the Radical party. He was preceded by a noisy band of music and by flags, while above the crowd rose a board, inscribed ' Order.' There sat in the carriage his allies, Johnson, Moorhouse, Saxon and Swift. Hunt stood up in the barouche, eyeing the enormous multitude with astonishment and satisfaction. On the box sat an Amazon named Mrs. Fildes, bearing the standard of the Manchester Female Reformers, and waving a white handkerchief."

The band struck up " Rule Britannia " and " God Save the King," and it was observed that for the most part the men in the vast crowd took off their hats. Immediately Hunt mounted the platform the music ceased. It was proposed that he should take the chair, and the motion being seconded, it was carried by acclamation. A dead silence ensued, and the Orator advancing to the front of the hustings, addressed the great multitude. He said, " Gentlemen, I crave your indulgence while I proceed to state the nature and object of this meeting, and I particularly request that no gentleman will call silence, as it produces more disorder than any other circumstance, and perhaps will give our enemies the opportunity of causing a further encroachment on our rights and liberties. Gentlemen, for the honour you have done me in electing me chairman on this important occasion I return you my sincere and heartfelt thanks. I am happy to see such an immense concourse of people assembled, and I fearfully regret that I shall not be able to make myself heard by all of you, but those who are able to hear will, I hope, do so peaceably and quietly. It is useless to attempt to relate the proceedings that have occurred

prove the contrary. A placard which nobody could understand had been posted up all over the town, signed by *Tom Long* and *Jack Short* and some such contemptible beings. If any one is riotous, put him down, and keep him down."

At this moment, seeing cavalry moving in the distance, Hunt stopped his speech.

THE SCENE IN ST. PETER'S FIELD

in your town during the last ten days, or to state to you the cause of the meeting on Monday being postponed ; you are all acquainted with it. These wise magistrates who were the cause of preventing the meeting on Monday last, fancied they had achieved a glorious victory; but their pusillanimous conduct since, and the presence of such an immense and respectable assembly as now stands before me,

The Yeomanry galloped down Mosley Street and Peter Street, and ranged themselves, sword in hand, in front of the houses in Mount Street, on the south side of Peter's Field, quite close to where the magistrates were sitting at an open window. Hunt, in order to prevent the people scattering on the edge of the crowd near the horses, cried out that the coming of the Yeomanry was only a trick to frighten the meeting, and called on the people round the hustings to stand firm, and give three cheers.

The Yeomanry remained in front of the houses for about five minutes, during which time the Riot Act was read, but for what reason is unknown, as the crowd was quite quiet and peaceable. At the ending of the reading the Yeomanry waved their drawn swords and dashed straight into the crowd. But they were soon brought to a standstill owing to its density, their ranks were broken, and the troopers separated from one another, got wedged amongst the people, and could neither retire nor advance. As it has been pointed out, there was no danger in the situation, seeing the quiet temper of the crowd. The men could have remained where they were, until the meeting was over, and as the crowd dispersed, have arrested the speakers.

At this moment two squadrons of Hussars cantered up on the west side of the Field, indeed, most of the onlookers declared that the rush of the Yeomanry upon the people and the appearance of the Hussars were simultaneous. Then occurred the fatal mistake. From the window where the magistrates were looking down upon the vast concourse of people, it seemed that the Yeomanry were being knocked about and buffeted by the crowd, whereas they were only trying to press their horses forwards or backwards. There was general alarm amongst the magistrates, and Colonel L'Estrange asked what he should do.

"Good God, sir!" cried Mr. Hulton, one of the magiststrates, "do you not see how they are attacking the Yeomanry? Disperse the crowd!"

Colonel L'Estrange was there for the purpose of obeying the civil power. He gave the order "Forward!" the bugle sounded, and the three hundred and seventy Hussars dashed upon the sixty thousand closely packed people. Mr. Hulton left the window "because he would rather not see any advance of the military." A spectator of the terrible scene that followed, wrote:—

"The troops instantly dashed off at full gallop amongst the people, actually hacking their way up to the hustings. A cordon of special constables was drawn from the house occupied by the magistrates towards the stage, and fared as ill from the attacks of the soldiers as the people at large. A comparatively undisciplined body, led on by officers who had never had any experience in military affairs, and probably all under the influence both of personal fear and considerable political feelings of hostility, could not be expected to act either with coolness or discrimination; and accordingly, men, women, and children, constables and reformers, were all equally exposed to their attacks; numbers were trampled down and numbers were cut down. When they arrived at the hustings, sixteen banners and a cap of Liberty were torn or cut from the hands of those who held them, and Hunt, Johnson and Saxon, with several other persons, including three or four women, were taken into custody. Hunt was hurried along by constables to the house where the magistrates were sitting, crying out 'Murder!' as he was every instant struck by the bludgeons of numbers of constables who surrounded him. An attempt was made to knock his hat off, but unsuccessfully; and just as he was going up the steps a person struck him on the head with both fists."

When Hunt saw the cavalry charging into the crowd, he called out to those near the platform, "They are riding upon us! Stand fast!" The cry passed through the ranks of the Middleton men, "Stand fast!" The cavalry got confused, and could not, says the spectator quoted above, "with all the weight of man and horse, penetrate that compact mass of human beings; and their sabres were plied to hew a way through naked held-up hands and defenceless heads, and then chopped limbs and wound-gaping skulls were seen: and groans and cries were mingled with the din of that horrid confusion. 'For shame! For shame!' was shouted, and then, 'Break! Break! They are killing them in front and they cannot get away!' and there was a general cry, 'Break! Break!' For a moment the crowd held back as in a pause; then there was a rush, heavy and resistless as a headlong sea, and a sound like low thunder, with screams, prayers and imprecations from the crowd, moiled and sabre-doomed, who could not escape. . . . In ten minutes from the commencement of the havoc, the field was an open and deserted space. The sun looked down through a sultry and motionless air. The hustings remained, with a few broken and hewed flag-staves erect, and a torn and gashed banner or two drooping; whilst over the whole field were strewed caps, bonnets, hats, shawls and shoes, and other parts of male and female dress, trampled, torn and bloody."

The dead and the dying presented a horrible spectacle, "several mounds of human beings still remained where they had fallen, crushed down and smothered. Some of these still groaning, others with staring eyes, were gasping for breath; and others would never breathe more. All was silent save those low sounds, and the occasional snorting and pawing of steeds. Persons might sometimes be noticed peeping from attics and over the tall ridgings of houses, but they quickly withdrew, as if fearful of being observed, or unable to sustain the full gaze of a scene so hideous and abhorrent."

Another eye-witness says: "The shrieks of women and the groans of men were to be heard at some distance. Every person who attended out of curiosity immediately fled. The crush was so great at one part of the field that it knocked down some outbuildings at the end of a row of houses, on which there were at least twenty or thirty persons, with an immense crash. As I was carried along by the crowd, I saw several almost buried in the ruins. Others, in their anxiety to escape, had fallen down, and had been trampled upon by the populace."

That night the Manchester Infirmary was crowded with wounded and dying people, many of whom had been slashed on the heads, shoulders, or hands by the sabres of the cavalrymen. All the roads leading to Middleton, Leigh and Royton were crowded with people hurrying homeward, some wounded, some with their clothes torn to shreds; and the next morning within a radius of fourteen miles of Manchester, several hundreds of people were still lying in the fields, or by the roadside, overcome with fatigue, or unable to reach their homes because of the injuries they had received.

Orator Hunt and the other leaders were brought up before the magistrates, on a charge of high treason, but it was afterwards abandoned for one of having conspired to alter the law by force and threats, on the ground that "numbers constituted force, force terror, and terror illegality." Hunt was sent to gaol for two years and a half.

The Peterloo Massacre, as it was called in bitter parody of the Duke of Wellington's great victory at Waterloo five years previously, and the subsequent legal proceedings, roused a fever of indignation throughout the country. But the sympathisers suffered either rebuke or punishment. When the Common Council of the City of London presented a petition upon the matter to the Prince Regent (afterwards George IV.) he publicly re-

of the Government in no measured terms; whilst for attending a meeting of twenty thousand people at York and signing a

TO THE
WORKING CLASSES.

Fellow Workmen:—

Be wise in time. **ABSTAIN FROM GIVING ANY ASSISTANCE TO THE CHARTIST MOVEMENT;** be sure those who advise you otherwise are your worst, your bitterest enemies. Read these two statements of your **GAIN AND LOSS,** which of them depends upon your conduct now

LOSS.

If you side with these men, and IF YOU SUC-SEED in overturning the government, you will suc-ceed also in Closing our Factories, in Closing our Warehouses, in Closing our Shops. Having des-troyed our Trade, you may next succeed in upsetting our National Credit, your next success will be by throwing thousands upon thousands of your fellow-men out of Employ, and, finally by bringing your Wives and your Children to Want, and your Country to Distress and Difficulty, from which she may never recover.

GAIN.

Be peaceable and quiet, and your advantage will soon be abundance and prosperity.

You know that the French FAC-tories are most of them closed—there is no Trade and no Work—their pro-duce is therefore not likely to com-pete with your labour. Germany, Austria, Prussia, Italy, all the Manu-facturing Countries of Europe are similarly situated, and they cannot even produce necessaries for them-selves. Already our Manufacturers have orders to supply these wants, and to meet this demand, IF ORDER AND CREDIT is maintained here, your labour will be wanted.

Besides this, it is calculated that many Millions of Pounds Sterling are spent every year by English Travel-lers abroad; be peaceful, be orderly, and this money, owing to the dread-ful state of Europe, will be spent at home, and you will benefit by it.

Remember the Rich cannot suf-fer without the Middle Classes and the Men in Trade suffering too, and then comes your turn. But GOD knows the Poor cannot suffer long, alone.

Which of these two conditions will you go for? Decide at ONCE AND ACT ACCORDINGLY, but remember if riot is your choice, you will have to answer to the LAW FOR IT.

A WARNING BASED ON THE EVENTS OF PETERLOO

proved them in his most majestic manner. But Westminster, Norwich, Bristol, Liver-pool and Nottingham, undaunted by the royal disapproval, sent in addresses con-demning the magistrates and the coercion

requisition to the High Sheriff, Earl Fitz-william was deprived of his office of Lord Lieutenant of the West Riding of York-shire, and Sir Francis Burdett because of his fervent protests was proceeded against for libel. Another Lord Lieutenant, the Duke of Hamilton, openly expressed his sympathy and opinions by sending fifty pounds to the Manchester sufferers.

Many people on the other hand insisted that the Manchester magistrates had acted rightly, and the Regent expressed his " approbation and high commendation of the conduct of the magistrates and civil authorities at Manchester, as well as the officers and troops, both regular and yeomanry cavalry, whose firmness and effectual support of the civil power preserved the peace of the town on that most critical occasion."

The contention that the magistrates had acted illegally was wrong. They had acted according to the law. Yet it must be admitted that their management of the affair brought about the tragedy. It was an act of folly to send one hundred and forty Yeomen to break through a crowd of sixty thousand people in order to arrest the men on the platform, and then, before even a stone had been thrown, to read the Riot Act. Only a few people in the immediate vicinity of the house from which the magistrates were watching the meeting, could have heard the reading of the Act. The magistrates, we know, believed that the Yeomanry were being ill-treated by the crowd, but the people were too closely packed together to be dangerous, even if they had wished to be so. Having forbidden the meeting of August 9, the magistrates could easily have prevented the second one, on the 16th, taking place. If St. Peter's Field had been occupied by the soldiers, and the people from the country round turned back before they entered the town, there would have been no necessity for the mistaken and horrible charge of the soldiers. The inscriptions on some of the banners certainly gave the magistrates every cause to fear acts of violence upon the part of the Reformers, but the Peterloo Massacre will always remain a signal instance of prevention being better than cure.

AN EPITAPH IN BOLTON CHURCHYARD

" JOHN OKEY, the servant of God, was born in London 1608, came into this town 1629. Married Mary, the Daughter of James Crompton of Breaktmet, 1635, with whom he lived comfortable 20 years, and begat 4 sons and 6 daughters, since then he lived sole till the day of his death : in his time were many great changes and terrible alterations ; 18 years Civil Wars in England, besides many dreadful sea-fights, the Crown or Command of England changed 8 times, Episcopacy laid aside 14 years, London burnt by Papists and more statly built again, Germany wasted 300 miles, 200,000 Protestants murdered in Ireland by Papists, this town thrice stormed, once taken and plundered : he went through many troubles and divers conditions ; found rest, joy and happiness only in holiness, the faith, fear and love of God in Jesus Christ : he died the 29th of April, and lieth here buried, 1684."

THE FOUNDER OF THE MANCHESTER GRAMMAR SCHOOL

IN the middle of the fifteenth century, when Hugh Oldham, to whom Manchester owes its grammar school, was a boy, schools did not exist. The cathedrals and the monasteries gave a smattering of learning, but it was mainly for those who were destined to enter the Church or become monks, and was not intended for the sons of gentlemen. It was therefore the custom for the latter to enter the service of some great nobleman or ecclesiastical dignitary as pages, and here they were trained in all the accomplishments required of gentlemen of that period, and also educated. Hugh Oldham was born, it is believed, at Crumpsall; there are no records of his family, but that he was of gentle birth is shown by his admission into the household of Thomas Stanley, first Earl of Derby. This powerful nobleman had married Margaret, Countess of Richmond, the mother of Henry VII., a woman of high character, who, as one of her biographers says, " would seem to have taken an especial pleasure in superintending the education of the young." Very possibly she delighted in the society of youth. In the first year of her son's reign, we discover the facts of her not only being entrusted with the " keeping and guiding " of the unmarried daughters of Edward IV., but also of " her great charges" of the " young lords," the Duke of Buckingham and the Earls of Warwick and Westmorland. The Countess kept in her service a " learned man of Oxford " named Maurice Westbury, for the express purpose of instructing " certain young gentlemen at her finding." Among these " certain young gentlemen" were Hugh Oldham and his friend William Smith of

Widnes, who are supposed to have been trained at Knowsley and Latham under the direct superintendence of the Countess. Whether this tradition is correct or not, it is certain that both owed their after-advancement to her influence. When his training in Lord Derby's house was finished, Oldham went to Exeter College, Oxford, and from there to Queens' College, Cambridge. The Battle of Bosworth, which placed Henry VII. on the throne, was fought on the 22nd of August, 1485, and a month later, on the recommendation of the new king's mother, the Countess of Richmond, Oldham was appointed rector of St. Mildred's Church in Bread Street, in the City of London. During the next twenty years he passed from preferment to preferment, his all-powerful patroness never losing sight of his interests, until, in 1505, when he was made Bishop of Exeter, he reached the summit of his career. He is described as being " a man of more zeal than knowledge, and more devotion than learning, somewhat rough in speech, but in deed and action friendly."

Oldham's occupancy of the see of Exeter was marked by " continual suits " with the Abbot of·Tavistock, who resisted his right to visit the monastery. The increase in the number of monasteries and their absorption of money and land was, in the reign of Henry VII., already beginning to exercise the minds not only of statesmen, but of the most devout and pious. Grown arrogant, the abbots and abbesses insisted on the right of self-government, denying all authority on the part of the Bishops, and acknowledging no superior save the Pope. The Abbot of Tavistock, for instance, when Bishop

Oldham excommunicated him for contumacy, obtained Oldham's own excommunication from Rome. The invention of printing spread a revival of learning throughout the country, and there gradually arose an opinion that to place the opportunity of education before all classes by the founding of schools and colleges was of greater help to the country than to swell the already over-grown revenues of the monastic establishments.

Oldham's patroness, the Countess of Richmond, who was one of the most devout and pious women of her time, and a most devoted daughter of the Church of Rome, before her death in 1509, had devoted the large sums of money she had arranged to leave to priests and monks for the saying of masses for the repose of her soul, to the founding of St. John's College, Cambridge, and the further endowment of Christ Church, Oxford. She was persuaded to do this by her confessor, Bishop Fisher (who was afterwards made a Cardinal), who also experienced little difficulty in inducing the Countess to procure the dissolution of two monasteries and apply their revenues for the endowment or support of colleges and professorships at both Oxford and Cambridge.

Although he had risen to high ecclesiastical rank and had passed the greater portion of his life in the south of England, Oldham had ever a tender affection for his native county, and especially for Manchester, and ten years after he became Bishop of Exeter, and four years before his death, he determined to remedy the " educational destitution " from which the growing and already prosperous town suffered. About this time Leland described Manchester as " the fairest, best-built, quietest and most populous of all Lancashire." The example of his life-long friend and patron, the Countess of Richmond, may have set the worthy Bishop's

thoughts in the direction of school and college endowment, but in all probability his provision of education for all classes was the outcome of the growing opinion amongst the more thoughtful people of the age, that it was wrong to support monks and nuns and leave the lower classes in blank ignorance and superstition. In 1515 he built the Manchester Free Grammar School, buying the lease of some corn mills by the River Irk, a fulling mill near by, and " also sundry messuages " in Ancoats, the income of which was to form the endowment of the school. A large part of this income was derived from an ancient right vested in the owners of these mills on the Irk, " the right of soke," which compelled the inhabitants of Manchester to have their corn and malt ground at these mills and at these mills only. Such a monopoly in the course of time, as the town grew in size and the population increased, became a pressing injustice, but it continued until 1758, when a special Act of Parliament deprived the millers of this oppressive " right."

The two tenants of the mills appear to have both been very thin men when, in the last years of the reign of George III., public indignation against the monopoly of the two mills reached fever-heat, and John Byrom, the Manchester poet, put the situation very neatly in this epigram—

" Bone and Skin two millers thin,
Would starve the town or near it;
But be it known to Skin and Bone
That Flesh and Blood can't bear it."

Thus for two hundred and forty years Manchester boys were educated by the grinding of Manchester corn.

Bishop Oldham's reasons for the foundation of the school are quaintly set out in the statutes : " For the good mind which he had and bare to the country of Lancashire ; conceiving the bringing up in learning, virtue and good manners, of children in the same country should be the key and ground to have good people there, as also because, of long time past, the teaching, bringing up of young children to school, to the learning of grammar, hath not been taught here for the lack of sufficient school-master and usher there, so that the children in the same country, having pregnant wits, have been for the most part brought up rudely and idly, and not in virtue, cunning, erudition, literature and in good manners." Cunning is an odd word to use with regard to education, but it is here used in the sense of cleverness. The school was to be entirely free, with the exception that each scholar on entering was to pay the sum of a penny, which was to be given to "two poor scholars," who were to keep the school registers, and clean the school out once a week. By this stipulation of payment to "two poor scholars," the Bishop clearly designed that his school should be used by all classes. Beyond this all other payments were forbidden; "cock-penny" and "victor penny" were expressly prohibited as being encouragement to cock-fighting; so also was "potation-penny," a contribution by each scholar to a banquet given once a year by the head masters of "some ill-regulated establishments." Bishop Oldham's dislike of the monks is shown in the clause referring to the appointment of the head

BISHOP OLDHAM, FROM THE PORTRAIT IN CORPUS CHRISTI COLLEGE, OXFORD

master. He was to be a "convenient" (that is, suitable) "person and school-master, single man, priest or no priest, so shall he be no religious man" (that is a member of a religious monastic order or community), "having sufficient literature and learning to be a school-master, and able to teach children grammar, after the school use, manner, and form of Banbury in Oxfordshire." Banbury was the model grammar school of the time.

The Manchester school even included infants. One of the clauses in the Bishop's statutes reads, "Item—The High (head) Master for the time being shall always appoint one of his scholars, as he thinketh best, to instruct and teach, in the one end of the school, all infants that shall come there to learn their A B C primer, and forth till they begin grammar, and every month choose another new scholar so as to teach infants on the commandment of the said High Master. And if any scholar refuse so to teach infants the same scholar so refusing to be banished the same school for ever." From this last ordinance of Bishop Oldham's the system of monitors and pupil-teachers, which is so important a factor in modern education, may be traced.

For two hundred and fifty years the boys of Manchester were educated in the Grammar School built for them by the good Bishop of Exeter. In 1766 the buildings, which were inadequate for the increasing number of pupils, were pulled down and a new school was built.

Bishop Oldham's interest in education was expressed at Oxford as well as at Manchester. There is a story that he "had intended to have enlarged Exeter College (of which he was a graduate) in Oxford, as well in building as in revenues, but being denied a fellowship there he altered his determination." He was also reported to have withdrawn an offer to help his old friend of Knowsley and Latham days, Bishop Smyth, to found Brazenose College at Oxford, because "he was denied to have the nomination of a founder." But seeing that his Bishop's coat of arms was displayed in stained glass in the window of the library at Brazenose, there is every reason to doubt the story. Men "somewhat rough in speech," as the Bishop is described to have been, make many enemies, and when, as in his case, they enjoy the protection of the great ones of the earth, envy of their good fortune adds malice to the expression of wounded feelings created by the roughness of their tongues.

It is more than probable that Oldham assisted in the foundation of Brazenose, as he gave large sums of money to his friend, Bishop Fox, for the foundation of Corpus Christi College, his name only appearing as that of a benefactor. Bishop Fox, who had been one of Oldham's predecessors in the see of Exeter, then occupied the see of Winchester, and, unlike his old friend Oldham, had a lingering fondness for the monastic idea, and thought of making the new college at Oxford a seminary for the monks of St. Swithin at Winchester. This did not please the Lord Bishop of Exeter. "What, my lord," he cried, "shall we build houses and provide livelihoods for a company of bussing monks, whose end and fall we ourselves may live to see? No, no, it is more meet a great deal that we should have a care to provide for the increase of learning, and for such as who by their learning shall do good in the Church and Commonwealth!" "To this Bishop Fox at length yielded," says Holinshed, "and so they proceeded in their buildings, wherein Oldham, reserving to Fox the name of the founder, was contented with the name of a benefactor, and very liberally did contribute great masses of money to the same; and since (according to his wish and desire) the same college hath been, and is, the nurse of many notable, good scholars." In recognition of his liberality a statue was erected to Oldham in the College, one of the fellows of which must always be a Lancashire man.

Two years after the founding of Corpus Christi College, and four years after the founding of the Manchester Grammar School, Bishop Oldham died at Exeter, where he lies buried in a chapel he had built in the Cathedral.

Hall to the "Seven Stars" in Withy Grove, which was the oldest licensed house in England, dating back as far as the year 1356. Signs of this passage were found at the Hall, but the entrance has been blocked up. There were signs also of an underground passage at the "Seven Sisters," but this was believed to have been connected with Trafford Hall.

In the forties of the last century Ordsall Hall was still in the country, and in *Guy* itself free from such inscriptions. There was a legend that Runic writings and crosses were cut into the sides of the cave, but the last time I was there I was unable to find any trace of such markings. In fact, the dates accompanying the inscriptions did not go further back than some two hundred and fifty years. In the cave there was a rude bench cut out of the rock, and in one corner a low, narrow tunnel appeared. This, it was popularly

THE GUNPOWDER PLOT : THE CONSPIRATORS

Fawkes we have a charming picture of the landscape, as it appeared in Harrison Ainsworth's day. Near the Hall was Woden's Cave, which plays so important a part in *Guy Fawkes.* Writing of the former appearance of the country round Ordsall, an old Manchester man says: "From Ordsall lane the land to the west sloped upwards, and the outer entrance to the cave formed a pretty bay, overshadowed by trees and shrubs. The trees bore the initials of many of the loving couples who resorted to that sylvan spot to 'bill and coo,' being completely hidden there from the highway. Nor was the cave said, ran to 'Quaker Hall's' house. The entrance was barred by an iron grille, and all that could be seen, even with a light, was a sharply-curved passage, the entrance being filled with sacks of potatoes. Of all the striking changes in once hallowed spots, the metamorphosis of Woden's Cave is one of the strangest. The site of the cave had become utterly forgotten by the time it came into the possession of Alderman (now Sir William) Bailey, and it was then a coal-yard. Ultimately the land was sold to the Corporation for the purpose of forming the Emerald Street Playground. On levelling the broken land, a great portion of the rock having been carried away, a great cavity was found under the surface, and this cavity, it is conjectured, was the once mysterious and romantic cave immortalised by Harrison Ainsworth. A more depressing spot, with its sordid surroundings, than this playground can hardly be imagined—that is, when its past beauty is recalled."

Ordsall Hall originally possessed a moat, which was in existence so late as 1830, but forty years later all that remained of it was a small pond near the eastern end. This old home of the Radcliffes has had a happier fate than many other old halls, whose former sylvan surroundings have gradually been devoured by the necessities of the commerce and manufacture of Manchester and the surrounding towns.

OLD CURES FOR WARTS

"STEAL a piece of meat from a butcher's stall or his basket, and after having well rubbed the parts affected with the stolen morsel, bury it under a gateway at four lane ends, or, in case of emergency, in any secluded place. All this must be done so secretly as to escape detection ; and as the portion of meat decays the warts will disappear."

The following cure used to be prevalent in the neighbourhood of Manchester : "Take a piece of twine, and making upon it as many knots as there are warts to be removed, touch each wart with the corresponding knot. Then bury the twine in a moist place, saying at the same time : "There is none to redeem it besides Thee." As the twine decays the warts will gradually disappear.

A snail hung upon a thorn was a favourite · spell against warts, it being believed that as the snail wasted away so did the warts.

Another cure was to take a bag of stones equal in number with the warts to be destroyed, and throw the stones over the left shoulder. The warts were said to speedily leave the thrower. But this cure had a drawback, for whoever chanced to pick up one or more of these stones took with them as many of the warts as they picked up stones.

THE OLD INFIRMARY AT MANCHESTER

IT is now a hundred and sixty years ago since a hospital was first established in Manchester ; and at that time there were only three other such institutions in the provinces—at Liverpool, Shrewsbury, and Winchester. In 1752 Manchester had a population of thirty thousand. She owed the hospital to Mr. Charles White, a surgeon of high local reputation, and to Mr. Joseph Bancroft. These two gentlemen, seeing the crying necessity for some accommodation for the suffering poor, rented a small house in Garden Street, Shudehill, which they equipped with a few beds. The good work done by this humble institution attracted the attention of several men of position in the town ; they held a private meeting at which it was decided that a public meeting of the inhabitants should be called to consider the advisability of promoting a larger scheme. The meeting accordingly took place and four gentlemen were selected to collect funds. In a very short time they succeeded in collecting three hundred pounds in legacies and donations, as well as an annual income of five hundred pounds, promised in subscriptions. Upon this support a site was chosen, the choice of the committee falling upon a piece of ground at the top of Market Street known as Daub Hole Field, and belonging to Sir Oswald Mosley, then Lord of the Manor of Manchester. The site was one acre and twenty-five perches in extent, and was leased to the trustees for nine hundred and ninety-nine years at a yearly ground rent of six pounds. Later on, however, it was generously given to the hospital.

Three years after the meeting which put the claims of the sick poor before the Manchester people, the central portion of the infirmary was completed, particular care being taken that in the event of any extensions becoming necessary they could be carried out. The wisdom of this provision was demonstrated more than once in the history of the Infirmary.

The curious name of the site—Daub Hole Field—was believed to have come down from the time when the houses in Manchester were built of wattle and daub —that is, a wooden framework filled in with mud. In front of the site was an oblong piece of water which was said to have been the hole made by the continual excavation of clay to be used for the "daub" in building. This sheet of water was enclosed by railings and remained for over a century, serving as a great ornament to the front of the building. Fountains were

73

made in it, and even after the pond itself was filled in, these fountains were kept for some years, being ultimately done away with in the sixties of the last century.

The Infirmary was built to hold forty beds, with a prospective extension to eighty; but in 1766 the governors decided to add accommodation for lunatics, and the building therefore served the town also as an asylum, continuing to do so until 1847, when the insane were removed to Cheadle.

Twice in the eighteenth century extensions became necessary—in 1780 and 1788—a sign of the increasing population of the town. Eight years later we have an indication of the growth of the use of machinery, and of the services of the Infirmary, in a request sent to mill-owners by the Board of Trade asking that their machinery shall be so guarded as to prevent the clothes of the operatives being entangled in it. This request was made because so many accidents had been caused by unguarded machinery. About the same time there was a bad epidemic of typhus and typhoid fever in Manchester, and the need of a building for the isolation of infectious cases having been placed before the governors, a "house of recovery," as it was called, was immediately erected— one of the earliest instances of an isolation hospital in the country.

An interesting feature of the old Infirmary was the Harrogate and sulphur baths, which were at one time of great importance. About the end of the eighteenth century they were placed under the charge of William and Ann Howarth, and from that date were called " Howarth's Baths." William Howarth performed other services as well as looking after the sulphur baths, for in 1812 the governors came to an agreement with him that he should cup (i. e. bleed) the patients in the hospital gratuitously, and that " such

emoluments derivable from private patients as might accrue to him as cupper to the Infirmary should be divisible between himself and the Board in equal proportions." Cupping seems to have occupied the serious attention of the governors on more than one occasion ; and at one time Howarth, being asked by the Board to give instruction in the operation to pupils, flatly refused and resigned his place. Subsequently, however, he agreed to give the required teaching and was reinstated. There is a quaint record in the papers of the Infirmary in 1805 which says, " The Board agreed with Thomas Powell to shave the patients in the Infirmary at eight guineas a year in place of Old Martha, deceased "; and on the Coronation Day of George IV. this notice was put up : " This being the Coronation Day of George IV., the garden gates were closed to prevent the lunatics and other patients being disturbed through the passage of the loyal processions."

By the year 1824 Manchester had increased so much in size that representations were made to the governors of the insufficiency of the accommodation afforded by the Infirmary, with the result that many urgent cases had been refused admission. The building was therefore enlarged at a cost of seven thousand pounds. But at the end of another twenty years the Board were again called upon to consider urgently necessary extensions. Nearly two thousand square yards of land were taken from the lunatics' asylum, which resulted in the removal of the lunatics to Cheadle. Two wings were built, arranged to hold two hundred and twenty beds. This involved an increase of two thousand pounds a year in the upkeep of the Infirmary. Whilst the north wing was being built to correspond with one previously built on the south side, the great singer, Jenny Lind, fulfilled an engagement to sing at Manchester. Hearing of the needs of the Infirmary she promised to return and give two concerts in aid of its funds. This promise she most faithfully kept, and as the result of two concerts given by her, one at the Free Trade Hall and the other at the Concert Hall, over two thousand five hundred pounds was handed over to the Board.

It was in 1902 that the decision was made to remove the Infirmary from the site it had occupied so long, but the project had been mooted nearly forty years before, the Corporation in 1864 having made a proposal to purchase the site in order to build a new Town Hall upon it. But the Board refused the offer, giving it as their opinion "that the site should not be abandoned for any purpose whatsoever." Other times, other necessities.

AN OLD SCHOOL ADVERTISEMENT

Doctrina Vires promovet insitas,
Rectique Cultus pectora roborant.

CLASSICAL AND COMMERCIAL
EDUCATION,

AT

Leigh, near Manchester.

MR. BLUNDELL respectfully informs the Public, that he takes TWELVE Young Gentlemen, at

One Guinea Entrance.

Board, & Education in the Classics, Mathematics, Geography, Belles Letters, &c.

25 *Guineas per Annum*—*Washing not included.*

FRENCH, MUSIC, DRAWING, and DANCING, by approved Masters, at the usual Terms.

As the number is so limited, every attention will be paid to render it select and respectable.

N. B. The usual notice will be expected.

☞ A GOOD LIBRARY.

R. & W. Dean, Printers.

75

THE HIDDEN TREASURE

HULME HALL

AMONGST the ancient halls in and near Manchester which have disappeared was Hulme Hall, once the residence of the Lord of the Manor of Manchester. In the reign of Edward I. it was occupied by Adam, son of Adam de Rossendale. During the next century it belonged to the Prestwich family, with whom it continued for over two hundred years. The Prestwiches were people of considerable means, and in the reign of Elizabeth, the then lord of Hulme, Edmund Prestwich, received a letter from the Queen herself calling upon him to contribute fifty pounds as a voluntary contribution to the necessities of the State. His grandson, Thomas, was created a baronet for his loyalty to Charles I. in 1644, but later on suffered severely for his constancy to this monarch.

Sir Thomas made no secret of his adherence to the royal cause during the Parliamentary War, being encouraged, it was said, by his mother, who assured him that she had hidden treasure with which she would supply all his needs.

This wealth was supposed to be hidden somewhere in or about Hulme Hall. But unfortunately the old lady died suddenly, and having become speechless before her death, was unable to communicate her secret. In consequence, when her son was fined three hundred and thirty pounds by the Parliamentary sequestrators, he was obliged, owing to his other heavy losses in the Royalist cause, to mortgage Hulme Hall and its lands to Nicholas Mosley of Ancoats, and in 1673 the house and estate were bought by that family, the Mosleys thus becoming lords of the Manor of Manchester. A Mosley heiress carried the property into the Bland family, by her marriage with Sir John Bland, with whom it remained until 1751, when it passed by sale to George Lloyd of Manchester. Both the manor and the old hall were purchased by the Duke of Bridgewater in 1764, and it was ultimately pulled down by his trustees to make way for buildings in connection with the Bridgewater Canal.

All that now remains of Hulme Hall is

a series of wooden panels covered with carvings of grotesque figures. They were taken from the old house before its demolition, and after the many coats of whitewash with which they were covered although he called himself Sir John Prestwich his claim to the baronetcy was never fully acknowledged. The unfortunate Sir Thomas, who lost Hulme, and practically all else he possessed through his loyalty to

PANEL FROM HULME HALL, NOW AT WORSLEY

had been removed, they were fixed in the old hall at Worsley, whence they were removed to the new Worsley by the first Earl of Ellesmere, on its completion.

The last Prestwich of the old family of Hulme died in Dublin in 1796, but Charles I., survived his two sons. His cousin, of the same name, claimed the succession to the title, but the relationship was somewhat doubtful, and although his son, grandson, and great-grandson used the title, the right to its possession was seriously questioned in the case of the great-grandson.

Thomas Barrett, the Manchester antiquary, made close inquiries into "Sir" John's genealogy and wrote thus quaintly:

"As to my pedigree, which you desire me to furnish you with, I shall inform you that it stands in need of repairs, as it is almost worn out with age, insomuch that it wants the riches or lands that formerly were attached to it, and which are now much wanted to mend it: without these all is vanity."

OLD MAY=SONGS AT SWINTON

"ONE evening towards the close of April 1861," says Mr. Harland, in his *Ballads and Songs of Lancashire*, "I was surprised by a party of waits who had come into the garden (in the hamlet of Swinton and township of Worsley), and who serenaded the family in a song, the words of which I could not make out from their singing. There were four singers, accompanied by a flute and a clarionet, and they together discoursed most simple and rustic music. I could not at first make out what was evidently a local custom of some standing, as it was not Easter, or Whitsuntide, or May Day or any of the old popular festivals. My inquiries on the subject resulted in my obtaining from the dictation of an old Mayer the words of two songs, called by the singers themselves, "May Songs," though the rule is that they must be sung before May comes in. My chief informant, an elderly man named Job Knight, living in Swinton, tells me that he himself "went out" a-May singing for about fourteen years, though he has discontinued the practice for some years. He says the time the Mayers commence is usually about the middle of April, though some parties start as early as the beginning of that month. But the songs cease with the evening of the thirtieth of April. Job says he can remember the custom for about thirty years, and he never heard any other than the two songs which follow. There are usually, he says, four or six men, with a fiddle and sometimes a flute or clarionet. The songs are printed just as recited by Job Knight; and when I ventured to hint that one line (the third, in third verse of song II) was too long, he sang it over to show all the words were somehow brought into the strain. The first song bears marks of some antiquity; first in the double refrain or second and fourth lines in each stanza, which are poetically and musically far superior to the others; next in the picture of manners conveyed by the worshipful master of the house in his chain of gold, the mistress with gold along her breast, &c. The phrases, "house and harbour," "riches and store," also point to earlier times. The last line of this song appears to convey its object, and to point to a simple superstition that these songs were to draw, or perhaps drive " these cold winters away."

OLD MAY SONG

All in this pleasant evening together come we,
For the summer springs so fresh, green and gay ;
We'll tell you of a blossom that buds on every tree,
Drawing near to the merry month of May.

Rise up the master of this house, put on your chain of gold,
For the summer springs so fresh, green and gay.
We hope you're not offended, (with) your house we make so bold,
Drawing near to the merry month of May.

Rise up the mistress of this house, with gold along (upon) your breast,
For the summer springs so fresh, green and gay ;
And if your body be asleep, I hope your soul's at rest,
Drawing near to the merry month of May.

Rise up the children of this house all in your rich attire,
For the summer springs so fresh, green and gay ;
For every hair upon your head shines like the silver wire,
Drawing near to the merry month of May.

God bless this house and harbour, your riches and your store,
For the summer springs so fresh, green and gay ;
We hope the Lord will prosper you, both now and evermore,
Drawing near to the merry month of May.

So now we're going to leave you in peace and plenty here,
For the summer springs so fresh, green and gay ;
We shall not sing you May again until another year,
For to draw these cold winters away.

The second song was called " The Basiers " and was said to have been written by a Swinton man. Basier was the name given in this part of Lancashire to the auricula which is usually in full bloom in April. This curious word would seem to have come into existence from the Lancashire dialect pronunciation of " bear's ears," the name by which the auricula was first known when introduced into this country from Switzerland in 1567, because of the resemblance of the leaf to an ear.

NEW MAY SONG

When the trees are in bloom, and the meadows are green,
The sweet smelling cowslips are plain to be seen,
The sweet ties of nature, which plainly do say,
For the basiers are sweet in the morning of May.

All creatures are deemed, in their station below
Such comforts of love on each other bestow ;
Our flocks they're all folded, and young lambs sweetly do play,
And the basiers are sweet in the morning of May.

So now to conclude with much freedom and love,
The sweetest of blessings proceeds from above ;
Let us join in our song, that right happy may we be,
For we'll bless with contentment in the morning of May.

The last line was doubtless " For we're blest with content in the morning of May."

SILVER-TONGUED WROE

RICHARD WROE affords one of the rare instances of a prophet being honoured in his own country. He was the son of a yeoman, and was born at Radcliffe on the 21st of August, 1641. After being educated at the Manchester Grammar School he went to Jesus College, Cambridge, where he took his degree a year after King Charles II.'s restoration to the throne. Taking holy orders Wroe was appointed Chaplain to the Bishop of Chester, and was made a Fellow of the Collegiate Church of Manchester. He was likewise made a Prebendary of Chester Cathedral and presented to the vicarage of Bowden. Subsequently he became Vicar of Garstang and Rector of West Kirby in Wirral. On the Wardenship of the Collegiate Church at Manchester becoming vacant in 1683, Wroe petitioned the King that the appointment should be given to him, the Bishop of Chester, who was the official visitor of the church, strongly recommending his claims in two letters to the Archbishop of Canterbury. Considerable delay, however, intervened between his petition and his appointment, it being considered doubtful whether he could hold the Wardenship as well as other church preferment. Wroe and his supporters argued that the Wardenship was not a cure of souls but a dignity, the reasons being—

" 1st He is called in the Charter and the Statutes, *Guardiamus*, and *Præpositus Collegii*, but never Rector or *Vicarius Ecclesiae*.

" 2d He is onely instituted by ye Bishop

DR. WROE

of Chester, and then installed in Manchester Church without any induction; nay, there is a particular proviso in the statutes (that he shall not be inducted but onely instituted and installed) to preve it as 'tis conceiued, all pretence of making it a Cure.

" 3d The late warden, Mr. Heyrick, had yᵉ Rectory of Thorneton, in Cheshire, together with his Wardenship, and never had any dispensation as for two cures.

" 4th The last warden, Dr. Stratford, hath held it the best part of a year without any dispensation, whereas he had left his living here in London yᵉ next moment after his induction, had a dispensation been requisite as for two cures.

" 5th Add to this, in behalf of Mr. Wroe, yᵉ present Petitioner, that nis Vicarage of Bowden is contiguous to Manchester; yᵉ boundaries of yᵉ parish join; and that yᵉ Wardenship alone will scarce maintain itself in house and hospitality without some additional preferment."

Upon these arguments Wroe was appointed Warden on 1st May, 1684, being created a Doctor of Divinity two years later. He was an admirable scholar, a profound theologian and famous all over the county for his preaching. By the clergy he was called " The Chrysostom of Lancashire," and by the people, " Silver-Tongued Wroe." He had a beautiful voice, and the command of a perfect eloquence. Dr. Wroe died in 1718, and was buried beneath the choir of the Collegiate Church, having been Warden for thirty-four years.

GARROTTERS

URING the year 1865 a veritable reign of terror existed all over Lancashire. In lonely streets and lanes pedestrians would suddenly be seized by the neck from behind by some ruffian, who had crept noiselessly after them, and while they were struggling in his iron embrace, an accomplice would rob them of everything they possessed. It was a form of attack which rendered the victim, even if he were a strong man, helpless on the instant. Sometimes the victims were left senseless on the ground and some of them received injuries from which they never recovered. The police had the greatest difficulty in dealing with this crime, for as a rule the garrotters worked in gangs of three—two men and a woman. Whilst one man choked the victim, and the other robbed him, the woman kept watch to warn them of the approach of the police. The suddenness of the attack, the amazing celerity with which the victim was half strangled and robbed, also made identification of the garrotters extremely difficult. When these scoundrels were caught, heavy punishments were meted out to them, but for the most part they were hardened criminals for whom imprisonment had neither fear nor disgrace. Meanwhile the cases of garrotting grew more numerous and more daring, and so serious a danger to the public safety did the matter become that Justice Lush at the assizes held at Manchester in the summer of 1865, proceeded to the utmost severity the law allowed. Twenty-three garrotters were had up before him, he sent every one of them to penal servitude for longer or shorter periods according to the brutality they had shown towards their victim. In addition, every single one of them was ordered to be flogged, some of the most desperate three times, others twice, and the remainder once.

"The scene which was witnessed in the Court," says Superintendent Bent, in his book on crime in Lancashire called "Criminal Life," "when the sentence was passed, is one that neither I myself, nor probably any one who saw it, will ever forget. It fell to my lot to assist the prison warders to handcuff some of the prisoners, upon whom the law was shortly to bring to bear one of its strongest arms of punishment. I never saw human beings more utterly cowed. The dread of pain is to such persons their only fear, and from that dread they will shrink like a whipped cur. So it was on this occasion. I shall never forget how . . . I was besought by them for a bit of my boot lace, that they might put it between their teeth while they were being flogged because they said it would to some extent alleviate the pain."

Superintendent Bent was not present at the flogging, but an eye-witness told him that, "as the thong fell on the bare shoulders of the ruffians who had not hesitated to inflict unknown cruelty upon their victims, it was piteous to hear their cries for mercy. A few of them, putting on the air of bravado which desperate men driven to earth sometimes assume, would protest during the first stroke or two that they would be able to bear the blows without shrinking. 'Lay it on, my mother could do more than that; you would not do for a schoolmaster,' and similar epithets were indulged in ; but as the blows continued to fall, first there would be silence, and then the cry for mercy would break forth, ending in utter collapse."

This drastic method speedily put an end to garrotting, for these unspeakable scoundrels frankly admitted that they would rather be twice "boated," that is sent to penal servitude, than once "backed," which is in criminal parlance being flogged.

MASSED MARRIAGES

CARVING IN MANCHESTER CATHEDRAL

DURING Lent it was the custom to double the marriage fees at the Collegiate Church, Manchester, the result being that at Easter, there were so many people to be married that the scene has been described as " unequalled elsewhere in England." It certainly must have been amusing to the onlookers, judging from the following account of the Easter marriages in 1835 :

" I attended the old church at Manchester in order to witness the solemnisation of several marriages I had reason to suppose were then and there to take place. I had heard on the preceding Sunday, the banns proclaimed as follows :—For the first time of asking, seventy-five; for the second time, seventy-two; for the third time, sixty; total one hundred and seventy-nine. When all was ready, and the church doors opened, the clergyman and the clerk betook themselves to the vestry; and the people who were about to be married, and their friends, seated themselves in the body of the church, opposite the communion table, on benches which were placed there for the purpose. Not less than fifty were assembled, among whom I took my seat, quietly without being noticed. A party, who had arrived in a narrow *vis-à-vis* fly,

most exclusively paraded, in the meantime, up and down, as if unwilling to identify themselves with the humble candidates of matrimony, in another part of the church.

" The people at first took their seats in solemn silence, each one inquisitively surveying his neighbour ; but, as the clergyman and clerk were some time in preparation, the men first began to whisper one to another and the women to titter, till, by degrees, they all threw off their reserve, and make audible remarks on the new-comers. There was little *mauvaise honte* among the women ; but of the men, poor fellows! some were seriously abashed ; while, among the hymeneal throng, there seemed to prevail a sentiment that obtains, pretty generally, among their betters, namely the inclination to put shy people out of conceit with themselves. Thus, at the advance of a sheepish-looking bridegroom, he was immediately assailed on all sides with, ' Come on, mon! What are thou afraid of ? Nobody 'll hurt thee.' And then a general laugh went round, in a suppressed tone, but quite sufficient to confound and subdue the new-comer. Presently a sudden buzz broke out, ' The clergyman's coming,' and all were perfectly silent.

" About twelve couples were to be married, the rest were friends and attendants ; the former were called upon to arrange themselves altogether round the altar. The clerk was an adept in his business, and performed the duties of his office in a mode admirably calculated to set the people at their ease, and direct their proceedings. In appointing them to their proper places, he addressed each in an intonation of voice particularly soft and soothing, and which carried with it more of encouragement, as he made use of no appellation but the Christian name of the person spoken to. Thus he proceeded. '*Daniel and Phœbe—this way Daniel—*

take off your gloves, Daniel. William and Anne—no, Anne—here, Anne—t'other side, William. John and Mary—here, John —oh, John !' And then addressing them altogether—'Now, all of you, give your hats to some person to hold.'

"Although the marriage ceremony appeared to me to be very generally addressed to the whole party, the clergyman was scrupulously exact in obtaining the accurate responses from each individual."

CARVING ON A SEAT IN THE CHANCEL, MANCHESTER CATHEDRAL

AN ADVERTISEMENT FOR A BELLMAN IN 1840

BELLMAN
OF
MANCHESTER AND SALFORD.

NOTICE IS HEREBY GIVEN,

That **WILLIAM SHERRAN**, Post-Office Keeper, of *New Windsor*. *Salford*, and of No. 3, *Old Millgate, Market-Place, Manchester*, is duly **APPOINTED** to the Office of **BELLMAN** of the Towns of MANCHESTER and SALFORD; (the appointment to which exclusively belongs to Arabella Penelope Eliza Hoare, wife of Peter Richard Hoare, of Kelsey Park, in the County of Kent, Esquire, as one of the descendants of the Chetham Family, formerly of Clayton Hall and Turton Tower, in this County.) *Any Person found Trespassing after this Notice upon his Rights and Privileges will be Prosecuted.*

BARRETT, RIDGWAY, & FORD,
Solicitors for Mr and Mrs. Hoare.

NORFOLK-STREET, NOV. 17, 1840.

J. AND J. THOMSON PRINTERS MARKET-STREET, MANCHESTER

83

MANCHESTER AMAZONS

IN December 1814, a middle-aged woman, named Sarah Taylor, applied for parish relief at the Churchwarden's Office in Fountain Street, the churchwardens at that time being responsible for the poor of the parish. In giving the history of her life—a recital insisted upon by the authorities before granting relief—she made a strange revelation. She said that she was the daughter of a Manchester bricklayer, and that whilst very young she had helped her father in his work, wearing boy's clothes for the sake of convenience. Male attire evidently pleased her more than her proper dress, for at the age of fourteen, being unusually tall for her age, she enlisted in the Fifteenth Light Dragoons under her father's name—William Roberts. Recruits were urgently needed at the time, and their examination was of the most cursory nature ; " William Roberts " was therefore passed without question. She became an excellent rider, and being sedate in her conduct, she remained in the regiment for twenty-one years, as private, corporal and sergeant ; her real sex never being suspected.

At the end of twenty-one years she was offered her discharge, but preferring to remain in the service she was transferred in the year 1800 to the Thirty-seventh Regiment of Foot, which was then stationed in the island of St. Vincent. Shortly after she joined her new regiment she fell ill of yellow fever, and, believing she was dying, confided her secret to a sergeant's wife. When she recovered, her secret being no longer her own, a soldier's life was impossible. So, making the best of the situation, and not wishing to give up her military associations, she donned her natural dress and married a private in the regiment, by whom she had three children. Wherever the regiment went there followed the intrepid erstwhile

" William Roberts," and finally, together with her husband, she was captured by the French and confined in prison for two years. They were released by the Peace of 1813. Shortly afterwards her husband died suddenly, and in consequence she was obliged to leave the regiment. Being entirely without means she went to the house of her parents in Lee Street, Newton Lane. She claimed a pension in reward of her long and faithful service in the Army, but in the meantime was compelled to seek relief from the parish. How she succeeded in concealing her sex for twenty-one years is a mystery, as she was wounded several times during foreign campaigns, one of which was the expedition against Napoleon in Syria. But of all her sufferings she declared none had exceeded those in the French prison.

Another case in Manchester of a woman passing herself off as a man is even more remarkable. In 1839, owing to a quarrel between a married couple called Stoakes over household expenses, it transpired in evidence that the husband, Henry Stoakes, was in reality a woman. Early in life she had discarded female clothing for that of man, and was apprenticed as a boy to a builder in the West Riding of Yorkshire. In 1816 she was married at Sheffield, and thirteen years later removed to Manchester, where the " husband " followed the trade of a bricksetter. She was an excellent workman, and, being particularly clever in fixing ovens and boilers, was in constant employment. " Henry Stoakes " also acted as a special constable, " performing the duties with ease and efficiency." After twenty-eight years of " married life," arose this quarrel, which disclosed the secret and ended in the separation of the pair. Like " William Roberts," " Henry Stoakes " never seems to have been suspected. He lived in Cumberland Street, Deansgate.

THE TRAGEDY

OF

MADAME

MALIBRAN

MADAME MALIBRAN

F EW musical festivals have created
so much interest in Manchester
as the Festival held in September
1836. The whole town was excited
months beforehand by the preparations.
"Carpenters swarmed in the Collegiate
Church (it was not a cathedral then),"
says Mrs. Linnæus Banks, "erecting
immense galleries, rising almost to the
roof, in preparation for the oratorios."
The Festival ended with a fancy dress
ball, the largest ever given in Manchester.
Mrs. Linnæus Banks, then a girl of sixteen, was present at the ball, and thus
describes the arrangements made for it :—
" At that time the Portico confronted the
Assembly Rooms in Mosley Street, the
back of the Assembly Rooms and the
back of the theatre were on opposite
sides of Back Mosley Street, consequently
all three buildings abutted on Charlotte
Street. In preparation for the ball upper
windows were taken out of all three, and
the spaces were converted into doorways
for long passages on strong supports to
bridge over the intervening streets. The

narrow window space limited the width of
the passages somewhat, but as there were
in each case two, one for entrance, the
other for return, the systematic arrangement more than doubled the accommodation. Then alongside the three
buildings a supper-room was erected on
immense beams and trestles high up over
Charlotte Street, the very solidity of these
supports denoting what a crush was
expected."

The Festival opened with an ordinary
ball upon Monday evening the 12th
September, on Tuesday, Wednesday,
Thursday and Friday mornings there
were oratorios and sacred music in the
Collegiate Church, and on Tuesday,
Wednesday, and Thursday evenings there
were secular concerts, vocal and instru-
mental, in the old Theatre Royal in
Fountains Street; on Friday night the
great fancy dress ball brought the Festival
to a close. The band numbered one
hundred and four, and the chorus two
hundred and twenty-four. Curiously
enough, there were no contraltos in the

chorus, fifty-three male altos drawn from places so far apart as Liverpool, Oldham, Chester, Huddersfield and Sheffield taking their places: in the performance of the *Messiah* the air " O thou that tellest " was taken by an alto. The great attraction of the Festival was the engagement of Madame Malibran de Bèriot, or Madame Malibran, as she was more generally known, then one of the first singers in the world. With her were Mrs. Henry Bishop, Mrs. W. Knyvett, Clara Novello, then aged eighteen, Mrs. Alfred Shaw, Madame Caradori, Braham, Henry Phillips and the great Lablache, all stars in the operatic and concert world. Never before had Manchester heard such an array of talent at one and the same time.

Malibran, like so many of the great singers, had achieved her fame early. She was the daughter of the celebrated singer and teacher of singing Manuel Garcia, and sister of the Manuel Garcia who carried on their father's traditions of teaching for so many years in England. She was born in Turin in 1808, and in her early years showed the strangest dislike to music in any form, and especially to singing. But as a French writer has said, " with a father and professor such as was the great singer Manuel Garcia she either had to become an artiste or die." His methods were drastic. Often the passers-by in the street in which Garcia lived in Paris, would hear the most piercing cries, and in response to their frightened inquiries would be told by the neighbours:

" Oh, it is nothing. It is Monsieur Garcia, who is making his daughter sing."

Although she had only sung in a private salon in Paris, Maria Garcia made her début in London at the old King's Theatre. She was engaged to sing interludes. A few days after her first appearance, the great singer Pasta fell ill. In forty-eight hours Maria learnt the part of Rosina in the *Barber of Seville* and sang it in place of the *diva*. Her success was instantaneous, and although she was only sixteen she at once took her place amongst the great singers of the world.

When the opera season of 1824 in London was over, Garcia went with all his family to New York, where he had been engaged to direct the opera house. He made Maria the principal singer, working her incessantly, and without the least consideration, in all the operas then in vogue. Her success in New York was as brilliant as in London. Maria Garcia was very attractive ; she had a good figure and expressive eyes ; a French merchant called Malibran, long settled in America, fell in love with her and proposed marriage. Although Malibran was fifty and his daughter seventeen, Garcia forced her to accept him because of his supposed wealth. Maria made no secret of her repugnance, but was compelled to obey her father.

A few weeks after the marriage Malibran went bankrupt. Half crazy with rage and mortification Garcia fled from New York, leaving the theatre to manage itself, and his daughter in one of the most desolate situations in which a girl just beginning her married life can be placed. But Madame Maliban—as she was hereafter called—had a high courage. She organised an opera troupe and gave performances which not only added to her reputation but brought in a goodly sum of money. This she divided between her family and her husband's creditors. But it was an impossible situation, more especially as she had no affection for Malibran, and in 1827 she left him and went to Paris. In the following year she made her début before the French public at the Opera. Again her success was instant, and during the next eight years her life was one of triumph, London, Brussels, Paris and all the great cities of Italy laying their laurels at her feet.

In 1830 her husband suddenly made his appearance in Paris, and, anxious to share in his wife's prosperity, summoned her to return to him. Madame Malibran refused, and the unworthy husband was only saved from invoking the aid of the law by the intervention of friends. In 1835 the marriage was declared null and void by the Paris Courts, and in the following March Madame Malibran married a Belgian violinist of great renown, called de Bèriot. But, as will be seen, the great singer was not fortunate in her husbands.

The version of her tragic death in Manchester only six months after her marriage as given in the official account of her life differs very materially from the accounts of Manchester people who knew all the circumstances. Officially it is stated that a month after her marriage Madame Malibran came to London to fulfil an engagement, and that whilst riding one day, her horse threw her. Her foot caught in the stirrup and she was dragged along the ground for some distance. In order to relieve de Bèriot of all anxiety she sang that same night. Shortly afterwards she sang in Brussels and at Aix-la-Chapelle, and then went to Paris to rest. Whilst in Paris she suffered from nervous attacks and violent headaches, " sad precursors," says the account, " of the malady which killed her."

The true story is very different. This version was clearly given in order to " whitewash " de Bèriot, who sadly needed it. Miss Leach (afterwards Mrs. Wood), who was considered the best soprano in Lancashire, had been engaged for the Festival to support Madame Malibran in the oratorios, and also to lead the trebles in the choruses ; her testimony therefore was that of an eye-witness. She said that at the early morning rehearsal of the principals it was whispered that Malibran was very ill and suffering from the pains of maternity ; it was considered doubtful whether she would be able to appear at the performance. De Bèriot was consulted, and " remonstrated " with, but he in the most brutal manner commanded Malibran to go on with the rehearsal, as he was not going to sacrifice so much of her salary for the sake of saving her a little further pain. This speech so exasperated Miss Leach that she offered, through the conductor, to assist Madame in every way she could, more especially in taking up the higher notes, leaving Madame to reserve her strength for the lower notes. This offer was at once thankfully accepted by Malibran, and the two ladies immediately began to practise the parts together ; and after repeating them several times satisfied all present that the attempt was feasible and could not be detected. So when the great trial came on, and Malibran rose for the task, Miss Leach leaned forward so that her voice would go over Malibran's shoulder, and the whole piece was such a success that no one in that vast audience suspected the ruse which had been practised upon them.

" I was told afterwards," adds Mr. John Wood, " that some members of the chorus were highly indignant at Miss Leach craning her neck in such a manner as if she were listening to detect any flaw in her notes, but the surprise was greater when Malibran turned at the finish and bowed her thanks for the assistance she had received. But it was only at the close of the performance, when Malibran in leaving the platform, clasped Miss Leach with both her hands and sobbed her acknowledgments (she could not speak) that the whole truth became known, and then Miss Leach was greeted with a burst of applause for her generous action." This would be on Wednesday morning. In the evening Malibran sang at the concert in the theatre. It was for the last time. Manchester had never heard such glorious singing. A duet in which she sang with Madame Caradori—from the long-forgotten *Andronico* of Mercadante —was encored, and with such rapture that refusal was impossible. The Committee of the Festival, which issued a statement after Malibran's death, said : " The duet, as repeated, was sung by her (Madame Malibran) as well as by Madame Caradori, with increased effect ; and when in the last triumphant shake, she almost electrified the audience, many felt for her what she would not anticipate for herself, that she was exerting herself beyond her physical strength. But her high spirit carried her away ; and she evinced her general character when she declared immediately afterwards, that whilst she was on the stage her spirit surmounted all difficulties."

Scarcely, however, had she left the stage when she was seized with serious illness. Two doctors were hastily summoned out of the audience ; they found it necessary to resort to bleeding, and the great singer, whose voice was never to enchant the world again, was removed to her hotel, the Mosley Arms in Piccadilly.

But despite her illness her first thought was for her husband, who was playing a concerto at this same concert ; and although in great suffering she sent an inquiry from the hotel to know how his performance had been received.

The statement of the Committee tells us that on the Thursday morning Madame Malibran felt so much better that she insisted on singing ; despite the advice of the doctors, she said, " I will go, lest

people should think it is a sham," and after consulting with her husband, they gave way, thinking this the lesser evil than exciting her by opposition. De Bèriot seems to have made no attempt to dissuade his wife from singing. However, when she reached the Collegiate Church Malibran was seized with hysterics, and had to be taken back to her hotel, where she was attended by three doctors. On Sunday her own medical attendant, Dr. Belluomini, who had been sent for, arrived, and the three Manchester doctors were told that their services were no longer needed.

On the following Friday Malibran died after intense suffering, and the same night de Bèriot, accompanied by Dr. Belluomini, left for Brussels, leaving his wife's dead body in the hotel. Ugly rumours had been current as to the treatment of Madame Malibran by the doctor and her husband, and this inexplicable flight, and the callous desertion of her dead body to be buried by strangers, was naturally taken as proof that the rumours were true. It was said that the two men fled in order to escape criminal proceedings, and also that de Bèriot had hurried post-haste to Brussels the moment the breath had left his wife's body, in order to get possession of her property. The statement of the Committee entirely disposes of the first rumour, since on medical evidence it exonerates Dr. Belluomini from the suggestion of unskilful or neglectful treatment. De Bèriot's cruel and unfeeling conduct in forcing his wife to sing had become generally known, and a strong feeling had grown up against him. The Festival Committee would appear to suggest that fear was the cause of his flight, it being stated that when asked to go to the house of a member of the Committee when his wife died, de Bèriot most gratefully accepted the offer, but Dr. Belluomini strongly opposed the suggestion, saying "his (de Bèriot's) life would be endangered if he remained in the town." Whether extraordinary thing for a husband to leave his dead wife's body in a hotel in a foreign land, entirely to the care of

BURIAL OF MALIBRAN IN MANCHESTER COLLEGIATE CHURCH

fear or cupidity was the cause of the sudden departure to Brussels, it was an strangers. In the official account of Malibran's life no mention is made of de Bèriot's desertion, it only says that during the nine days of her illness he never left her side, whilst the actual cause of her illness and death are entirely suppressed.

When the news of the great singer's death became known the feeling in Manchester was profound. A public funeral was given by the town, and on Saturday, October 1st, she was buried in the south aisle of the Collegiate Church. On that day Manchester might have been mourning some national calamity, so universal were the signs of mourning. The next day a funeral sermon was preached in the same church. "Look back," said the preacher, "but a few brief days, and we behold her in the pride of her fame and the bloom of her youth, standing up in this place amid admiring thousands to magnify the name of the Eternal Jehovah in strains which few human tongues could rival, and with an intense expression of devotion which, as it went to the hearts of those who heard her, we may now sincerely hope and believe came directly and warmly from her own. Europe was then too narrow for her fame, and wealth too contemptible for her ambition. A few days more and all this is passed away. Public admiration of her talents is succeeded by public lamentation for her fate."

Some time afterwards de Bèriot erected a mausoleum in the cemetery at Laecken near Brussels, and placed in it a beautiful statue of his wife. Thither the coffin containing her remains was taken from the vault in the Collegiate Church, a somewhat tardy tribute of devotion.

Writing of the sad event some sixty years later, one who heard Malibran sing for the last time said, "I shall never forget the almost electric thrill that went through the house at Malibran's magnificent shake upon the upper E flat, but (ill as she was) she was carried fainting from the stage." Another person gives us the general feeling in Manchester. "Had he (de Bèriot) thought of his wife as much as she thought of her husband, Manchester would not have been in mourning nine days afterwards. I remember seeing the funeral in the 'Old Church,' where only such a short time before her magnificent voice had been heard, and the strings of private carriages at least half a mile long, also the disinterment three months later, and the coffin containing the remains of the incomparable songstress and charming woman taken away for re-interment abroad."

De Bèriot, who was six years younger than Malibran, died in 1870, having made a brilliant reputation as a violinist, but his amazing behaviour after the death of his wife left an indelible stain upon his reputation.

MIDDLETON AND THE ASSHETONS

A STRIKING feature in the history of Lancashire is the continuance of old families in one place for centuries, and then the passing of their estates and houses through a daughter for lack of a male heir. Thus for three hundred and twenty-seven years the manor of Middleton was owned by the Asshetons, their tenure beginning with a Sir Ralph in 1438, who married Margaret Barton, the heiress of Middleton, and ending with a Sir Ralph in 1765, whose daughter married Harbord Harbord, afterwards Lord Suffield, and carried the estate into that family. And throughout those centuries the history of the Assheton family was the history of Middleton.

The first Sir Ralph had a sinister reputation, still preserved, as the " Black Knight of Assheton " ;[1] but his grandson was one of the heroes of Flodden Field (1513), and led the famous Middleton bowmen on that memorable day. He received the honour of knighthood for his valorous services, and returning home, dedicated his standard and his armour to " St. Leonard of Middleton," placing them in the parish church which bore the name of that saint. Part of this armour still remains.

In the civil war between Charles I. and the Parliament, the Middleton clubmen fought under Colonel Assheton at Bolton-le-Moors in 1643, on the Parliamentarian side, and it was at Middleton that the remnant of the Royalist troops were defeated in 1651 after their retreat from the disastrous battle of Worcester in which the Earl of Stanley—the Martyr Earl—was taken prisoner.

Colonel Assheton's son, Ralph, did not share his father's views, and when he succeeded to the Middleton estates, in 1650, openly espoused the cause of

Charles II. He was rewarded with a baronetcy by that monarch on his restoration in 1660. Only two baronets succeeded him, his son, and his grandson, and then the ancient family died out, save for two daughters, one of whom married Lord Suffield.

Samuel Bamford relates the following anecdote of the last Sir Ralph Assheton's kindness to the poor of Middleton : " This Sir Ralph very materially relieved the necessities of nearly all the old and infirm people of the township. They were supplied with meal, broth, and broken meat on certain days of the week. A large ark of meal, with a wooden piggin for measure, always stood ready to supply the accustomed dole to the applicants. Some were allowed to help themselves both to meal and broth ; but once an old woman, named Dane, did not notice a leg of mutton which slipped into her can of broth, and she was walking off with it when, the mutton being missed, she was followed and the joint recovered. Notwithstanding this astounding act of 'inattention' as she called it, the family continued to receive their usual allowance, only they were not permitted to ladle broth for themselves."

The Middleton estates continued in the Suffield family until 1848, when they were sold, and thus ended the centuries-long connection of the Assheton family with the place. They were purchased by Messrs. Peto & Betts, the great railway contractors, whose sensational failure in 1861 brought the ancient estates of the Asshetons once more to the hammer.

Middleton Church is of great antiquity but the exact date of its foundation is unknown. A church existed here, however, in the early part of the reign of Henry III., for there are deeds still in existence of that date in which " Peter,

[1] See " The Black Knight of Assheton."

parson of Middleton," and "Thomas, clerk of Middleton," appear as witnesses. It was the curious custom to place the gravestones in the churchyard flat upon the ground.

Formerly a structure of wood surmounted the church tower, as shown in the illustration. Various reasons have been given for this unusual erection, one being that it was feared that the ground was not sufficiently strong to bear the weight of a stone tower of that height.

senting a tonsured priest wearing his vestments and holding a chalice in which is the wafer marked with the sacred monogram, in his hands. The Latin inscription below records that this is the resting-place of "Master Edmund Assheton, Rector of this Church," who died on August 20, 1522. He was a brother of the Sir Richard Assheton of Flodden Field, who was perhaps the greatest of all the Asshetons. The part played by the Middleton bowmen in that battle is

MIDDLETON CHURCH

But, as the soil is clay, the reason scarcely holds good. In all probability the addition was made to improve the proportions and appearance of the building, and wood was used instead of stone from motives of economy. Within the church, which was partly rebuilt by the hero of Flodden Field and his wife, are many memorials of the departed greatness of the Assheton family. Amongst these are brasses of a Richard Assheton and his wife, dated November 7, 1618. Their six sons are shown on another brass, all kneeling except a baby which is in swaddling clothes; on a third brass are figures of their two daughters.

Another monument shows that the custom of putting younger sons into family livings is of very old standing. On a slab in the chancel is a brass repre-

perpetuated by a group of figures in the north window representing persons of note in the neighbourhood who led the Middleton bowmen, under Sir Richard. There are the chaplain, Henry Taylor, and seventeen warriors clad in blue jackets, all kneeling, each bearing his bow on his left shoulder, and their quivers, full of arrows, slung upon their backs. The inscription below, which gave the names of the seventeen men, has been sadly broken and mutilated, only a name here and there being decipherable. Through the defacing of the inscription the Battle of Flodden appears as having taken place in 1505 instead of 1513, a circumstance which has led many antiquarians to doubt whether this window was in reality raised to local heroism on that occasion. But there is little doubt that the date originally placed upon the inscription was either 1515, two years after the battle, or 1525, which was the year after Sir Richard Assheton enlarged the church. The inscription begs the parishioners to pray "for the good estate of Sir Richard Assheton, and··those who glazed this window, and whose arms and pictures are shewn above, 1505."

Middleton Hall, the old home of the Asshetons, fell into decay in the latter part of the eighteenth century. Part of it was then pulled down and rebuilt, but in 1845 it was entirely demolished, a cotton mill being erected on the site.

Terrible scenes occurred at Middleton in 1812, during a Luddite riot against the introduction of machinery into the cotton mills. Luddism had its rise in Leicestershire, and rapidly spread to Lancashire, its object being destruction of all machinery which superseded or diminished manual labour. The name is said to havebeen taken from a youth named Ludlam, "who when his father, a frame-work knitter in Leicestershire, ordered him to 'square his needles,' took his hammer and beat them into a heap. The mill-breakers used to assemble in parties of from thirty to fifty, according to the supposed necessities of the case, under a leader styled General Ludd, when, armed with swords, pistols, firelocks,

hammers and axes, they proceeded to the scene of destruction. A guard was appointed, and when the work was accomplished, the names of those present were called over· by the leader, after which the men dispersed to their own homes. The outrages assumed such daring proportions that eventually it became necessary to assemble a large military force to aid the civil authorities in preventing the destruction."

At Middleton, the people rose, not in thirties or fifties, but to the number of several thousand, and gathered round the power-loom weaving manufactory of Messrs. Daniel Burton & Sons in the centre of the town. Warning, however, had reached the mill of the intended attack, and preparations had been made. The mob was given notice of what would happen, but believing in superior strength, attempted to rush the mill. A sharp fusillade from the windows was the immediate answer. Four men were instantly killed, and many wounded. This tragic defence saved the mill, but the next day the people wreaked their vengeance upon the mill-owners, by attacking the house of Mr. Emanuel Burton, half a mile away. They set it on fire and utterly destroyed it. The situation in Middleton became alarming, a strong force of cavalry was at once dispatched from Manchester, which after consider-

Ꜣin iacet magister Edmundus Assheton Rector istius ecclesie qui obiit vicesimo die mensis augusti anno domini millimo ccccc vicesimo secundo cuius animae ꝑꝛ ... animae picietur deus Amen

BRASS ON THE TOMB OF EDMOND ASSHETON

able trouble, succeeded in awing the rioters into tranquillity.

Amongst the records of the Assheton family we find that the Parliamentary Colonel Ralph Assheton had a son called Richard, who died young in 1630. It was declared that the boy had been bewitched to death by a man called Utley, "who for this crime was tried at the assizes at Lancaster, and executed there." A brother of this same Colonel Assheton, William, who was rector of Middleton from 1633 to 1659, may be called the originator of the many systems of life assurance which now exist amongst all classes of the community, by starting a scheme for providing pensions for the widows of clergymen.

THE OWDHAM RECRUIT

WHEN I're a young lad, sixteen
    years ago,
    I lov'd a pretty lass, and followed the plough;
But somehow or other I was ne'er content,
Till I like a *noddy* for a sodger went.
There were such shouts of mirth and glee,
For I thowt I should a Captain be.
Bud ah! by *gum!* I wur varra much mista'en,
And monny a time I wished mysel' at t'
    plough-tail again.

So we march'd and march'd abeawt Owdham
    streets,
Where they tried to persuade me it was my
    turn to treat;
I treated them all till we geet drunk as *foos,*
Between serjeant, me, and corporal, there
    wur nod mich to chuse;
I thowt that my *brass* wod never ha' been done,
Thinks I but we shall live a life of rare fun.
Bud ah! by gum! I wur varra much mista'en,
And monny a time I wished mysel' at t'
    plough-tail again.

But when my brass were o spent and dun,
They pushed me about for a bit of roaring
    fun;
By gum, they'd like to *throttled* me; eh,
    what a sin;
With a collar stiff as steel just stuck under
    my chin,
They cut my hair so close, sure, and gathered
    such a crop,
They made me soon i' th' regiment a real
    dandy fop.

Bud ah! by gum! I wur varra much mista'en,
And monny a time I wished mysel' at t'
    plough-tail again.

I'st never forget what a fuss of me they
    made,
When we went to a *pleck* ut they coed their
    parade;
If I could look to pleeos um theer, may I
    indeed be brunt,
For they wanted all at once my *een,* left,
    reet, and front;
Then o in a row like fire potters we wur stood,
And my toes wouldn't turn in let me do wot
    I could;
I listed for a Captain; but, by gum, I wur
    mista'en,
And monny a time I wish'd mysel' at t'
    plough-tail again.

I wondered wot the *dickins* could ever be
    the matter,
For they shut me in the guard-house to live
    on bread and *watter;*
And when I offered then to quit that ugly
    place,
A soldier with his *bagnet* stood staring in my
    face;
I began then a-thinkin' that my case was
    verra bad,
For I're wur off by far than when i' th'
    awkward squad.
I listed for a Captain; but, by gum, I wur
    mista'en,
And monny a time I wished myself at t'
    plough-tail again.

"HOT CHELSEA BUNS"

Hot Chelsea Buns

Bridge, where he cried his wares, "Hot Chelsea Buns! Hot Chelsea Buns!"

The "Chelsea Bun-Man" was eagerly waited for by the children, and it was seldom that he returned to his shop with anything but an empty tray. A snowy cloth was spread over the tray, which was slung round the Bun-Man's neck by a strap. An ingenious device of charcoal, burning in a tin box beneath the tray, justified the Bun-Man's boast that the last cake he sold in Manchester was as hot as the first one he had sold at Salford when he started on his round. In wet weather the cakes were kept dry by a huge gingham umbrella, which the Bun-Man carried, tucked under his arm, when it was fine. He had a loud and particularly sonorous voice, and a peculiar way he had of saying "Thank you, ma'am," was famous all over Manchester and Salford. For many years he was so regular on his rounds, entering Manchester by the Blackfriars' Bridge and returning to Salford by the Victoria Bridge, and "so true to time that he served the purpose of a public clock."

Salford's "Chelsea Bun-Man" was a favourite subject for artists, chiefly those who made silhouettes, and his likeness was frequently to be met with upon jugs, basins and beer-mugs. To all those who desired to make a sketch of him, or even a caricature, this local celebrity was most willing to sit. But when a comic singer gave an imitation of him—voice, buns and all—at Benjamin Lang's music-hall, near the Victoria Bridge, the Bun-Man considered that the bounds of respect had been passed; and calling upon the singer he gave him such proof of his annoyance that the imitation was not repeated. The Chelsea Bun-Man died in 1863, his loud "Hot Chelsea Buns! Hot Chelsea Buns!" and "Thank you, ma'am," being heard in the streets till within a short time of his death,

O NE of the most familiar and certainly one of the most popular figures in Salford during the childhood of the grandfathers and grandmothers of many Salford folk, was the "Chelsea Bun-Man." These delicious buns had originally been made by a baker called James Robinson from the recipe of the Old Bun House at Chelsea in London, but it was his son-in-law and successor who became a local celebrity under the title of "The Chelsea Bun-Man." He first had a baker's shop in Posey Street, but later he moved to John Street, Salford, where "he compounded and baked those delicious morsels which he rendered so familiar to our eyes, ears, and palates in the thoroughfares of Manchester and Salford," says Mr. R. W. Procter in his *Memorials of Bygone Manchester*. His favourite stand was on Old Salford

THE BOGGART'S CLOUGH

THE BOGGART'S CLOUGH

THE Boggart's Clough, or as it should properly be called the Boggart-hole Clough, possessed an unhappy reputation in the days before it was made into a recreation ground for Manchester people. It was the abode of a " boggart," an impish, invisible sprite, which had singled out the inhabitants of a farmhouse at the top of the Clough for particular torment. Night after night the ghostly visitant made his appearance, and each night he varied his tricks. Sometimes he would strip all the bedclothes off the beds, pulling them off again as often as the shivering and frightened occupants replaced them. Sometimes the cream was found churned in the morning, at others it was upset all over the ground. The maids would wake up to find themselves either on the floor or with their heels on the pillows; the children would be wakened out of their sleep, and scream with terror. Indeed, they seemed to be especial objects of dislike to the " boggart," for the curtains of their beds would be pulled violently to and fro—those were the days when every bed had curtains—then a heavy weight, like that of a human body, would squeeze them nearly to suffocation. In addition, loud footsteps, as of a person wearing clogs, were heard clattering up and down the stairs in the dead of night, and all the earthenware and pewter dishes and plates appeared to be dashed upon the kitchen floor. But in the morning they were all found intact upon the shelves of the dresser. And every night there were sounds of shrill, impish laughter. Sometimes the Boggart had a kindly mood. Then they found the pans and kettles all scoured, and many other domestic affairs carried out by unseen hands. But such kindly moods were invariably followed by some trick more than usually impish, such as the snatching away of the children's bread and butter as they were putting it to their mouths, or the knocking to the ground of their porringers of bread and milk.

The staircase to the upper rooms ascended from the kitchen, and beneath it a cupboard had been made by a partition of boards. In one of these boards was a large round knot, which by some means or other had been displaced. One day the youngest of the farmer's children, whilst playing with a shoe-horn stuck it into the knot-hole; it was instantly ejected with great force and struck the poor child upon the head. Whether the hole had been made by the Boggart for the purpose of watching the family, tradition does not go so far as to say, but at any rate it was called the Boggart's Peep-hole, and on one point the tradition is explicit—whenever the shoe-horn or any other object was placed in the knot-hole it was promptly ejected, invariably hitting the person who had put it there upon the head. Apparently familiarity bred contempt, and the knot-hole became a source of amusement to the servants and others. They called it "laking wi' t' Boggart." An old tailor used to aver that the horn was often "pitched" at his head, or that of the apprentice whilst they were seated on the kitchen table, when they were working at the farm, as used to be the custom with country tailors.

At last matters reached a crisis, and the farmer and his wife, unable to bear the nightly torment any longer, decided to take another farm, and leave the Boggart the master of the situation. Accordingly another farm was taken, the furniture was packed and the family were ready to depart. There was only one more night to pass in the old home, and this was spent upon straw beds. That night they all slept in peace and quietness, and in the morning they told each other that seeing they were in earnest the Boggart had made up his mind to part with them in a quiet and friendly manner. Immediately after breakfast the wagons containing the furniture began to move, the farmer with his wife and children following the last one.

"Thank God," said the farmer, as they turned from the door, "we're flittin' at last."

"Yes," cried a voice they knew only too well, from the depths of a churn placed on the last wagon, "Yes, and I'm flittin' wi' ye."

"Od rot thee!" cried the dismayed farmer, "and if I'd known thou'd be flittin' too I wadn't ha' stirred a peg! Nay, nay," he said to his wife, "it's no use, we may as weel turn back again to th'owd house as be tormented in another not so convenient."

The story goes that they unpacked the furniture and returned to the house, and that the Boggart, having apparently realised the insecurity of his comfortable quarters, became less tormenting and never again disturbed the peace of the family.

This legend was used by Tennyson in one of his *English Idylls*, "Walking to the Mail," which was published in 1842.

"His house, for so they say,
Was haunted with a jolly ghost, that shook
The curtains, whined in lobbies, tap't at doors,
And rummaged like a rat; no servant stay'd;
The farmer vext packs up his beds and chairs
And all his household stuff; and with his boy
Betwixt his knees, his wife upon the tilt,
Sets out, and meets a friend who hails him,
'What!
You're flitting?' 'Yes, we're flitting,' says the ghost.
(For they had packed the thing among the beds).
'Oh, well,' says he, 'You flitting with us too—
Jack, turn the horses' heads and home again.'"

"We entered the cleft," says a traveller in Lancashire in 1844, "and looked in vain for the abode of the Boggart, but were abundantly repaid by the beauty of the scenery. Coming from the other end of the dell, a boy met us, of the true Lancashire breed, his breast uncovered, his head bare and uncombed, his eyes and mouth full of broad quiet fun, with something like cunning in his look, and signs of health and strength from head to foot.

"Hast thou seen the Boggart?" we inquired. "There's noa Boggart neaw," replied he, with an archness of meaning that language is quite unable to convey.

THE OLD MAN AND HIS WIFE

This is a modern version of a ballad written in the reign of Edward IV., called "A Ballad of a Tyrannical Husband," the original of which is in the Chetham Library at Manchester.

THERE was an old man who lived in a wood,
    As you may plainly see;
He said he could do as much work in a day
    As his wife could do in three.
"With all my heart," the old woman said,
    "If that you will allow,
To-morrow you'll stay at home in my stead,
    And I'll go drive the plough.

"But you must milk Tidy the cow,
    For fear that she go dry;
And you must feed the little pigs,
    That are within the sty;
And you must mind the speckled hen,
    For fear she lay away;
And you must reel the spool of yarn,
    That I spun yesterday."

The old woman took a staff in her hand,
    And went to drive the plough;
The old man took a pail in his hand,
    And went to milk the cow.
But Tidy hinched and Tidy flinched,
    And Tidy broke his nose;
And Tidy gave him such a blow,
    That the blood ran down to his toes.

"High, Tidy! ho, Tidy! high,
    Tidy! stand thou still;
If ever I milk you, Tidy, again,
    'Twill be sore against my will."
He went to feed the little pigs,
    That were within the sty;
He hit his head against the beams,
    And he made the blood to fly.

He went to mind the speckled hen,
    For fear she'd lay astray;
And he forgot the spool of yarn,
    His wife spun yesterday.
So he swore by the sun, the moon, and the stars,
    And the green leaves on the tree,
If his wife didn't do a day's work in her life,
    She should ne'er be ruled by he.

A TRAGIC LAUNCH AT MANCHESTER

AS the launch of a vessel on the Irwell had never been witnessed near Manchester, the announcement of the New Quay Company that they would launch a new flat, the *Emma*, with full rigging on February 19, 1828, caused great excitement in the town. "The weather on the appointed day," says an eye-witness, "is clear and breezy, with occasional gleams of sunshine. We press forward with the throng, assured of witnessing an agreeable novelty. Desertion is common in the mills, warehouses and other places of business. Thoughtless apprentices give themselves a field day, regardless of the drill that awaits their return. When we arrive at the selected spot, the vessel stands, full-rigged, upon the stocks, and two or three hundred individuals are on board, the majority being young women, many of them decorated in their holiday attire. The spectacle is of the gayest description. Flags and small streamers are flying along the Quay, as likewise from the vessels in the river. The booming of cannon answers the mirthful occasion; while the band of the Ninth Regiment, playing in the yard, adds to the general hilarity."

The *Emma* was duly launched amidst loud cheering, the two ladies who broke the bottle of wine upon her bows being, oddly enough, on the vessel itself. But, to the horror of the huge crowds, the *Emma* glided straight across the river, and striking the Salford bank, heeled over on her side, precipitating all those on board into the water. It was a terrible spectacle, this mass of struggling human beings literally drowning one another in their frantic efforts to escape.

Several men, hastily stripping off their clothes, jumped into the river and brought body after body to the shore, some already dead, some only senseless. As soon as they had handed their charge to those on the bank, who instantly applied all the methods then known for resuscitation, these brave men dived back into the water for further rescue. One of them, Richard

STATUE TO OLIVER CROMWELL

99

Walker, after saving three people, was drowned by one of the victims clinging tightly round his neck when they were within close reach of the bank. A fishmonger, who had his stall in front of the Salford Town Hall, when he saw the *Emma* turn upon her side, immediately tore off his clothes, and placing them by the river side, went to the rescue. After some hours in the water, during which time he saved many lives, he returned, utterly exhausted, to the place where he had left them. But they had vanished! They had been stolen! One would think that even the most abandoned thief would have some regard, in that time of supreme tragedy, for a man who was actually risking his life. The exposure to the cold of a February day, after the hours of heavy exertion in the water, brought on an illness which caused the brave man's death a few months afterwards.

In all thirty-eight people were drowned, and of those who were resuscitated it is recorded that " where brandy, constant friction, and the hot bath proved useless, . . . an incision was made in the windpipe, thus enabling the lungs to be inflated by bellows. As a last resource, the blood of a man, or of a dog, was transferred into the veins of the patient."

One of the two sisters who christened the *Emma*—daughters of William Brereton Grime, the agent of the New Quay Company, and who were both rescued from the river—in later life became one of the benefactors of Manchester as Mrs. Heywood. The first statue of Oliver Cromwell erected in the country was presented by Mrs. Heywood to the City Council. It bears this inscription—

The Gift of
Elizabeth Salisbury Heywood
to the citizens of Manchester
August 1875.

THE BLACK KNIGHT OF ASHTON

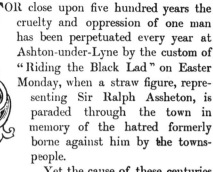

(*Reproduced by permission of Messrs. Lupton, Ashton-under-Lyne.*)

FOR close upon five hundred years the cruelty and oppression of one man has been perpetuated every year at Ashton-under-Lyne by the custom of "Riding the Black Lad" on Easter Monday, when a straw figure, representing Sir Ralph Assheton, is paraded through the town in memory of the hatred formerly borne against him by the townspeople.

Yet the cause of these centuries of obloquy was a weed!

Sir Ralph Assheton, who married Margaret Barton, the heiress of Middleton, and so established a branch of his family in that place, was the son of Sir John Assheton, lord of the manor of Ashton. He was made Vice-Constable of England and amongst the many privileges granted to him for his lifetime was that of "guld-riding." The "guld" was a species of marigold "which grew amongst the corn—it was often called the 'corn-marigold.'" It had a poisonous effect upon all corn, and in order that it should be extirpated, and so preserve the harvests, a law was passed enacting that in the spring, the lord of the manor should inspect the fields of all his farmers, and that wherever a stock of the "guld" was found growing amongst the corn the farmer should be fined a wether sheep, the animal going to the fold of the lord of the manor. This annual inspection was called "guld-riding."

The custom had apparently fallen into disuse, for in the time of Sir John Assheton a large portion of the lower lying land near Ashton, called Low Carr, was overrun by the weed. His son, Sir Ralph, acting upon his privilege of "guld riding," "on a certain day in the spring, made his appearance in this manor, clad in black armour (whence his name of the Black Lad) mounted on a charger, and attended by a numerous train of his followers, in order to levy the penalty arising from the neglect of clearing the land from "*carr gulds*." Such an interference by one who was not actually their lord was considered as rank tyranny by his father's tenants. They refused to give their sheep in payment of the fine. Lords of the manor in those times had power of life and death; the Vice-Constable of England, too, had summary powers. At some distance from the Castle at Ashton was a place called the Gallows Field, where the lord of the manor had set his gibbet. The unhappy peasants, who had allowed the *carr gulds* to invade their cornfields and had refused to pay the fine demanded by Sir Ralph, discovered that his rights led them to the castle dungeons, and from the dungeons to the gallows.

There was a reign of terror in Ashton. The yearly visitations of the Black Knight, as he was called, sent thrills of fear quivering through the whole community, a fear which was expressed in this prayer—

> "Sweet Jesus, for Thy mercy's sake,
> And for Thy bitter passion,
> Save us from the Tower axe
> And from Sir Ralph Assheton,"

which was varied with—

ton, who succeeded their father, Sir John, abolished the usage of "guld-riding" for ever, and set aside a small sum to perpetuate by an annual ceremony the dreaded visits of the Black Knight. There could have been little love lost between the brothers. The Easter Monday "Black Lad" procession at Ashton-under-Lyne is the only case in which family hatred has been perpetuated for nearly five hundred years.

ASHTON HALL

> "Oh, save me from the burning stake,
> And from Sir Ralph de Assheton."

Sir Ralph has not lacked defenders who contend that his enforcement of the old law against *carr gulds*, was inspired by a zeal for improving agriculture. Be this the case or not, he carried out the law with a cruelty so bitter and harsh that he left an ineffaceable memory amongst his father's tenants.

It is significant that when Sir Ralph died his half-brother Sir Thomas Asshe-

Once upon a time the straw figure of the Black Lad was set up as a target after the procession was over, and literally shot to pieces.

The lot of the tenant under the feudal lords was anything but easy, and in Ashton-under-Lyne the manorial rights were rigidly enforced. Service was then given instead of rent, the tenants in Ashton taking their tenements for twenty years on these conditions :—

1. To render certain services to the lord of the manor.

2. To contribute a prescribed sum to a Yule or Christmas-day feast, to be held in the lord's mansion, and at which they and their wives were guests.
3. To plough and harrow in the lord's land a certain number of days in the year.

the lord at the death of the head of the family.

The last stipulation, by which upon the death of a farmer the lord claimed his best beast, was called a heriot. It was a cruel exaction; and as the Church took the second best beast, the widow of a poor man was deprived perhaps of her

THE GAOLER'S CHAPEL, ASHTON HALL

4. To lead a fixed quantity of turf from the Moss to the lord's residence.
5. To shear four days in harvest and cart corn one day, and to grind their corn at the lord's soke-mill, giving the lord one six-teenth part of the grain so ground.
6. To pay their rents half-yearly (June 24 and Nov. 11).
7. To pay the best of their beasts to

principal means of livelihood. There used to be many traditions in Ashton of the hardships inflicted by this feudal custom, of which a story told by Dr. Hibbert-Ware concerning Dukinfield, is an illustration. "A tenant's boy, on the death of his father, driving an only cow to the manor-house of Dukinfield, being met by the lord (Sir Robert Dukinfield), with whose person and rank the boy was unacquainted, was questioned whither he was taking the beast,

THE DUNGEONS, ASHTON HALL

" 'I am driving it to Dukinfield for the heriot,' said the boy. 'My father is dead. We are many children and have no cow but this. Don't you think the Devil will take Sir Robert when he dies?'

" The lad was fortunately addressing a humane landlord.

" 'Return home,' said the knight, 'take the cow back to thy mother! I know Sir Robert. I am going to Dukinfield myself, and I will make the matter up with him.' "

Unhappily instances of this kind were unknown at Ashton, the lords of the manor there, and the Church, both exacting their toll from their dead tenants, no matter how poorly off they had left their families. In the course of time these crying injustices, carried out in the name of the law, were gradually fathered upon the Black Knight, who consequently was made much blacker by tradition than he actually was. Sir Ralph Assheton, beyond his spring inspections for corn-

marigolds and the punishments he inflicted thereupon, had no rights or authority in the manor of Ashton-under-Lyne, these belonging to his father and his half-brother. But tradition has laid every act of feudal severity in the district at his door.

Local tradition has assigned the Black Knight a permanent residence at Ashton Hall, and has made it the scene of his judgments upon the trembling peasants. But it could only have been his home up to the time of his marriage with the heiress of Middleton, when he went to Middleton Hall and founded another branch of the Assheton family. Tradition has drawn moving pictures of Sir Ralph, seated in knightly magnificence at Ashton Hall, brow-beating poor widows who could not pay the heriot, or sallying forth with a band of armed attendants to pillage and oppress his humble neighbours. But for once tradition is sorely at fault. Sir Ralph was by no means popular with his own family, and it is very doubtful if he ever stayed at his paternal home after his appointment as Vice-Constable of England and his consequent revival of the " guld-riding."

The descendants of Sir Ralph's half-brother, Sir Thomas, reigned at Ashton Hall until 1516, when the estate passed to the eldest of the last Sir Thomas Assheton's three daughters, Margaret, who had married Sir William Booth. One of her descendants, George Booth, was created Lord Delamere about a hundred and fifty years later, and his son, although a staunch supporter of the Parliament in the great struggle with Charles I, was made Earl of Warrington in the reign of James II. The title became extinct on the death of his son,

who left only an heiress, Lady Mary Booth. She married Henry Grey, fourth Earl of Stamford, who added her family name to his own. Their son, George Grey-Booth, was given a second earldom in 1796— that of Warrington — and thus Ashton came into the possession of the Earls of Stamford and Warrington.

Ashton Hall was pulled down a few years ago. The original hall was built in the fifteenth century. At one time it was used as a prison, and the illustrations, which are reproduced from old drawings, show the old hall with its gables and latticed windows, the portion of the building turned into dungeons, and the ruins of the gaoler's chapel.

HORSE=BREEDING AT SALFORD

IN the reign of Queen Elizabeth an Act of Parliament was passed to keep up the breed of horses, and also to prevent them from being sold abroad. Lord Burghley, the great Minister, himself sent a letter to the magistrates of, the Salford Hundred requiring the strict enforcement of the new law which ordained that every landowner should keep a certain number of mares for breeding. The reply of the Salford magistrates has been preserved in the Harleian MSS. and is given below. As well as giving Lord Burghley the information that the law was being obeyed, it shows the landowners in the Salford Hundred at that time, and the extent of their possessions.

" HUNDRED DE SALFORD. The Present-m^{tes} of the Jurates there whoe Saye that concerninge the Carryinge or conveying of horses and mares out of this Realm theye finde nothinge. And as touchinge thincrease and breedinge of horses, geldinges and mares the Jurates saye that the Right and ho. Edward Therle of Derby

hath ij parkes wthin the said hundreth. The one Contayninge in Quantity three myles Compas, and the other one myle, and hath mares for breede accordinge to the statute. Edmunde Trafford esq^r hath ij parkes wthin the said hundrethe eyther of them contayninge in Quantitie twove myles Compas, and hath mares for breede accordinge to the Statute. Robert Worsley knight hath one parke in the said hundredth contayninge in Quantity ij miles in Compasse, and hath mares for breede, accordynge to the Statute. John Byron Esqre hath one parke in the saidde hundreth contayninge in Quantitie ij myles in Compas and hath mares for breede according to the Statute, John Bothe esq^r hath one parke in the said hundreth contayninge in Quantitie ij myles Compas and hath mares for breede accordinge to the Statute. Richard Asshton of Middleton esq^r nowe the Queens Ma^{tes} warde, hath one parke wthin the said hundrethe Contayninge in Quantity ij myles compas."

"JEMMY DAWSON"

WHEN the Young Pretender, Charles Edward, came to Manchester in 1745, among the many young men who enlisted beneath his banner was James Dawson, the son of a doctor in that city and a graduate of St. John's College, Cambridge. He was given a commission as captain in the Manchester Regiment. After the disastrous defeat of the Young Pretender's army, the Manchester regiment surrendered at Carlisle, the officers believing that, as they had been given French commissions by the Pretender, they would be treated as prisoners of war and would be exchanged. This plea, however, did not hold good. They were considered as rebels and traitors who had taken up arms against their lawful sovereign, and were sent in wagons strictly guarded to London, where they were led in triumph through the streets. Captain Dawson was engaged to a young lady, and on both sides the attachment was unusually deep and tender. Her name was Katherine Norton. It was said that "she was an orphan and that her parents had been of illustrious rank," and that whilst travelling with a maiden aunt she had made Dawson's acquaintance at Cambridge.

The Manchester officers were tried in London, on July 16, 1746, and after a three days' hearing were condemned to death as traitors; the execution of nine of them, including Dawson, being fixed for the 30th of the same month. On the appointed day the nine were dragged on three hurdles from the New Prison at Southwark to the gallows at Kennington. Near the gallows was a block and a pile of faggots, for the executions were to be carried out with all the ancient barbarity appointed for the death of traitors. No clergyman was present, as they had been condemned to die "without the benefit of clergy," and for nearly an hour after they had been removed from the hurdles to the fatal cart the condemned conducted their own devotions. Then the faggots were set alight, the cart passed under the gallows, a noose was placed round each man's neck, and the cart was driven on, leaving the nine men struggling and writhing in the air. Before life was extinct they were cut down and stripped naked. Each body was placed upon the block; the hangman severed the head with a stroke of a cleaver, and placed it in a coffin; he then cut out the bowels and the heart, and threw them into the fire, crying out as he accomplished his revolting task, "God save King George!" to which the watching crowd replied with a loud shout.

Miss Norton gave a supreme proof of her love for the unfortunate Dawson by following him from the prison to the gallows. "When it was ascertained," says Mr. Robert Chambers in his *History of the Rebellion of '45*, "that Captain Dawson was to suffer death, the inconsolable young lady determined to witness the execution, and she accordingly followed the sledges in a hackney coach, accompanied by a gentleman nearly related to her, and one female friend. She got near enough to see all the dreadful preparations without betraying any extravagant emotions; she also succeeded in restraining her feelings during the progress of the bloody tragedy; but when all was over, and the shouts of the multitude rang in her ears, she drew back her head again into the coach, and crying, 'My dear, I follow thee! I follow thee! Sweet Jesu, receive both our souls together!' fell upon the neck of her companion and expired in the very moment she was speaking."

The following ballad by Shenstone was written shortly after the death of these two devoted lovers—

> Come listen to my mournful tale,
> Ye tender hearts and lovers dear;
> Nor will you scorn to heave a sigh
> Nor will you blush to shed a tear.

And thou, dear Kitty, peerless maid,
  Do thou a pensive ear incline ;
For thou canst weep at every woe,
  And pity every plaint but mine.

Young Dawson was a gallant youth,
  A brighter never trod the plain ;
And well he lov'd one charming maid,
  And dearly was he lov'd again.

One tender maid she lov'd him dear ;
  Of gentle blood the damsel came,
And faultless was her beauteous form,
  And spotless was her virgin fame.

But curse on party's hateful strife,
  That led the faithful youth astray,
The day the rebel clans appear'd :
  O, had he never seen that day !

Their colours and their sash he wore,
  And in the fatal dress was found ;
And now he must that death endure
  Which gives the brave the keenest wound.

How pale was then his truelove's cheek
  When Jemmy's sentence reach'd her ear !
For never yet did Alpine snows
  So pale, nor yet so chill appear.

With faltering voice she weeping said :
  " O Dawson, monarch of my heart,
Think not thy death shall end our loves,
  For thou and I will never part.

" Yet might sweet mercy find a place,
  And bring relief to Jemmy's woes.
O George, without a prayer for thee
  My orisons should never close.

" The gracious prince that gives him life,
  Would crown a never-dying flame,
And every tender babe I bore
  Should learn to lisp the giver's name.

" But though, dear youth, thou should'st be
  dragged
To yonder ignominious tree,

Thou shalt not want a faithful friend
  To share thy bitter fate with thee."

O then her mourning coach was call'd,
  The sledge mov'd slowly on before ;
Though borne in a triumphal car,
  She had not lov'd her favourite more.

She follow'd him, prepared to view
  The terrible behests of law ;
And the last scene of Jemmy's woe
  With calm and steadfast eye she saw.

Distorted was that blooming face
  Which she had fondly lov'd so long ;
And stifled was that tuneful breath
  Which in her praise had sweetly sung ;

And sever'd was that beauteous neck
  Round which her arms had fondly closed ;
And mangled was that beauteous breast
  On which her love-sick head reposed ;

And ravish'd was that constant heart
  She did to every heart prefer ;
For though it could its king forget,
  'Twas true and loyal still to her.

Amid those unrelenting flames
  She bore this constant heart to see ;
But when 'twas moulder'd into dust,
  " Now, now," she cried, " I'll follow thee.

" My death, my death alone can show
  The pure and lasting love I bore ;
Accept, O Heaven, of woes like ours,
  And let us, let us weep no more."

The dismal scene was o'er and past,
  The lover's mournful hearse retired ;
The maid drew back her languid head,
  And, sighing forth his name, expired.

Though justice ever must prevail,
  The tear my Kitty sheds is due ;
For seldom shall she hear a tale
  So sad, so tender, and so true.

SELLING A WIFE

FROM time to time cases in the police court show that there is still a belief, especially amongst colliers, that a man may legally sell his wife. Formerly the error was widespread amongst the lower classes in Lancashire, it being thought to be a purely legal transaction if the wife was taken to the place of sale with a halter round her neck, and the buyer was given a written receipt by the husband for the money paid. Quite late in the nineteenth century a man pleaded in a Lancashire county court that he was not liable for his wife's debts as he had sold her to another man for half-a-crown long before the debts in question were contracted, and *had given a receipt for the money!*

OLD MANCHESTER

THERE died in Manchester, some fourteen years ago, at the age of ninety-two, a lady, Mrs. Louisa Potter, who had lived there all her life. before the reader than any bookish description.

"If you ask me," she said, "to tell you of the changes I have seen in Man-

OLD MARKET STREET, MANCHESTER

Retaining vivid powers of observation and memory to the end, Mrs. Potter's recollections of the Manchester of her youth, as recorded in the *Manchester Guardian* two years before her death, bring the old conditions more clearly chester, I must say at once that, within my recollection, the place has changed altogether. I might almost say that I remember it as a village, for with all its size the Manchester of my youth, judged by the standard of to-day, was little more.

How could it be anything else, you modern people would say, when it sent no member to Parliament, had no omnibuses, no cabs, no suburbs, very little light in the streets, no police except the decrepit old watchmen, scarcely a public building, and not even the thought of a bishop. We all lived in the town in those days, either that or quite in the country some three or four miles away. Mosley Street was occupied exclusively by dwelling-houses. Such a thing as a warehouse or a place of business in Mosley Street wasn't known when I was a girl. Next, I think, to King Street, it was the best residential quarter in the town. I remember seeing one of the houses advertised for sale, together with the garden. This garden, you may be surprised to learn, extended ever so far in a line with what is now Market Street. And in King Street there was a very pretty rookery."

The houses inhabited by the "genteel" families in St. James's Square, Prince's Street, Mosley Street, Piccadilly, Norfolk Street, Brown Street and Portland Street, were fine and handsome, "many with noble staircases and rooms richly decorated with pilasters, carving on wood, and festoons of stucco flowers." The most imposing of these mansions, Mrs. Potter said, was on the site of the old Town Hall, the present Reference Library; "the house had two wings and a cupola, and there was a courtyard in front reached by a grand flight of steps. The courtyard was paved, I think, with diamond-shaped slabs of black and white marble. In the riots of 1819 the house came to be used as a barracks, and very formidable it looked with cannon at each end of the

OLD HOUSES IN THE MARKET PLACE

OLD HOUSES IN SMITHY DOOR

terrace and the sentinels pacing up and down in front."

At that time King Street ended at Police Street, the only communication with Deansgate being through Back King Street. Market Street Lane was a narrow irregular street, its houses having projecting black-and-white upper storeys, and gabled roofs. At the lower end, near the Exchange, the footpath was only eighteen inches in width.

The Cathedral was all shut in by old tumbledown houses, the only approach into Strangeways being down Hunt's Back; beyond that was the country, with houses and gardens at intervals.

The interior of the Cathedral must have been somewhat startling. Mrs. Potter says, " To begin with, the ceiling was blue, with ornaments of gold, and very pretty it looked. But the angels with which the church was adorned—what would modern taste have said to them, I wonder? Those strange effigies wore blue coats, red waistcoats, gold-coloured knee-breeches, and powdered wigs!"

Graveyards received scant attention, and the gravestones outside the Collegiate Church were allowed to lie where they fell. Mrs. Potter said they were sometimes taken away. She remembered a panic in the town because one morning the loaves of a certain baker appeared with the impression of a skull and cross-bones upon them. The baker had helped himself to a gravestone to serve as flooring for his oven.

She remembered the pillory in the Market Place, but never saw it used, and the scold's " bridle " or " brank," which was kept at the Town Hall. Its last wearer was a dwarf, called Charlotte, whose boast was that she could drink twenty-four noggins of gin on end.

"Preference" parties were the great distraction of the Manchester ladies, at which a game called "quadrille" was played. "We always began with tea," said Mrs. Potter, "and very weak it escort the ladies home. Sedan chairs were not very much in use, though I remember my mother going in one. Some people had their own. For my part, I always thought it must be extremely unpleasant to be shut up in such boxes. But there were no one-horse cabs then, you know—nothing but coaches and pair

SALFORD CROSS (TAKEN DOWN IN 1824)

generally was, for at that time the commonest tea cost 6s. 8d. a pound, and such tea as was served at parties would cost from 10s. to 12s. 6d. White sugar was 1s. 6d. a pound, and the coarsest brown sugar 9d. The teapot, you see, could be an expensive luxury in those days. Cake and wine would be served in the middle of the evening, and at the close, carriages or coaches would be announced, or servants would be in waiting with lanterns to —and if you posted anywhere it was enormously expensive."

Mrs. Potter remembered Harrison Ainsworth coming to their house in Adelphi Terrace to escort his mother home from one of the card parties; and she was present at the performance of his first play, given in the cellar of his father's house[1] when he was about sixteen. Artificial flowers were used for table decora-

[1] See "William Harrison Ainsworth."

111

tions, never real ones. The first white camellia in Manchester was brought to Mrs. Potter's father from China, and was regarded as a great curiosity. She remembered, too, the introduction of dahlias. As this was brought about by Lady Holland, they were called "Georginas" in compliment to her Christian name, but this was speedily displaced by the word dahlia, taken from the name of the Swedish botanist Dahl.

In 1887 there was a Jubilee Exhibition in Manchester, a striking feature of which was a representation of Old Manchester. Mrs. Potter said it was just like a visit to the scenes of her childhood. The Salford Cross (which was taken down in 1824), and the old bridge, she remembered perfectly. When passing through the mimic Market Street, Mrs. Potter remarked to the architect:

"These cobble stones make me think of Market Street as I used to know it."

"Well," he replied, "you are right. They are the same stones!"

When Market Street had been repaved the old cobbles had been kept.

An Act of Parliament, obtained in 1866, for the building of the Town Hall and Albert Square, entirely changed that

VIEW OF OLD MARKET STREET

112

quarter of the city. Princess Street had been in existence since 1740, but in 1785 it was the end of Manchester upon that side. The original street only extended from Cross Street to Cooper Street, from there to Portland Street it was called Bond Street, and from Portland Street century the then owner of Garratt Hall married young, and lived there with his wife and family for several years. Then he was called to London on business. He announced his safe arrival, and from that time nothing more was heard of him, despite the anxious search made by his

THE WOOL-PACK PUBLIC HOUSE

to the River Medlock it was known as Old Garratt.

In an angle formed by the Medlock and Shorter's Brook stood an old black-and-white house, called Garratt Hall, which had belonged successively to the Trafford, Gerard and Mosley families. Before its demolition the same fate befell the old house which happened to so many of the halls near Manchester. It was divided into tenements for workpeople.

A curious story was told of this house. Early in the first half of the eighteenth

relations and the authorities. It was believed he had met his death in one of the appalling slums then abounding in London. His wife devoted herself to the education of their children.

Years passed, until the eldest son came of age. In order to prove his right of inheritance certain documents had to be produced. No trace of them could be found anywhere. It was thought probable that the missing man might have taken the papers with him to London and deposited them in safe keeping. An advertisement was therefore inserted in the London newspapers, so skilfully worded that only the holder of the documents in question would understand its meaning.

After a considerable lapse of time a mysterious answer came to Garratt Hall, laying down certain conditions, one being that the heir himself should go to London. The young fellow obeyed and, arriving at

Upon his taking the oath, the stranger confessed that he was the missing father.

On his arrival in London he had taken a lodging, and falling in love with his landlord's daughter, had passed himself off as a bachelor. After a short wooing he married her, and abandoning Garratt Hall, his estate, his wife and children, became the partner of his father-in-law,

OLD BUILDINGS IN DEANSGATE, NEAR PARSONAGE LANE

the house indicated, was told by a man who received him that he must agree to being blindfolded. This being done, he was put into a sedan chair, and after many turnings and twistings was set down, and his eyes unbandaged. He found himself in a sitting-room with an elderly man, who made him take a most solemn oath that he would not divulge how he obtained the deeds. At the same time he was told he would receive a message, when he might make the secret known.

who was a shopkeeper. He told his son he had never repented his action. He had either forgotten the documents or was not aware of their importance, for it was only when he realised the risk his son ran of losing his patrimony, from the advertisement, that he took the extreme step of making the truth known.

The son returned to Garratt Hall in possession of the papers. Many years elapsed before he received the promised message of his father's death. The story was then told to a few friends, and thus it became known, the son having most faithfully kept his promise of silence.

Even when Manchester had secured her manufacturing supremacy — which was about 1835—the lord of the manor controlled the markets, and appointed his officers to regulate all matters appertaining to them. Water was only obtainable from private wells or from a company, who supplied what was called "store-pipe water." Only the main thoroughfares were lighted with gas; oil lamps, which had to be trimmed every day, and were lighted with a torch, being the only illumination in the side streets. The police staff consisted of four beadles, four keepers of the lock-up, fourteen "assistants" or "runners" to the police, four street-keepers, a comptroller, a clerk, assistant clerk, committee clerk, a cashier and a messenger.

In 1795 the Post Office was near the Bull's Head, the staff consisting of a lady postmistress and two clerks. But its receipts were eleven thousand pounds more than those of any other provincial post office.

Taverns were numerous in old Manchester, but they were not the public-houses of to-day. Restaurants were unknown, the taverns supplied their place, the landlords themselves personally presiding at the dinner-table. On market-days the taverns were crowded with merchants, manufacturers and other commercial men who had driven into the town. The leading taverns had large stables, where the patrons of the house could put up their horses and conveyances. The bar-parlours served as clubs to the residents, those institutions being then unknown, and were frequented by men of the highest standing in the town—"there was no shamefaced hesitation in those days as to the respectability of public-houses."

The Bear's Head, the Seven Stars, and the Vintner's Arms in Smithy Door were the leading taverns, but there were many more equally as popular. Some of the landlords were great "characters." One of them, John Shaw, who kept John Shaw's Punch House in the Shambles, had served in the Army, and had acted as a Sheriff's officer. He became famous in the town for a particular brew he made of punch, then the favourite beverage. Shaw was a rigid disciplinarian. His punch was served in china bowls of two sizes, one called P., the other Q.; the first costing a shilling, the second sixpence. It was a fixed rule that no customer should drink more than one shilling bowl or two sixpenny bowls; further orders were refused. Another rule was the closing of the house at eight o'clock. Immediately the hour had struck, Shaw would enter the bar-parlour and announce the time. Once, after an election, Colonel Stanley, the successful candidate, was entertaining some of his supporters at Punch House, and when Shaw warned him it was eight o'clock, he begged for an extension of time.

"Colonel Stanley, you are a law-maker, and should not be a law-breaker," was the inexorable Shaw's reply, "and if you and your friends don't leave the room in five minutes, you will find your boots full of water."

At the end of five minutes an old servant, called Molly, appeared with a mop and a bucket of water. The new M.P. and his friends departed hastily.

Smithy Door led from the Market Place to Old Bridge Street. Its curious name is said to have been derived from the following incident. A blacksmith, who had a forge in Old Bridge Street—which was long ago called Smithy Bank—summoned one of his customers for debt in the Court of Requests. Proof of the debt was demanded, whereupon the blacksmith went to his smithy, took down the upper portion of the door, on the back of

When Victoria Street was made, an ancient building with an oriel window and a portion of the upper part of a

OLD BUILDINGS, STRANGEWAYS BRIDGE

which he had chalked his accounts, and carrying it into the Court triumphantly, proved and won his case.

statue of the Virgin Mary, was discovered in the upper part of Smithy Door. By many authorities this building was believed to have been the Sanctuary House established in the reign of Henry VIII. by Act of Parliament. By this Act Manchester was constituted " a place of privilege and tuicion for terme of life to all offenders and malefactors of whatsoever quality, kind or nature their offences might be, for the which saide offences and crimes, the paines and punishment of death shall ensue by the statute laws and customes of the realme."

This privilege to criminals was so harmful to the town, that after a year Manchester's right of sanctuary was abolished by another Act, the right being transferred to Chester.

The first Exchange was built by Sir Oswald Mosley, the lord of the manor, in 1729, but it was a failure owing to its being used for a market as well as for commercial transactions. A traveller, visiting the town in 1764, wrote, "Instead of affording a convenient walk for the merchants, it is crowded with butchers' stalls."

In 1792 the first Exchange was pulled down, the second one being built in 1805. It had a circular front ornamented with fluted columns. At the back was the Post Office, and when increasing business made enlargement necessary, in 1839 it was absorbed into the Exchange. A further extension took place in 1850, at a cost of £86,000. But sixteen years later this proved entirely inadequate for the rapidly increasing trade of the town. The present magnificent building was opened in 1871.

What was known as the Old Exchange is sometimes confounded with the two early Exchanges. It was a building in King Street, erected by Lady Ann Bland —" a handsome room upon pillars, with a space beneath to walk in "—early in the eighteenth century. It seems to have been used chiefly as an Assembly Room. The first circulating library in Manchester was established there in 1765, under the title of the Manchester Circulating Library. The illustration shows the ticket of membership. It was afterwards removed to Exchange Buildings, Ducie Street, and only came to an end in 1867, when its many thousands of volumes were sold by public auction.

MEMBER'S TICKET FOR THE FIRST CIRCULATING LIBRARY IN MANCHESTER

POETS' CORNER, MANCHESTER

THERE stands in "ye Milne-gate" at Manchester, a quaint old shop, once an inn, which had for its sign "Poets' Corner," so given because it was the meeting-place of a little band of Manchester poets and writers during the 'forties and 'fifties of the last century. But before the little hostel was singled out for their reunions by the Manchester *literati*, it was called the Sun Inn, as witnesses the invitation to the first of these gatherings.

> "Sun Inn, Long Millgate, Manchester,
> "*January 1st*, 1842.

"DEAR SIR,

"It is proposed by a few gentlemen, admirers of the Manchester poets, that a friendly Poetical Soirée should be held at the Sun Inn, Long Millgate, on Friday the seventh instant. A little plain dinner will be provided at three o'clock precisely.

"Mr. C. Swain, Mr. J. C. Prince, Mr. J. B. Rogerson, Mr. Rose, Mr. S. Bamford, etc., are expected to be present, and your company will be esteemed a favour by, dear Sir,

"Yours most respectfully,
"W. EARNSHAW.

"P.S.—A reply, on or before Wednesday, would oblige."

Charles Swain, one of the "Manchester Poets," had a considerable reputation in his time, not only in his native city, but in London. These lines from an "In Memoriam" poem to his friend Henry Marsden, are good examples of his facile style, and sincere, pleasing, though somewhat platitudinous verse. It expressed the spirit of the generation in which it was written.

"Is there a childhood in that sphere
 To which thy soul hath fled;
Do we begin the spirit-year,
 New born from out the dead?

Tread we eternity at first,
 As we trod time of yore;
Or, does immortal glory burst
 At once from God's own shore?

Oh, gate of death! Oh, gate of life!
 Oh, mystery sublime!
With everlasting wonders rife,
 And marvels of all time;
Say, shall affections still remain?
 Shall memories endure?
And links of friendship's endless chain
 Eternity secure?

Shall truth find truth—and love find love,—
 Within that better world?
Shall all the tears and pains we prove,
 Be ever earthward hurl'd?
Shall friend meet friend in that blest hour,
 Before their Saviour's sight,
And feel that Death no more hath power
 To separate or blight?"

In such respect was Charles Swain held in Manchester that when he died in September 1874, the Mayor ordered the flag at the Town Hall to be hoisted half-mast.

These meetings of the poets were passed in literary discussions, the reading of verses, and very often when musicians, singers and players, either amateurs or professional, were present, with old English songs and recitations. The majority of the "poets" were engaged in various trades and occupations; literature was their relaxation. Thus Mr. J. B. Rogerson, referred to in the letter of invitation, held a post in connection with the Harpurhey Cemetery. And the Starkie, a strolling player, the Baines, a comic singer, of whom he wrote in 1855,— "Starkie and Baines were both interred in Harpurhey Cemetery, and I read the service over them," were doubtless two of the many guests who had entertained and been entertained by the Poets' Corner.

The editor of *Brierley's Journal* gave an amusing anecdote of this same Starkie, who seems to have been of some celebrity in Lancashire. "We knew Starkie well," he says. "He was engaged with a travelling booth then (1841) stationed at Hollinwood when we first knew him. He had a prevailing fondness during nonworking hours for visiting the homes of hand-loom weavers in that locality, and cultivating the sociabilities peculiar to that class of people. On one of these visits—we were present at the time—he conceived a notion that he could weave, and got upon a loom for the purpose of making a trial of his skill. Unfortunately the seat-board had been made for a much lighter man, Starkie being stout and heavily built. He had no sooner seated himself and placed his feet upon the treadles than the board snapped in the middle, and the tragedian disappeared as if down the 'trap' of a stage. His exclamation was, as he lay in the treadle-hole, 'How are the mighty fallen!'"

Another poet of the little Manchester band was William Rowlinson, whose ballad, "Sir Gaulter," has already been given in these pages. It embodied a tradition of the Northen Boat House, but when it appeared in the old ballad form, in the *Phœnix*, a weekly periodical which had a short but a brilliant existence, it was believed by many to be a genuine old ballad. Rowlinson after being a clerk in a warehouse became a traveller for a directory. All these Manchester poets felt the burden of the daily labour which prevented the exercise of their talent. Rowlinson wrote to a friend, "I should be the happiest dog alive if I possessed a little competency . . . but my destiny has been otherwise cast; the weird sisters have spun my thread of coarse and dark materials."

But the most remarkable of all these men was John Critchley Prince, whose trade was that of a reed-maker. In 1841 he published *Hours with the Muses*, a work which bordered upon genius, and showed the true poet's command of the music of words. This verse, from the "Poets' Sabbath," alone shows the heights to which Prince could have risen if he had been free to devote his time to writing, instead of having to make reeds for his daily bread:

"My heart's religion is an earnest love
  Of all that's good, and beautiful, and
    true !
My noblest temple is this sky above—
This vast pavilion of unclouded blue :
These mountains are my altars, which
    subdue
My wildest passions in their wildest
    hours ;
My hymn is ever many-voiced and
    new,—
From bird and bee, from wind and
    wave it pours.
My incense is the breath of herbs, leaves,
    fruits and flowers."

Hours with the Muses made a considerable stir amongst the literary folk of Manchester. It ran through two editions, and the reed-maker became the most talked-about, the most flattered and the most entertained man in the town. A lodge of Oddfellows and another of Ancient Shepherds were named after him. But it was rightly felt that the author should be placed in a position—to quote his own words—"above the fear of poverty, while pursuing for its own sweet sake, the exalted and refining profession of song." Various influential friends therefore tried to get him a Government post. Mr. Picton tells us, "After much correspondence and personal pressure a snug Government post, with immediate possession was obtained. The first announcement did not reveal the precise character of the appointment ; but of course we all knew what a post under Government was —ample salary with ample leisure, and finally a retiring pension for public services!"

Not possessing the means to pay his fare by train or coach to London, Prince set out on foot to take up the appointment. When he arrived there he found his "Government post" was that of a postman at Southampton! No wonder that he wrote from London in June 1842, "I find my earliest friends the most faithful after all. Is it not lamentable that after being feasted, flattered, lionized and promise-crammed for twelve months, I am now compelled to sink down into a penny postman at fifteen shillings per week? It stings me to the quick. I have, however, learned a lesson I shall not forget, and by which I hope ultimately to profit.

"I am grieved that I shall have to tear myself away from many in Manchester whom I respect, but there are others from whom it is well to part.

"I go to my new appointment (at Southampton) to-morrow. I do not know how I shall like it—not very well I am sure, though I shall there be really and truly a *man of letters*. I trust you still occasionally find solace in the exercise of your fancy and imagination. Let me tell you that you are happy in the possession of a calling which yields you bread *independent of the pen*. You will excuse my brevity, as I am not 'i' the vein.'"

When Prince arrived at Southampton he found that he had to commence his duties at five o'clock in the morning, and that "the delivery of letters would be relieved by an occasional pull at a handcart." So far from his new position giving him leisure for his poetry, he had even less time, and certainly less wages, than when following his trade in Manchester. Therefore he left Southampton after a few days and returned to his shop in Long Millgate. The "patrons" who had secured

this "Government post" for him were aggrieved, and considering him foolish in rejecting a certainty, however small, they washed their hands of him. Prince's head was undoubtedly turned by the praise and flattery which welcomed *Hours with the Muses*, and as his letter, already quoted, shows, he felt the difference between the promise of his "patrons" and its reality very bitterly. The bitterness affected his poetry; he never again reached the high level of the *Hours*. Ultimately he left Manchester and settled at Ashton-under-Lyne where he carried on his old trade, as is shown by his business card.

JOHN CRITCHLEY PRINCE
REED MAKER & HEALD KNITTER
PENNY MEADOW
ASHTON-UNDER-LYNE
Orders executed and repairs done promptly,
at the most Reasonable Prices.
February, 1851.

Prince died in 1866, having, unhappily, long outlived his fame, although he was only fifty-eight. One of his admirers has every justification in saying that if a small pension could have been given to him instead of the situation as a postman "the provincial favourite would in all probability have become a national poet." His genius was strangled by his poverty.

Samuel Bamford, whose name also appears in the invitation to the first gathering of the Poets' Corner, was a working man, who in his earlier life went through many hardships because of his advocacy of Parliamentary reform.

But, unlike most poets and reformers, he was rewarded in his lifetime, the Bamford Testimonial in 1847 bringing him a substantial sum of money, and a place being found for him at Somerset House. When he died at Moston, in a little cottage where his every want was provided by his admirers, the whole neighbourhood expressed its feeling of reverence and esteem by giving him a public funeral, and five years after his death a monument was erected over his grave and that of his wife and daughter, in Middleton Churchyard by public subscription.

Upon the first side of the monument is this inscription :—

BAMFORD
ANN, died October 15th, 1834 in the 25th year of her age.

She wept that we so soon must part,
She knew that death was near her heart ;
Yet lovely in her tears she smil'd,
A mournful radiance sadly mild,
Like sun gleam on a ruin wild,
So Heaven illum'd our dying child.

JEMIMA, died September 23rd, 1862, in the 74th year of her age.

Oh ! bless'd was her abiding care,
That watch'd me with affection's eye,
To warn of spy's perfidious snare,
To comfort in adversity.

SAMUEL, for promoting a reform of the Commons House of Parliament and a repeal of taxes on food, he was twice arrested on charges of high treason ; he was five times taken in custody before the Privy Council ; he was on five different occasions escorted in chains or manacles to various and distant parts of the country ; he stood a trial of ten days, and conducted his own defence in a manner and with a testimony which brought credit to himself and the cause he represented ; notwithstanding which the Jury found him guilty, and he was again sent to prison.

Died April 13th, 1872,
in the 85th year of his age.

On the other three sides of the monument are these inscriptions :—

Erected by public subscription in his native town. 1877.

" Bamford was a Reformer when to be so was unsafe, and he suffered for his faith."
JOHN BRIGHT.

SAMUEL BAMFORD
Born 18th February, 1788.
Died 13th April, 1872.

An early advocate of Civil and Religious Liberty, Free Trade, and Parliamentary Reform.

Author of " Passages in the Life of a Radical," and other Works in Prose and Verse.

The last of Bamford's poems was written in his seventieth year. The simplicity and homeliness of this " Farewell to my Cottage " are found in all his other poems.

" Farewell to my cottage that stands on a hill,
To valleys and fields where I wander'd at will,
And met the young spring with her buskin of dew,
As o'er the wild heather a joyance she threw ;
'Mid fitful sunbeamings, with bosom snow-fair,
And showers in the gleamings, and wind-beaten hair,
She smil'd on my cottage, and buddings of green
On alder and hawthorn and woodbine were seen—
The crocus came forth, with its lilac and gold,
And fair maiden snowdrops stood pale in the cold—
The primrose peep'd coyly from under the thorn,
And blithe look'd my cottage on that happy morn,
But spring pass'd away, and the pleasure was o'er,
And I left my cottage to claim it no more.
Farewell to my cottage—afar I must roam,
No longer a cottage, no longer a home.

For bread must be earned, though my cot I resign,
Since what I enjoy shall with honour be mine ;
So up to the great city I must depart,
With bodings of mind, and a pang at my heart.

There all seemeth strange, as if foreign
the land,
A place and a people I don't understand;
And as from the latter I turn me away,
I think of old neighbours, now lost, well-
a-day.
I think of my cottage full many a time,
A nest among flowers at midsummer
prime;
And honeybine garland o'er window and
door;
As prim as a bride ere the rebecks begin,
And white as a lily without and within.
Could I but have tarried, contented I'd
been,
Nor envied the palace of lady the queen,
Fair children would often come near us
to play
Or sent on an errand well pleasèd were
they;
A pitcher of water to fetch from the
spring,
Or wind-broken wood from my garden to
bring:
Quite happy when pleasing dear Mima or
me—
For I was their " uncle," and " granny "
was she.
And then as a recompense sure if not soon,
They'd get a new posy on Sunday forenoon,
Or handful of fruit would their willing
hearts cheer;
I miss the dear children—none like them
are here,

Though offspring as lovely as mothers ere
bore
At eve in the park I can count by the
score.
But these are not mine—of a stranger
they're shy,
Though I can but bless them as I pass
by;
When ceasing their play my emotion to
scan,
I daresay they wonder ' what ails the old
man.'

Of mine some have gone in their white
coffin shroud,
And some have been lost in the world
and its crowd;
One only remains, the last bird in the
nest,
Our own little grandchild, the dearest and
best.
But vain to repeat, though we cannot
subdue
The feelings to nature and sympathy
true.
Endurance with patience must bear the
strong part—
Sustain when it cannot give peace to the
heart;
Till life with its yearnings and struggles
is o'er,
And I shall remember my cottage no
more."

POETS' CORNER

JONE O' GRINFILT'S RAMBLE

THE authorship of this song, which was one of the most popular ever sung in Lancashire, has been attributed to various writers, amongst them James Butterworth, the author of " Rochervale." Samuel Bamford, in his *Walks through South Lancashire*, says that the song took amazingly. It was war time, and he records how, having volunteered himself, he stood at the bottom of Miller Street, Manchester, with a cockade in his hat, " viewing with surprise the almost rage with which the very indifferent verses were purchased by a crowd that stood around a little old-fashioned fellow with a withered leg, who, leaning on a crutch, with a countenance full of quaint humour, and a speech of the perfect dialect of the country, sang the song, and collected the halfpence as quickly as he could distribute it." The late Mr. John Harland discovered the actual author—a cripple called Coupe. He came upon this cripple singing at Ashton-under-Lyne, and being anxious to find out the origin of a song of which it was said more copies had been sold in rural Lancashire than any other, he invited the singer to a neighbouring tavern. Over a friendly pipe and pot of ale, the ballad-monger was easily led to talk, Mr. Harland jotting down his words in shorthand. This at first caused the cripple much concern.

" It was a cold and rainy day in winter." says Mr. Harland, " the door was accordingly shut, the fire stirred up to a warm glow. The cripple sat basking before the fire, with his lame leg thrown across his crutch, his other foot on the fender, when, after putting a quid of tobacco into his mouth, and taking a swig of the ale, he went on gaily with his narrative for some minutes, until, glancing towards the paper, and seeing uncouth figures multiplying upon it, he sprang on his one foot, and with a look of astonishment not unmixed with concern, he exclaimed—

" 'Heigh! Heigh! theer, I say! Wot mack o' letters art 'o settin deawn? Dust o' think 'at nobody knows wot theaw'rt drooin? Busithe (But see thee) I'd ha' thee to know 'at I know wot theaw'rt doin' az well az theaw duz thisel. Theaw pretends to rule th' plannits, dust o'? Busithe I con rule um az weel az theaw con, an' thet I'll let-te know iv theaw awses (attempts) to put ony o' thi tricks o' me.' A hearty laugh, a brief explanation, and, more than both, a kindly invitation to the drink and tobacco, soon brought the guest to his seat again, and to his wonted jovial humour. He then said there were thirteen 'Jones o' Grinfilt,' produced within a short time; but the original one was composed by Joseph Lees, a weaver residing at Glodwick, near Oldham, and himself—Joseph Coupe—who at the time of its composition was a barber, tooth-drawer, bloodletter, warper, spinner, carder, twiner, stubber, and rhymester residing at Oldham. He said they were both in a terrible predicament, without drink, or money to procure any, after having been drinking all night. They had been at Manchester to see the play, and were returning to Oldham the day following; when in order to raise the wind they agreed to compose a song, to be sung at certain public-houses on the road where they supposed it would be likely to take, and procure them what they wanted—the means of prolonging their dissipation. A storm came on and they sheltered under a hedge, and the first verse was composed by him (Coupe) in that situation. Lees composed the next verse, and they continued composing verse and verse until the song was finished as afterwards printed. But it took them three days to complete it, then they 'put it i' th' press,' and he said :—

"'We met ha' bin worth mony a hunthert peawnd, iv widdin ha' sense to ta' care o' th' brass.'"

This was the original "Jone o' Grinfilt's Ramble," the first verse of which was composed by the cripple under the tree :—

" Says Jone to his woife on a whot summer's day,
 ' Au'm resolut i' Grinfilt no longer to stay ;
 For aw'll goo to Owdham os fast os aw can,
 So fare thee weel Grinfilt, an' fare thee weel Nan ;
  For a sodger aw'll be, an' brave Owdham aw'll see,
  An' aw'll ha'e a battle wi' th' French.

' Dear Jone,' said eawr Nan, un' hoo bitterly cried,
' Wilt be one o' th' foote, or theaw meons for t' ride ? '
' Ods eawns ! wench, aw'll ride oather ass or a mule,
Ere aw'll keawer i' Grinfilt os black os th' owd dule,
  Boath clemmin', un starvin', un never a fardin',
  It 'ud welly drive ony man mad.'

' Ay, Jone, sin we coom i' Grinfilt for t' dwell,
Wey'm had mony a bare meal, aw con vara weel tell.'
' Bare meal ecod ! ay, that aw vera weel know,
There's bin two days this wick 'ot wey'm had nowt at o'.
  Aw'm vara near sided, afore aw'll abide it,
  Aw'll feight oather Spanish or French.

Then says my Noant Marget, ' Ah ! Jone, theawn't so whot
Aw'd ne'er go to Owdham, boh i' Englond aw'd stop.'
' It matters nowt, Madge, for to Owdham aw'll goo,
Aw'st ne'er clem to deeth, both sumbry (somebody) shall know ;

Furst Frenchman awfind, a w'll tell him meh mind,
Un if he'll naw feight, he shall run.'

Then deawn th' broo aw coom, for weh livent at top,
Aw thowt aw'd raich Owdham ere ever aw stop ;
Ecod ! heaw they staret when aw getten to th' Mumps,
Meh owd hat i' meh hont, un meh clogs full o' stumps ;
  Boh aw soon towd 'um, aw're goin' to Owdham,
  Un' aw'd ha'e a battle wi' th' French.

Aw kept eendway thro' th' lone, un' to Owdham aw went,
Aw ax'd a recruit if they'd made up their keawnt ?
' Nowe, nowe, honest lad ' (for he tawked like a king),
' Goo wi' meh thro' th' street, un' the aw will bring
  Wheere, if theaw'rt willin' theaw may ha'e a shillin'.'
  Ecod ! aw thowt this war rare news.

He browt me to th' pleck, where they measurn their height,
Un' if they bin reight, there's nowt said abeawt weight ;
Aw ratched meh un' stretched meh, un' never did flinch :
Says th' mon, ' Aw believe theaw'rt meh lad to an inch.'
  Aw thowt this'll do ; aw'st ha'e guineas anoo'.
  Ecod ! Owdham, brave Owdham for me.

So fare thee weel, Grinfilt, a soger aw'm made ;
Aw gotten new shoon, un' a rare cocade ;
Aw'll feight for Owd England os hard os aw can,
Oather French, Dutch, or Spanish, to me it's o' one ;
  Aw'll mak' 'en to stare, like a new started hare,
  Un' aw'll tell 'em fro' Owdham aw coom."

In many of the old copies the song ends here, but in others there are several more verses, of which the two following will serve as an example :—

" When aw went for a soger, aw ment for
to ride,
So they browt meh a tit, un' aw gat on
at wrang side,
Aw geet at wrang side, boh aw soon
tumbled o'er ;
Meh officer said aw should niver ride
more.
Aw thowt, that's quite reet, aw con goo
o' meh feet
Os fur os aw wish fur to goo.

Soa they browt meh a gun, un' cawd lift
un' reet,
Theaw mun howd up thy yed, un keep
slippin' thy feet ;
Oh ! they wheelt me abeawt till aw leant
to one side,
Un' meh officer said aw could noather
walk nor ride."

On the conclusion of peace Jone returns
home :—

" Soa neaw aw'm at whoam, an' th' loom's
set agate,
Wee'm plenty o' praties, an' dumplins to
ate ;
And now peace is made th' weyvers may
laugh
At Billy's brown loaf, made o' bran un' o'
chaff."

Of the many imitations of this popular
ballad, " Jone o' Grinfilt's Return," describing his return without having gone
to the war ; " Jone o' Grinfilt Junior,"
describing the terrible distress of the
hand-loom weavers after the Battle of
Waterloo, and " Jone o' Grinfilt going
to th' Rooshan War," were the greatest
favourites. For considerably over half a
century the imaginary " Jone o' Grinfilt "
always had a ballad ready for any happening of local or national importance.

THE OLD FERRY AT BIRKENHEAD

"THE MANCHESTER AND DEE CANAL"

A SHIP Canal for Manchester was the dream of some of its inhabitants so long ago as 1825, and a proposal was seriously contemplated of cutting such a canal to the River Dee. Such a project did not fail to stir the pens of local humorists, and more especially that of Mr. Benjamin Oldfield, who provided much fun and laughter for his fellow-citizens by his skits and caricatures. In December 1825, he published a broadsheet called, *The Manchester Times and Stretford Chronicle*, in which amongst other " squibs " the humour of which cannot now be appreciated, as they applied to contemporary happenings, is the following amusing gibe at the proposed canal.

" NATIVE OYSTERS.

" Jno. Sprat, Fishmonger, having lately purchased an extensive Plot of Land by Chorlton Row, for the purpose of making a Reservoir, and having also made arrangements with the *Manchester and Dee Ship Canal Company* for a constant Supply of Sea Water, begs to inform his Friends and the Public that he hopes very soon to be able to supply them with real Native Oysters, fresh from the Beds every day.

" J. S. intends during the season to visit London, in order to select a few scores of prime oysters to breed from."

The following announcement in the same broadsheet is more subtle in its humour, but none the less caustic in its punning satire.

" MANCHESTER AND DEE SHIP CANAL.

" The Committee of the Manchester and Dee Ship Canal Company have great pleasure in announcing to Shareholders that their hopes are not *de*-funct, nor their exertions *de*-creased ; that everything continues to go on *swimmingly*, and that the difficulties, anticipated and pro-

pagated by persons opposed to this *great undertaking*, are proved to be such as can easily be overcome. With regard to the procuring of a sufficient supply of water all doubts are removed, as the Committee are not only in treaty for, and confident of obtaining, the whole of the *Colnbrook stream in* Hulme, but have also the promise of its *waste water* from no fewer than four PUMPS in the neighbourhood of Chorlton, all of which are situated within two miles of the intended line of canal. The supply from these sources would doubtless be found amply sufficient, but in addition the Committee intend to erect at *Daw*-pool an engine of twenty Ass power, which will of itself be calculated to raise sufficient water to create a second DELUGE. With respect to the passing of the Bill (alluding, of course, to the Act of Parliament, not the Attornies' Bill), the Committee feel confident of success : in the lower House the two members for NEWPORT are pledged to support it, and although in the House of Lords LIVERPOOL will of course be hostile to it, the Committee have the assurance of MANCHESTER, PORTLAND, and many other Peers, that their utmost and united exertions will be used in its favour.

" As there are only a few shares remaining unsold, those who wish to became Shareholders must apply early.

" *Ship Tavern,*
" *Water Street.*"

Fifteen years later Manchester was still dreaming of a Ship Canal, and in 1840 a local poet signing himself as "Poor Jack," set forth a vision which has become a reality in our own time. The song was published in a handbill by Wilmot Henry Jones, of Market Street, Manchester, a " character " in literary Manchester in the early days of Queen Victoria's reign.

"THE *MARY*: A YARN.

"Air: *The Ram of Derby.*

"The Union Jackie's flying,
  By the Company's wharf, Old Quay,
And *Mary* of Dublin lying
  Unloading her Murphies to-day.

In the Irish Sea I hail'd her,
  As I stood in the packet boat;
With equal pride I never saw
  A merchant sloop afloat.

'Your name?' 'The *Mary*, Captain Hill.'
  'Your cargo?' 'Praties, sir!'
'Where from?' 'Dublin.' 'Whither
  bound?'
'The port of Manchester.'

Eighteen hundred and forty,
  October the twentieth day,
At half-past four in the evening
  She anchored by the quay.

It always does my heart good,
  To see the Union Jack,
So here's success to *Mary*,
  And soon may she come back.

And soon may scores of others
  Perform the trip with her
And trade and commerce double
  In noble Manchester."

In the same year a coasting vessel, the
Queen, arrived at Warrington, by the
canal. These lines were also printed and
published by Wilmot H. Jones—

"MANCHESTER AS IT MIGHT BE.

" Ye Manchester merchants let politics be,
  The *Queen* is at Warrington, up from the
    sea ;
And Forrest and Gill like Columbus of old,
  Have shown you the true way to gather
    the gold.
Your Mayors and your Councillors leave
  in the stocks,
And deepen your rivers and dig out your
  docks,
Import your own cargoes close up to your
  doors,
And warehouse and bond upon Man-
  chester floors :
Your home and your foreign trade both
  shall increase,
And yours be the quarters of Commerce
  and Peace :
To London stand next in the budget of
  State,
And *Queens* by the score shall scarce carry
  your freight."

On Friday Evening the 16th Instant will be by particular Desire.
AND UNDER THE IMMEDIATE PATRONAGE OF

SIR WILLIAM GERARD, Bart

FOR TWO NIGHTS ONLY.

At the Assembly-Room, Gerard's Arms Inn, Ashton,
On FRIDAY and SATURDAY next, the 15th and 16th of JULY. 1825

Mr. INGLEBY hopes to have an opportunity of amusing the Ladies and Gentlemen of Wigan, having given universal satisfaction in this town through the three Kingdoms.

Mr. I. wishes the Public to understand, that he is not one of those WOULD-BE Conjurors, but the REAL MAN himself.

INGLEBY,

SENIOR,

PROFESSOR OF ALL THE PROFESSORS IN THE CABALISTIC ART
LATE OF THE LYCEUM, LONDON

IN THE COURSE OF HIS PERFORMANCE HE WILL TAKE A

Plate of Sea Sand,

And by blowing on it, will change it into as many different colors as the audience may please to request.

HE WILL POSITIVELY ALLOW ANY GENTLEMAN TO TAKE AWAY

The Life of any Animal under the size of a Calf,

And with one blast of his magic breath it shall RISE and WALK as well as ever.

He will present different Boxes, with different Tricks, particularly one, which the Company may lock or unlock, which shall be full or empty as many times as the Company shall think proper.

The Company shall lay down any number of WATCHES they please, which he will make to STOP or GO by speaking one word.

HE WILL TAKE ANY GENTLEMAN'S WATCH,

BREAK IT INTO TWENTY PIECES,
And it shall be immediately returned to its owner as good as when first presented !!!

At a Game of Whist he will take the 13 Tricks.

He will give two Gentlemen each a Card to put under their Feet, standing the Distance of ten Yards from each other, when he will COMMAND ONE CARD TO ANOTHER, by saying only the simple Word—Pass.

WELL-MADE PANCAKES,

Fit for any Gentleman's table.

Mr. INGLEBY will discover any Gentleman's Thoughts,

He will perform the Flight of fifteen Miles a Minute,

HE WILL TAKE

TWO NEW-LAID EGGS,

OUT OF ONE WILL COME A CHILD,

Eating half a dozen Knives and Forks.

In the course of the Evening, a SONG, by

MRS. INGLEBY,

THE INVISIBLE HEN,

Doors to be opened at Seven and to begin at Eight o'Clock.
Front Seats, 2s. 6d.——Children Ditto, 1s. 6d.——Back Seats, 1s. 6d.

Tickets to be had at the Bar of the above Inn

ATKINSONS, PRINTERS, WIGAN

A BRUTAL HUSBAND

A STRANGE scene, which had a romantic ending, once occurred on the stage of the old Theatre Royal at Manchester. A charming and well-known singer, called Miss Paton, had been married according to the Scottish law to Lord William Lennox, but although he made her engagements and took her salaries, he would not allow her to use his name on the play-bills. So tight a hold did Lord William keep upon the money earned by his wife, that if she had not made a private arrangement with her managers she would not have had a penny of pocket-money.

One morning at rehearsal, before beginning her first song, Miss Paton advanced to the footlights and asked Mr. Wood, the conductor of the orchestra, if he would pitch the accompaniment a note lower, as she had a cold, and it would strain her voice to reach the high notes. Mr. Wood at once acquiesced, but Lord William, who always attended the rehearsals, interposed with an oath and said, " You shall sing it as usual." His wife remonstrated, saying she was utterly unable to take the high notes.

Lord William pretended that her cold was non-existent and insisted upon her singing " as he pleased," at the same time telling the conductor to take no notice of her but to " strike up as noted." Again Miss Paton pleaded her inability, Mr. Wood warmly supporting her, and pointed out to Lord William the risk his wife ran in straining her voice. For answer, Lord William, who had a riding whip in his hand, uttered a brutal oath, and began to lay it about her shoulders savagely. This was more than the conductor could stand. Leaping out of the orchestra, he tore the whip from Lord William's hand, and thrashed him round and round the stage until the whip broke ; then he threw the pieces in the bully's face.

This amazing scene was witnessed by the whole company and the employees of the theatre, who, as Lord William slunk away, vigorously applauded Mr. Wood.

Miss Paton refused to return to Lord William Lennox, and some time afterwards, the Scottish marriage having been set aside, she married her protector. Mrs. Linnæus Banks tells us, " I was in the theatre when, as Mr. and Mrs. Wood, the pair made their reappearance. As may be supposed, the house was crowded. The play was *Guy Mannering*. Mr. Wood was cast for Bertram. He was supposed to serenade Julia Mannering from his boat on the lake, and his voice was heard (I think joining in a duet with hers) before he entered at the ' practicable ' French Window. No sooner did he show himself than the prolonged and deafening applause caused him to bow and bow— and retreat. And this was thrice repeated, indicating the drift of public opinion, before the play was allowed to proceed. I saw them many times after that in various operas, *Love in a Village* for one. Mr. Wood had not much voice, but it was said she had trained him to make the best of it."

"THE '45"

IN 1745 the House of Stuart made its final attempt to regain the English throne when Prince Charles Edward, the son of the Old Pretender and grandson of James II., landed in Scotland, which had ever been favourably affected towards his family. Six thousand men flocked to his standard, and at the head of these he marched into England, and by way of Cumberland and Westmoreland entered Lancashire. His first halt was at Lancaster, the second at Preston, where thirty years previously his father's cause had been lost.

By the advices he had received from his agents the Young Pretender was led to believe that the inhabitants of every place through which he passed would hurry to his support. He was woefully deceived, and taking counsel with his commanders they came to the conclusion that the lack of enthusiasm was due to their rapid march. They determined therefore to make a halt, fixing upon Manchester, in order to give time for recruits to come in. A sergeant, with a drummer and a "sprightly girl," entered Manchester on November 28, and such was the panic caused by the news of the Pretender's approach, that the three may be said to have actually captured the town. No opposition was made to their entry, and in less than an hour they were beating up for volunteers. In the course of the afternoon they succeeded in getting some thirty recruits, to each of whom a white cockade was given, as well as the promise of five guineas. The same night at about nine o'clock the vanguard of the rebel army arrived to the number of about a hundred horsemen; they gave out to the terrified townspeople that quarters would be required for ten thousand men, an exaggeration of the strength of the rebel army which was given in order to excite enthusiasm for the Pre-

tender's cause. On the following day the main army reached Manchester, having halted at Wigan and Leigh for the night. "Regiment after regiment, with their glittering firelocks, their tartan sashes and gay and picturesque dresses, marched over the Old Bridge and into St. Anne's Square, then lately laid out, where they halted." At this very moment the body of the first rector of St. Anne's, the Rev. Joseph Hoole, was being committed to the grave. The bagpipes were instantly hushed, and the officers doffing their bonnets stood reverently by whilst the coffin was lowered into the grave. "White cockade and black scarf were at one in the presence of death. Many a white cockade was laid low ere a month was gone."

The same afternoon the Young Pretender, "Bonnie Prince Charlie," marched into Manchester, "dressed in a Stuart plaid, belted with a blue sash, and a blue bonnet over a light wig, and a white rose in his cap," and took up his quarters at the house of Mr. Dickenson in Market Street Lane, which was at once grandiloquently called "The Palace." The Prince's aide-de-camp was quartered upon Mr. Johnson, a rigid Hanoverian whose horses had been seized as they were being removed for safety. A letter from Mr. Johnson was also taken, in which he described the Stuart army as rebels; in consequence he was placed under arrest in his own house. Nevertheless he was bidden to a party of the officers given by the aide-de-camp. "King James" was the first toast; then Mr. Johnson was asked to give his toast.

"His Majesty King George," he replied stoutly. Several of the officers sprang to their feet in indignation and half drew their swords. For a moment it seemed that the loyal Mr. Johnson would pay for his temerity with his life, when one of the elder officers said, with happy readiness:

" He has drunk our Prince, why should not we drink *his?* Here's to the Elector of Hanover ! "

No time was lost after the Prince's arrival in proclaiming his father—King James III., the town crier being sent round the town to call out the order that persons owing townspeople. One of the clergy of the Collegiate Church, Mr. Clayton, however, preached a most eloquent sermon upon the arrival of the Prince, and a young man, called Thomas Coppock, the son of a tailor, who had been educated at the Manchester Grammar School and had only recently left Brasenose College and been ordained, was appointed Chaplain to

"THE PALACE," MR. DICKENSON'S HOUSE IN MARKET STREET LANE

duties to the Crown, or who held public moneys in their hands, were to pay them to the Secretary, Lord George Murray, at "The Palace," whose receipt would be their discharge. Then the bellman was sent round a second time to announce that there would be an illumination in honour of the Prince's arrival. Part of the town was illuminated, bonfires were lighted and the bells rang joyful peals. But there was very little real enthusiasm, the unfortunate borough-reeve, James Waller, being forced most reluctantly to convey the orders of the Prince to the His Royal Highness. Poor Coppock, he suffered a sad fate as the reward of his spiritual ministrations !

The recollection of the terrible punishment meted out to those who had taken part in the 1715 Rebellion, made the majority of the leading Manchester men, even those with Jacobite sympathies, chary of openly committing themselves. Whether the arrangement was suggested to Charles Edward, or whether it arose from his anxiety to save the authorities from any future charge of responsibility in the event of his failure, we do not

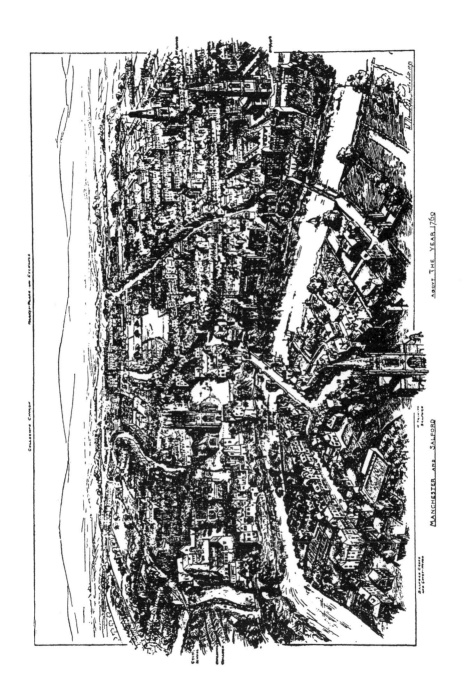

MANCHESTER AND SALFORD

ABOUT THE YEAR 1760

know, but a green silk curtain was hung across the audience-room in Mr. Dickenson's house; the Prince, his aide-de-camp, and his secretary sat upon one side of the curtain, the persons summoned to the audience being upon the other side. A voice gave the Prince's directions: whether it was that of the Young Pretender himself, or one of his attendants, the person on the other side of the curtain could not tell, but whilst he obeyed the instructions so given, he was able to say that he had taken no direct orders from the Prince.

On November 30, 1745, the whole of the Jacobite army, with its artillery of sixteen pieces of cannon, its baggage, consisting of a number of covered wagons and a hundred laden horses, was assembled in or near Manchester. Recruiting went on busily, two or three hundred young men being enrolled in a newly-created regiment, named in honour of the town, the "Manchester Regiment," of which Francis Townley was appointed colonel and commander. The headquarters of the regiment were at the Bull's Head; officers and men wore the white cockade, the former carrying a broadsword by their side and a brace of pistols in their girdle. One of the captains was James Dawson, whose tragic fate and that of his sweetheart were kept alive for many years by a ballad which was immensely popular in Lancashire.[1]

Although the green curtain settled the question of responsibility, the Young Pretender did not refrain from meeting his Jacobite sympathisers, and the receptions he held at Mr. Dickenson's house were thronged with people wearing tartan favours, " anxious to be presented, and to have the honour of kissing the Prince's hand."

Although a Roman Catholic, the

[1] See " Jemmy Dawson."

Prince attended service at the Collegiate Church.

" Colonel Townley's Manchester Regiment mustered in the churchyard, the men, in their blue and white cockades, gathering round their flag, which bore on one side the inscription, ' Church and Country,' and on the other, ' Liberty and Property.' The nave of the church was crowded with armed men, whose gaily coloured attire and glittering claymores, targets and other accoutrements produced a striking effect. The townspeople occupied the side aisles, and the ladies were ablaze with tartan ribbons, scarves and furbelows. The Prince occupied the Warden's seat in the choir, his retinue being accommodated in the stalls close by. Warden Peploe, a staunch Whig, had withdrawn from the town, and Coppock, the tailor's son, who had been appointed chaplain of the Manchester Regiment, supplied his place, preaching from the text ' The Lord is King; the earth may be glad thereof.' When the service was concluded the Manchester Regiment had the honour to be reviewed by their prince, the young Chevalier; and Colonel Townley selected the Collegiate churchyard for the field of review."

The Young Pretender was only two days in Manchester, leaving for the South on 1st December; but before his departure, finding so small a return from his order as to the payment of duties owing to the Crown, he levied a contribution of three thousand pounds upon the town, as well as requisitioning the horses within reach. "The conduct of the Highlanders," it was said, "was in some instances rapacious, wasteful and offensive; but in general the troops conducted themselves with moderation, and the behaviour of their officers was conciliatory and even courteous."

Liverpool was strongly Hanoverian,

and her regiment, the Liverpool Blues, had been busy in breaking down the bridges over the Mersey in order to hinder the progress of the Jacobite forces. Charles Edward issued this proclamation:—

" To the Inhabitants of Manchester. His Royal Highness being informed that several bridges have been pulled down in this country, he has given orders to repair them forthwith, particularly that at Crossford; which is to be done this night by his own troops, though his *Royal Highness* does not propose to make use of it for his own army, but believes it will be of service to the country; and if any of the forces that are with *General Wade* be coming this road, *they may have the benefit of it.* Manchester, Nov. 30, 1745."

A temporary bridge was built over the Mersey at Cheadle, of trunks and branches of poplar trees, across which the guns and horses were taken, but the Prince bravely taking the lead waded across the river at the head of his men, "immersed to the middle in water." On the opposite bank were drawn up a number of Cheshire Jacobite gentlemen, and with them a venerable old lady, Mrs. Skyring, of whom the following touching story of loyalty and devotion to a lost cause is told:—

" As a child she had been lifted up in her mother's arms to view the happy landing at Dover of Charles the Second. Her father, an old Cavalier, had after-

THE YOUNG PRETENDER, " BONNIE PRINCE CHARLIE"

wards to undergo not merely neglect but oppression from the thankless monarch; still, however, he and his wife continued devoted to the royal cause, and their daughter grew up as devoted as they. After the expulsion of the Stuarts, all her thoughts, her hopes, her prayers were devoted to another restoration. Ever afterwards she had with rigid punctuality laid aside one half of her yearly income to remit for the exiled family abroad, concealing only the name of the giver, which, she said, was of no importance to them, and might give them pain if they remembered the unkind treatment she had formerly received. She had now parted with her jewels, her plate, and every little article she possessed, the price of which she laid in a purse at the feet of Prince Charles, while straining her dim eyes to gaze on his features, and pressing his hand to her shrivelled lips, she exclaimed with affectionate rapture, ' Lord, now lettest thou thy servant depart in peace.' "

It is said that when news came, a few days later, of the Prince's retreat from Derby, old Mrs. Skyring, who was nearly ninety, died from the shock.

At Macclesfield the Manchester Regiment was drawn up in the churchyard, in order that arms might be distributed to such as had not received them at Manchester. Some of the men had grown dispirited, and numbers would have deserted but that they were persuaded by their fellow-townsmen to remain faithful. Several actually did desert, but were caught; two of them were tied together with a rope to a horse's tail and " obliged to run many miles without shoes, and in great torment."

From Macclesfield the Jacobite army moved to Derby, which it reached on December 4. The Young Pretender's swift descent upon England had taken the authorities by surprise, but an army was hastily dispatched from the South under George II.'s son, the Duke of Cumberland, whilst another under General Wade was following the Jacobite forces swiftly from the North. The Young Pretender and the Duke of Cumberland reached Derby almost simultaneously, and the whole of the 5th December was spent by both armies in preparation for the battle which was expected to take place on the following day. That battle might have changed the history of England. But during the night of the 5th word reached the Jacobites that General Wade was rapidly approaching. They therefore risked being caught between the two Hanoverian armies. The Prince and his younger officers were eager to attack the Duke of Cumberland, but the suggestion prevailed that they should retreat to Scotland and there avail themselves of the reinforcements newly arrived from France. Most unwillingly Charles Edward gave the order to retreat, and nine days after it had marched out of Manchester with drums beating and colours flying, his army re-entered the town.

When the news of the retreat reached Manchester some of the militant Hanoverians sent the bellman round the town, ordering people to provide pickaxes for breaking up the roads, and to arm themselves with weapons to attack the insurgents. Upon this summons a large number of men collected, but the magistrates, foreseeing that the town must inevitably be the scene of heavy fighting, ordered them to disperse. The Jacobites therefore entered the town unmolested. But the Duke of Cumberland was pressing hotly upon them. They stayed therefore only one day, but levied a contribution of five thousand pounds upon the inhabitants, threatening to sack the town if half of the sum were not paid by mid-day on the 10th. When the money was not forthcoming the next morning, " Mr. James Bayley, sen., of Hope Eccles, a gentleman between seventy and eighty years of age, was seized as a hostage and only liberated on condition that the money should be raised and paid to Secretary Murray at the 'Palace' in two hours. Mr. Bayley went to the Old Coffee House, and it was arranged that he and John Dickenson of the 'Palace,' where the Prince had previously fixed his quarters, should give promissory notes, payable in three months, to such persons as would advance them money to meet the demand. By this method the two thousand five hundred pounds was paid within the time specified."

On the 10th the Young Pretender reached Wigan; the next day he gained Preston, and on the 13th entered Lancaster, reaching Carlisle by way of Kendal on the 19th. Here Charles Edward stayed one day only, leaving about four hundred men to garrison the town whilst he with his main body went on into Scotland. Of the four hundred men left to defend Carlisle one hundred and twenty represented the Manchester Regiment, its members having shrunk by repeated desertions on the road. Colonel Townley commanded them, and with him were John Dawson, Syddall, the Deacon brothers, and Coppock, whom Charles Edward had dubbed Bishop of Carlisle. When he left them the Young Pretender promised to send reinforcements. Two days after his departure, the Duke of Cumberland and General Wade, who had joined forces, appeared before the town and immediately opened the siege.

The little garrison made the most spirited and gallant resistance, daily expecting the help promised them by Charles Edward. But the reinforcements never came, and meanwhile the Hano-

The officers of the Manchester Regiment were sent to London for trial, together with many of the privates. They came up for trial in July 1746, and seventeen of them were condemned "To be severally hanged by the neck, not till they were dead, but cut down alive, then their bowels to be taken out and burnt before their faces, their heads to be severed from their bodies and their bodies

Engraved by Leeds Cheetham

A View of the Old Coffee House &c

verians had been joined by the Liverpool Blues and other regiments. After eleven days' resistance a white flag intimated the wish of the garrison to capitulate on terms. To this the Duke of Cumberland replied that the only condition he could grant was that the rebels should not be put to the sword but reserved for the King's pleasure. The garrison had no choice but to accept these terms, and surrendered the town.

severally divided into four quarters, and these to be at the King's disposal."

The Battle of Culloden, which ended the hopes of the Stuarts, had taken place in April 1746. By his terrible treatment of the prisoners the Duke of Cumberland earned a lifelong infamy and the name of "The Butcher." It is said that it was by his persuasion that George II. caused the horrible punishment of hanging, drawing and quartering to be revived in the case of the Jacobite rebels. Thomas Coppock suffered the same fate at Carlisle in October 1746.

After the execution in London the heads of Thomas Deacon and Syddall were preserved in spirits and taken to Manchester, where they were exposed for a week upon the Exchange, "execrated by many as a disgrace to their town and country—reverenced by others as martyrs." Thomas Deacon's father never afterwards passed the Exchange without doffing his hat and making a profound obeisance, an example which was followed by several ardent followers of the Pretender.

Prince Charles Edward's retreat from Derby to Scotland is memorable in the history of warfare, for he covered nearly two hundred miles in midwinter in fourteen days and without any material loss of either men, baggage, or cannon.

The full story of the '45 can be enjoyed in 'The Manchester Rebels', £4.95 from all good bookshops

A VIEW OF PRESTON IN 1745

A BUSY HOUSEWIFE

"WHEN mun I come to see yo'?" one woman asked another. "Wall, dunnot come o' Monday, for I've t' cloas to side."

"Will t' day after do?"

"Eh, nowe! That's weshin' day. An' t' Wednesday's smoothin' day, an' Thursday's bakin' day, an' t' Friday's clennin' up day."

"Well, what about t' week-end?"

"Eh, but I'se ha' to goo an' buy in o' Sett'day, an' o' Sunday I allus go t' church, so I dunno gradely when yo' can come."

THE ACTORS' BRIDGE

THE OLD WOODEN BRIDGE AT BLACKFRIARS

THE coronations of King James II., of William and Mary, Queen Anne, and the two first Georges were not celebrated in Manchester, but for the coronation of George III., in 1761, there was a spontaneous outburst of loyalty. Processions of merchants, tradesmen, manufacturers and artisans, headed by the Mayor and corporation, paraded through the town in honour of the event, and at night there were brilliant illuminations and a ball at the Exchange Assembly Rooms. In this coronation year the old Blackfriars Bridge was built by a company of actors from Drury Lane and Covent Garden. They had taken the theatre in the Riding School, in what was then called Water Street, Salford, but is now Blackfriars Street, where they set up in opposition to the Manchester Theatre;

then under the management of James Whiteley. In order to attract Manchester folk to their performances they built a wooden foot-bridge across the river, the approach being through a narrow passage, called the Ring o' Bells entry, leading from Deansgate and thence by a flight of twenty-nine steps to the bridge. Aston in his *Metrical Records of Lancashire* has the following :—

" In the years seventeen sixty and sixty and one,
The town by the players was well play'd upon ;
Old Whiteley possession had got of the town,
And the two London houses join'd force and came down,
And no place being vacant that was near to the centre,
They determined in Salford to try their adventure ;

137

Erected a building, erected a stage,
To act o'er the passions of man and the age ;
And to tempt the Mancastrians, made steps
   down the ridge,
And over the river threw Blackfriars
   Bridge."

After the players' departure the bridge remained for nearly sixty years. It was taken down in 1820, and replaced by a stone bridge at the cost of nine thousand pounds, an Act of Parliament allowing the subscribers to draw tolls from both foot passengers and vehicles. The tolls were abolished in 1848, and the bridge made free.

MAY DAY IN OLD MANCHESTER

THE parade of their cart-horses, held by the big colliery and brewery firms, and also by the railway companies in Manchester on May Day every year, when prizes are given for the best-groomed animals, is a survival of an old custom. In the days when the only communication between different parts of the country was by road, Manchester was one of the chief coaching centres, and in celebration of this importance there were great doings in the city on May Day. The great coaching establishments, which carried the royal mails south, east, west, and north, all the livery stables which provided the chariots, post-chaises and "high-flyers" which people of more ample means were wont to hire in preference to travelling by the public coach, turned out all their spare horses and vehicles for a grand procession through the streets. Mail and other coaches were freshly painted for the occasion, the horses had new harness, the guards and coachmen new liveries. The coachmen were especially resplendent, with great cockades of coloured ribbon stuck in their hats, and huge bouquets stuck in the front of their coats. Cockades and nosegays were also fastened to the horses' harness. As nearly every coach was drawn by a team of four horses, the cavalcade was of great length and took a considerable time to pass through the large crowds which had flocked from all the country round, for, in addition to the coaches and chariots, there were lorries, wagons, drays, and carts, drawn by splendid draught horses, their manes and tails plaited with gaily coloured ribbons as they are to-day. The procession, the progress of which was enlivened by the guards blowing merry tunes upon their bugles, was closed by the milk carts of the town, the dresses of the drivers being all covered with ribbons.

The custom of plaiting the manes and tails of cart horses with coloured ribbon has come down from the Middle Ages, when the tails and manes of the knights' chargers were plaited with strips of cloth, representing their owners' colours.

THE RADCLIFFE OTTER HUNT

THE scenes of the following ballad are laid in the Irwell and upon its banks from Prestwich to Clifton and Radcliffe. The hunt probably took place in the eighteenth century, otters being rarely seen in the Irwell after that time. Two otters, however, were taken in the Bollin near Bowdon in 1849. The otter is supposed to tell his own story.

I am a bold otter, as you shall hear,
  I've rambled the country all round ;
I valued no dogs, far or near,
  In the water nor yet on the ground.

I valued no dogs, far or near,
  But I roved through the country so wide,
Till I came to a river so clear,
  That did Clifton and Prestwich divide.

As through the wild country I rambled,
  I liv'd at extravagant rate ;
On eels, chubs and gudgeons I feasted ;
  The fishermen all did me hate.

Yet still up the river I went,
  Where the fishes my stomach did cheer,
Till a challenge from Radcliffe they sent me,
  They quickly would stop my career.

Next morning, those dogs did assemble ;
  Jack Allen,[1] he swore I must die ;
It made me full sorely to tremble,
  To hear those stout hounds in full cry.

It was near Agecroft Bridge I oft went,
  Where with me they'd had many a round,
So closely they stuck to the scent,
  That they forced me to take to fresh ground.

Jack Allen, the darling of hunters,
  And Ploughman, the glory of hounds ;
You may search all the country over,
  Their equals are not to be found.

Although I my country did leave,
  It was sorely against my own will ;
They pursued me with courage so brave,
  That they prov'd a match for my skill.

Then into a bag they did put me,
  And up on their backs did me fling ;
And because that in safety they'd got me,
  They made all the valleys to ring.

Then right for old Radcliffe did steer,
  And soon at Bob Hampson's did call,[2]
And hundreds of people were there,
  To drink and rejoice at my fall.

The same afternoon they contriv'd
  With me more diversion to have ;
Put me into a pit where I div'd,
  Just like a stout otter so brave.

And yet I remain'd so stout,
  Though they swam me for three hours or more,
The dogs they could not force me out,
  Till with stones they did pelt me full sore.

Thus forcing me out of the water,
  Because that my strength it did fail ;
And then in a few moments after
  Jack Ogden[3] laid hold of my tail.

And so now they had got me secure,
  They right to the "Anchor" did steer ;
But my lot was too hard to endure,
  And my death was approaching too near.

Next morning to Whitefield they took me,
  To swim as before I had done :
When out of the bag they did put me,
  Alas ! my poor life it was gone.

And so now this old otter you've killed,
  You may go to Bob Hampson's and sing ;
Drink a health to all true-hearted hunters,
  Success to our country and king.

[1] Jack Allen was a well-known huntsman of the Radcliffe Otter hounds.
[2] A popular ale-house.
[3] Jack Ogden was a well-known character.

❖❖❖❖❖❖❖❖❖❖❖❖❖

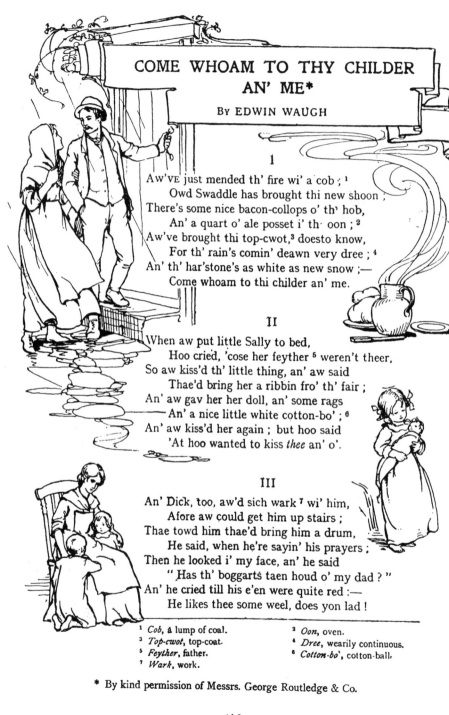

COME WHOAM TO THY CHILDER AN' ME*

By EDWIN WAUGH

I

Aw've just mended th' fire wi' a cob ; [1]
    Owd Swaddle has brought thi new shoon ;
There's some nice bacon-collops o' th' hob,
    An' a quart o' ale posset i' th' oon ; [2]
Aw've brought thi top-cwot,[3] doesto know,
    For th' rain's comin' deawn very dree ; [4]
An' th' har'stone's as white as new snow ;—
    Come whoam to thi childer an' me.

II

When aw put little Sally to bed,
    Hoo cried, 'cose her feyther [5] weren't theer,
So aw kiss'd th' little thing, an' aw said
    Thae'd bring her a ribbin fro' th' fair ;
An' aw gav her her doll, an' some rags
    An' a nice little white cotton-bo' ; [6]
An' aw kiss'd her again ; but hoo said
    'At hoo wanted to kiss *thee* an' o'.

III

An' Dick, too, aw'd sich wark [7] wi' him,
    Afore aw could get him up stairs ;
Thae towd him thae'd bring him a drum,
    He said, when he're sayin' his prayers ;
Then he looked i' my face, an' he said
    " Has th' boggarts taen houd o' my dad ? "
An' he cried till his e'en were quite red :—
    He likes thee some weel, does yon lad !

[1] *Cob*, a lump of coal.   [2] *Oon*, oven.
[3] *Top-cwot*, top-coat.   [4] *Dree*, wearily continuous.
[5] *Feyther*, father.   [6] *Cotton-bo'*, cotton-ball.
[7] *Wark*, work.

* By kind permission of Messrs. George Routledge & Co.

IV

At th' lung-length,[1] aw geet 'em laid still ;
    An' aw hearken't folks' feet 'at went by ;
So aw iron't o' my clooas reet well,
    An' aw hanged 'em o'th maiden to dry ;
When aw'd mended thi stocken's an' shirts,
    Aw sit deawn to knit i' my cheer,
An' aw rayley did feel rayther hurt,—
    Mon, aw'm one-ly [2] when theaw artn't theer.

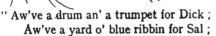

V

" Aw've a drum an' a trumpet for Dick ;
    Aw've a yard o' blue ribbin for Sal ;
Aw've a book full o' babs,[3] an' a stick'—
    An' some 'bacco an' pipes for mysel' ;
Aw've brought thee some coffee an' tay,—
    Iv thae'll *feel* i' my pocket, thae'll *see* ;
An' aw've bought tho a new cap to-day,—
    But aw al'ays bring summat for *thee !*

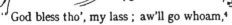

VI

" God bless tho', my lass ; aw'll go whoam,[4]
    An' aw'll kiss thee an' th' childer o' round ;
Thae knows, that wherever aw roam,
    Aw'm fain to get back to th' owd ground ;
Aw can do wi' a crack o'er a glass ;
    Aw can do wi' a bit of a spree ;
But aw've no gradely [5] comfort, my lass,
    Except wi' yon childer and thee.''

---

[1] *Th' lung-length*, the long length, the end.
[2] *One-ly*, lonely.   [3] *Babs*, babies, pictures.
[4] *Whoam*, home.   [5] *Gradely*, proper, right.

CHARLES WORSLEY

MANCHESTER'S FIRST MEMBER OF PARLIAMENT

THE first member of Parliament for Manchester, Charles Worsley of Platt, not only played an important part in his own county during the Commonwealth, but he was an actor in one of the most momentous scenes of English history. When Oliver Cromwell dissolved the Rump Parliament in 1653, Worsley commanded the files of musketeers who were brought into the House of Commons to eject the members, and it was into his hands that Cromwell gave the mace, the symbol of the power of Parliament, with the famous words, "What shall we do with this bauble? Take it away!"

The Worsleys of Platt were a younger branch of an old Lancashire family, the Worsleys of Worsley. The younger branch had gone into trade, and, amassing a considerable fortune for those times, Charles Worsley's grandfather had bought land in Rushholme ; his father, Ralph Worsley, having greatly extended the business of "haberdasher" or linen-drapér, was able to buy the estate of Platt out of his profits in 1625, three years after Charles Worsley was born. Charles Worsley's grandmother was a sister of Alice Clarke, the wife of George Clarke who founded the Manchester Charity, which still bears his name.

Ralph Worsley was a Puritan of the narrowest and most bigoted kind, his opinions upon religion and politics verging upon fanaticism. Charles I. ascended the throne the year after Charles Worsley's birth, and from the outset there were differences between the king and the Parliament, the king seeking to govern by "right divine," the Parliament seeking to restrain his tyranny and protect the rights of the people.

Thus Charles Worsley's childhood and youth were passed in the most stirring times in our country's history, and he grew up as staunch a Puritan and Parliament man as his father.

When he was twenty, the Civil War broke out, and a month after King Charles had raised his standard at Nottingham (August 1642) the Earl of Derby, on the king's behalf, made an unsuccessful attack upon Manchester. In the repelling of the attack, and the subsequent strengthening of the fortifications of the town, young Worsley took an active part, being rewarded two years later by an appointment as captain in the army of the Parliament, which had its Lancashire head-quarters at Manchester. He is described as being a "godly and handsome youth." So great was his zeal in training his men, and in making recruits, that when Charles I. was executed in 1649 he had risen to the rank of a lieutenant-colonel. In the following year, when war broke out between the Commonwealth and the Scotch, the young lieutenant-colonel was summoned to join Oliver Cromwell in Scotland, with his regiment. Ralph Worsley seems to have been inordinately proud of his son's military title, for from the moment that he notes in his diary, " At Cheetham Hill was the first muster of Lieutenant-Colonel Worsley's soldiers. The second in the same place August 2, 1650," he sets out every stage of the young man's march towards Edinburgh, always mentioning the " Lieutenant-Colonel." On August 19, " Lieutenant-Colonel Charles Worsley set forwards towards the north with his regiment ;" on the 24th " Lieutenant-Colonel Worsley came to Skipton;" on the 2nd September he was at Dereham, on the 3rd at Newcastle, on the 9th at Berwick, and on the 12th he arrived at Edinburgh, nine days after the battle of Dunbar in which Cromwell had been so signally victorious. He had not lingered upon the way, but the appalling state of the roads made quick marching impossible, hours being wasted every day in getting the baggage wagons out of the ruts in which they sank above their axle-trees. Thus it was that Worsley only reached Newcastle on the day that Cromwell routed the Scottish army, a victory which was snatched in the face of imminent defeat.

Charles II., accepting the conditions laid down by the Scottish Presbyterians, had landed in that country, when an army was immediately raised to support his claim to the throne of England. John Richard Green gives a vivid picture of the march of the Parliamentary forces, and the Battle of Dunbar. " A month after Charles had landed on the shores of Scotland," he says, " the English army started for the north. It crossed the Tweed fifteen thousand strong, but the terror of his massacre in Ireland (that is, Cromwell's) hung round its leader, the country was deserted as he advanced, and he was forced to cling for provision to a fleet which sailed along the coast. David Leslie, with a large force, refused battle, and lay obstinately in his lines between Edinburgh and Leith. A march of the English army round his position to the slopes of the Pentlands only brought about a change of the Scottish front ; and as Cromwell fell back baffled upon Dunbar, Leslie encamped on the heights above the town, and cut off the English retreat along the coast by the seizure of Cockburn's path. His post was almost unassailable, while the soldiers of Cromwell were sick and starving, and their general had resolved on an embarkation of his forces when he saw in the dusk of evening signs of movement in the Scottish camp. Leslie's caution had at last been overpowered by the zeal of the preachers, and his army moved down to the lower ground between the hillside on which it was encamped and a little brook which covered the English front. His horse was far in advance of the main body, and it had hardly reached the level ground when Cromwell in the dim dawn flung his whole force upon it. ' They run ! I profess they run !' he cried, as the Scottish horse broke after a desperate resistance, and threw into confusion the foot who were hurrying to its aid. Then, as the sun rose over the mist of the morning, he added in nobler words, ' Let God arise, and let His enemies be scattered ! Like as the mist vanisheth, so shalt Thou drive them away !' In less than an hour the victory was complete. The defeat at once became a rout ; ten thousand prisoners were taken, with all the baggage and guns ; three thousand were slain, with scarce any loss on the part of the conquerors."

Although Worsley had no opportunity of proving his courage and military ability upon the field of battle, his execution of the duties assigned to him after the victory at Dunbar, seem not only to have attracted the attention of Cromwell, but also to have inspired his confidence, for two years later we find the young man, then only thirty, appointed to the command of Cromwell's own regiment of foot. In October 1652 Ralph Worsley records in his diary: "My son, Lieutenant-Colonel Charles Worsley, with his wife, did set forward from Platt to ride to London," apparently in order to take up his new duties: it was in the following April that the historic scene occurred in the House of Commons.

Parliament was making the discovery that the substitution of a republican form of Government for a monarchy is not an easy task; that whilst old institutions may be swept away with comparatively little difficulty, they cannot be so quickly replaced by new ones. After the battle of Worcester in 1641, which sent Charles II. into exile with a price upon his head, a Bill was brought forward to dissolve the existing Parliament and for the election of a new one. But the Parliament was tasting the sweets of a power even more absolute than that wielded by Charles I., and for the exercise of which they had fought against him, and finally beheaded him; and they declined to be dissolved, notwithstanding that the Bill for the dissolution had been passed by a majority of two. "Internal affairs were almost at a dead-lock. The Parliament appointed Committees to prepare plans for legal reforms, or for ecclesiastical reforms, but it did nothing to carry them into effect. It was overpowered by the crowd of affairs which the confusion of the war had thrown into its hands, by confiscations, sequestrations, appointments to civil and military offices; in fact, the whole administration of the state; and there were times when it was driven to

resolve not to take any private affairs for weeks together, in order that it might make more progress with public business. To add to this confusion and muddle there were the inevitable scandals which arose from it; charges of malversation and corruption were hurled at the members of the House; and some . . . were accused, with justice, of using their power to further their own interests. The one remedy for all this was, as the Army saw, the assembly of a new and complete Parliament in place of the mere 'rump' of the old, but this was the one measure the House was resolute to avert." So determined was the "Rump" Parliament to remain in power, that it insisted that not only should its members continue as members in the new Parliament—which thus deprived the places they represented of choosing representatives,—but that they were to constitute a Committee of Revision to "determine the validity of each election and the fitness of the members returned," a tyranny which the officers of the army, headed by Cromwell, declined to accept.

There was a conference between the leaders of the House of Commons and the officers of the army, which, after some fruitless discussion, was adjourned to the following day on the understanding that no decisive step should be taken. But when the conference re-assembled at Whitehall the next morning, the leading members of the House were absent, and Cromwell and the officers learnt that the Bill authorizing the tyranny to which they were so determinedly opposed, was at that moment being hurried through Parliament. "It is contrary to common honesty!" Cromwell cried, and calling Lieutenant-Colonel Worsley, bade him follow him with a company of his musketeers to the door of the Commons.

When he entered the House, Cromwell, "clad in plain grey clothes and grey worsted stockings," quietly took his usual place and listened to Sir Harry Vane's passionate argument in favour of the Bill. "I am come to do what grieves me to the heart," he said to a neighbour, but he made no protest until Sir Harry pressed the House to put aside its usual forms of procedure and pass the Bill at once—a suggestion as illegal and tyrannous as the Bill itself.

"The time has come!" Cromwell said to Harrison, the fiery soldier who had brought Charles I. a prisoner from Hurst Castle to London.

"Think well," Harrison answered, divining his great leader's intention; "it is a dangerous work!"

As if undecided, Cromwell listened for another quarter of an hour. But when the question was put to the House, "that this Bill do pass," he could no longer restrain his anger, and, rising in his place, he denounced the Parliament and its methods. "Your hour is come!" he cried. "The Lord hath done with you!" In the midst of the angry cries and protests that followed, Cromwell shouted: "Come, come, we have had enough of this," and, moving to the middle of the floor of the House, put his hat upon his head, adding, "I will put an end to your prating. It is not fit that you should sit here any longer! You should give place to better men! You are no Parliament; I say, you are no Parliament! I will put an end to your sitting!"

Then turning to the Serjeant-at-Arms he cried imperiously, "Call them in! Call them in!"

The Serjeant-at-Arms opened the door, and in marched Charles Worsley at the head of two files of Cromwell's musketeers. In vain the members protested against the intervention of armed force into their proceedings, but, awed by the presence of Worsley and his men, they were obliged to yield, and one by one they left the House. The Speaker, however, refused to leave the chair until Cromwell, pointing to him, said to Harrison, "Fetch him down!" and it was only under a threat from Harrison "to lend him a hand to come down" that he left his seat of office. One member, Algernon Sidney, at that time member for Cardiff, refused to go. His father, the Earl of Leicester, thus reports the scene. "It happened that day that Algernon Sidney sat next to the Speaker on the right hand. The General (Cromwell) said to Harrison, 'Put him out!' Harrison spake to Sidney to go out, but he said he would not go out, and sat still. The General again said, 'Put him out!' Then Harrison and Wortley put their hands upon Sidney's shoulders, as if they would force him to go out. Then he rose and went towards the door." Worsley's name was mis-spelt in this account.

When all the members were gone, Cromwell picked up the mace from the table and said, "What shall we do with this bauble? Take it away!" at the same time handing it to Worsley, who afterwards locked the door of the House, and took both the key and the mace to his lodging. Thus was the famous "Rump" Parliament summarily dissolved by the calling in of Worsley and his men. The mace, that emblem of the power of the Parliament, remained for nearly three months in Worsley's possession, as is shown by this entry in the proceedings of the succeeding Parliament: "July 8, 1653—Resolved that the Serjeant-at-Arms attending this House do repair to Lieutenant-Colonel Worsley for the mace, and do bring it to the House."

The successor of the "Rump" Parliament was nicknamed the "Barebones" Parliament from one of its members, a fanatical Puritan leather-merchant called

Praise-God Barebones. In the legal sense of the word it was not a Parliament, for its members were appointed by Cromwell, to the head of the government under the title of His Highness the Lord Protector of the Commonwealth of England, Scot-

"'WHAT SHALL WE DO WITH THIS BAUBLE? TAKE IT AWAY!'"

and were not elected by the constituencies. After an existence of five months, "finding their task of construction and reconstruction too much for them," the members of the "Barebones" Parliament resigned, their resignation being immediately followed by the appointment of Cromwell land and Ireland. In 1654 a new Parliament was elected, but this time the electors were allowed their own choice; all those who had property of the annual value of two hundred pounds being qualified to vote, but those who had borne arms for King Charles, and also their sons, were disqualified. Up to this time Manchester, despite its growing importance as a centre of the linen industry, had not been represented in Parliament. This injustice was now removed, and the town, being wholly Puritan in sympathy, elected "Charles Worsley of the Platt, Esquire," the commander of the Lord Protector's own musketeers, as its first member. Worsley made no great figure in Parliament, but the Protector must have been impressed by his administrative capacity, and also by his absolute loyalty to himself, for when he divided England into ten districts in order to counteract the plots against his government amongst the Royalists and the more advanced of his own party, he appointed Worsley to be Major-General of the district consisting of Lancashire, Cheshire and Staffordshire. These ten Majors-General were practically viceroys. "He looks," wrote Carlyle, "after the good of the Commonwealth, spiritual and temporal, as he finds wisest; ejects or aids in ejecting scandalous ministers, summons disaffected persons before him, demands an account of them; sends them to prison, failing an account that satisfies him, and there is no appeal except to the Protector in Council. His force is the militia of his county, horse and foot levied and kept in readiness for the occasion, especially troops of horse, involving of course new expense, which we decided that the plotting Royalists who occasioned it shall pay. On all Royalist disaffected persons the Major-General, therefore, as his first duty, is to lay an *income tax of ten per cent.*; let them pay it quietly."

The Royalists, or Malignants, as they were termed officially, gave the Major-General of Lancashire no trouble. "The Malignant party," he says in one of his reports, ": seem to submit to what is imposed with readiness. I hope we shall be able to pay our county troops out of what we have done already, and provide you a considerable sum for other uses." One of the duties of the Major-General was to lessen the number of ale-houses, partly for the "reformation of manners," and partly also because they were meeting-places of those disaffected to the Protector's rule; but the ale-houses meant revenue to the state, and Worsley was in some difficulty. "I find it," he wrote, "a difficult business how to observe my instructions as to ale-houses, and not weaken that revenue, though truly it's too visible that they are the bane of the counties. Yesterday and the day before I met the commissioners and the justices for the Hundred of Blackburn about these things specified in the orders" (issued by the Protector), "and we find that these ale-houses are the very womb that brings forth all manner of wickedness. We have ordered at least two hundred ale-houses to be thrown down in their Hundred, and are catching loose and vile persons." Publicans and brewers, bad constables, suspicious and idle persons, fared badly at the Major-General's hands, and it is curious to note that, "we have sent a great number of persons to gaol for being married contrary to the Act of Parliament" (against marriage with a deceased wife's sister), "and the persons which have so married them." Horse-racing, too, meant prison. "Sir," wrote one of Worsley's subordinates, "there being a horse-race appointed in this county the last week, being informed of it I sent a party of the troop. They apprehended the chief actors, and they took the horses which, I hear, since I came to Manchester are still in custody. I desire your direction what to do with both."

After nine months strenuous labours in the three counties, Worsley was summoned to London by Cromwell for a conference of all the Majors-General of the kingdom. "Indeed, sir, I am not well," Worsley wrote, "my intent was to have taken a little rest at my coming home, and some physic, but seeing that I have received this command I intend (if the Lord will) to be with you with all speed." His hasty journey to London seems to have tried his already failing health, for shortly after his arrival at St. James's Palace, where a residence had been given him by the Protector, he was taken ill and died, on June 12, 1656, being then only thirty-five years of age. He was buried in Henry VII.'s Chapel in Westminster Abbey, with the highest honours, his funeral being thus described by the *Public Intelligence*: "Westminster, June 13.—In the evening was solemnized the funeral of Major-General Worsley, which was performed with much honour according to his merit, his hearse being attended by the rest of the Majors-General and divers other persons of honour and many coaches. Before him marched four regiments of foot, ten troops of horse, and the Life Guards of his Highness—drums being covered with mourning, pikes trailed on the ground, and trumpets mournfully sounding after the military manner usual in such solemnities—who conducted his body to Westminster Abbey, where it was interred near Sir William Constable in the chapel of Henry VII.: three grand volleys being discharged at the interment."

To the sorrowing old father at Platt a message was sent by a friend that the Lord Protector and his Council have granted a pension of "one hundred pound a year for ever" to Worsley's children, and "two hundred pound in money" to his widow.

Of all the prominent men in the Commonwealth whose bodies were buried in Westminster Abbey, Worsley's remains alone escaped exhumation and desecration when Charles II. was restored to the throne. The bodies of Cromwell, Ireton and Bradshaw, the last a Lancashire man, were torn from their graves, dragged on hurdles to the place of execution at Tyburn, and there strung up on the gallows—a hideous spectacle of revenge and barbarity. But the body of Worsley escaped this ignominy, probably because it was generally believed that his grave, from its position in the chapel, was that of James I. When this grave was opened in the middle of the last century, it was proved beyond doubt that the body buried in it could not have been that of James, for the skeleton was that of a tall man, whilst James was below the middle height. Worsley was tall, and the teeth of the skeleton, which were fresh and white, were those of a man under forty. So, by a strange trick of circumstances, the dust of the first member of Parliament for Manchester lies mingled with that of the kings and queens of England buried in Henry VII.'s Chapel. As Major-General of Lancashire, Cheshire and Staffordshire, he had harried and fined the Royalists for their devotion to the cause of King Charles; he had pursued Roman Catholics with all the rigours of the law, and at an age when most men are starting upon their career he had gained distinction and high reward by his devotion to Cromwell and the Commonwealth. Yet the bones of this Lancashire linen-draper's son, this Republican, this Puritan, rest side by side with the bones of kings and queens who represented and upheld, both in politics and religion, all that Worsley throughout the whole of his life strove to pull down and sweep away.

JOHN DEE
THE NECROMANCER

ONE of the most extraordinary stories of the astrologers is that of John Dee, the Warden of Manchester College during the later years of the reign of Queen Elizabeth. who, Prince of Wales. His father held a small post in the Court of Henry VIII., where apparently he was but indifferently treated, a circumstance which recommended his family to the King's descendants.

Dᵗ Dee avoucheth his Stone is brought by Angelicall Ministry.

although he was generally reputed to be a sorcerer and a necromancer and to have dealings with evil spirits, had the support and patronage of the Queen to the end of her life. Dee was a Welshman, and always declared that he was directly descended from Roderick the Great, At the age of fifteen Dee was sent to Cambridge, where he says that for three years he studied eighteen hours a day, leaving only four hours for sleep, and two for meals and recreation. He became the foremost mathematician of his time, and at the age of nineteen, when Henry VIII.

founded Trinity College, Cambridge, he was nominated one of the original Fellows. From that moment dated the evil reputation which clung to him for the rest of his life. Besides being a Fellow, Dee was appointed " to be the underwriter of the Greek tongue," and in his own words. "Hereupon I did sett forth a Greek comedy of Aristophanes; with the performance of the Scarabaeus as flying up to Jupiter's palace with a man and his basket of victuals on her back, whereat was great wondereing and many vain reports spread abroad of the means how that was effected."

This was doubtless some clever stage effect, but the wondering audience saw nothing but magic in this flight of a great beetle from the stage. In the following year Dee went abroad, and when he returned, at the end of a few months, brought with him the first astronomer's staff of brass, invented by a German called Frisius, as well as an astronomer's ring of brass and two great globes constructed by Mercator.

By the time he was thirty-four Dee had taken his place among the foremost mathematicians, logicians and astronomers of Europe, many foreign noblemen coming to him for instruction during his visit abroad. Such, indeed, was his fame that when he gave public lectures on Euclid in the College at Paris, his audience was so large that many had to look in through the window; such lectures had never been given before in any University in Christendom, and when he returned to England Edward VI. gave him an annual pension of one hundred crowns; he was offered a good annual stipend by the University of Oxford to lecture on mathematical science in the University—an offer he declined. During the reign of Mary he was imprisoned for a short time on a charge of attempting to take away the Queen's life by poison or by magic, being seized at Hampton Court a short while before Princess Elizabeth herself was imprisoned there—but after a very brief period he was released. It was, perhaps, for this reason that, upon the accession of Elizabeth to the throne, Dee was taken into her service, the Queen saying of him : " Where my brother hath given him a crown I will give him a noble."

At the Earl of Leicester's command Dee drew up an astrologer's calculation as to the fitting date for the Queen's Coronation, and as everything passed off auspiciously on the day he declared to be propitious, according to the stars, he was firmly placed in Elizabeth's favour. But, as was the case with so many of those who rendered her services, Elizabeth's rewards lay more in promises than in performances. Over and over again Dee was promised this or that preferment when it became vacant by death or removal, but when the vacancy occurred the place was invariably given to somebody else.

Dee lived at Mortlake, on the Thames, where he gathered together a remarkable library of books dealing with all the sciences, and a large number of valuable manuscripts. He made several trips abroad, and upon his return from one of these to Hungary, in 1564, Elizabeth became his pupil in astronomy. Returning from another journey to the duchy of Lorraine, he was seized with a dangerous illness, whereupon Elizabeth sent two of her own physicians from Hampton Court, and " divers rarities to eat." The Queen clearly believed in his divination, and when she and the courtiers were greatly alarmed by the appearance of a comet, she sent for him to Windsor and listened eagerly for three days to his discourse upon the matter. On another occasion a waxen image of the Queen with a pin in its breast, being found in Lincoln's Inn Fields, he was hurriedly sent for to prevent any mischief happening to the Queen, it being then firmly believed by all classes that those of whom wax figures were made must speedily die. He was also called into conference with the by means of a magical mirror—a disc of highly polished cannel coal which he declared had been brought to him by angels, Elizabeth meanwhile demanding his constant services, for which she appears to have paid only with promises. On one occasion the Queen sent Dee word that he

DR. JOHN DEE

Queen's doctors " concerning Her Majesty's grievous pangs and pains caused by the toothache and the rheum," and was sent into Germany to consult the most learned physicians there as to the Queen's health.

Thus twenty years passed away, Dee writing monumental works on astronomy and mathematics and casting horoscopes should have an hundred angels " to kepe my Christmas withall." Two days later, he says in his diary: "The Queen's Majestie called for me at my door about half-past three in the afternoon as she passed by, and I met her at East Sheen gate, where she, graciously putting down her mask, did say with merry cheer, ' I thank thee,

Dee; there was never promise made but it was broken or kept.' I understood her Majesty to mean of the angels she promised to have sent me this day." Queen Elizabeth paid Dr. Dee several visits, all of which he carefully records. One occasion was in 1574, when "the Queen's Majestie with her most honourable Privy Council, and other her Lords and Nobility came purposely to have visited my library; but finding that my wife was within four hours before buried out of the house, Her Majesty refused to come in; but willed to fetch my glass so famous, and to show unto her some of the properties of it, which I did; Her Majestie being taken down from her horse by the Earl of Leicester, Master of the Horse, at the church wall of Mortlake, did see some of the properties of the glass, to her great contentment and delight." This glass had been given by Sir William Pykering to Dee, who had instructed him in "logic, arithmetic, and the use of astronomical instruments" in the Low Countries during his first sojourn abroad. Dee thus described the glass: "A man may be curstly afraid of his own shadow, yea, so much to feare, that you being alone nere a certaine glasse and proffer with dagger or sworde to foyne (fence) at the glasse, you shall suddenly be moved to give back (in maner) by reason of an image appearing in the ayre between you and the glasse, with like hand, sword or dagger, and with like quickness foyning at your very eye, like as you do at the glasse. Strange this is to heare of, but more marvailous to behold than these my words can testifie, nevertheless by demonstration optical the order and cause thereof is certified, even so the effect is consequent."

On another occasion Elizabeth came by coach, taking "the higher way of Mortlake field, and when she came right against the church, she turned down toward my house. And when she was gainst my garden in the field, her Majestie stayed there a good while, and then came into the field at the great gate of the field, where her Majestie espied me at my door, making several and dutiful obeisance unto her; and with her hand, her Majestie beckoned me to come to her, and I came to her coach side; her Majestie then very speedily pulled off her glove and gave me her hand to kiss; and to be short her Majestie willed me to resort oftener to her Court, and by some of her Privy Chamber to give her to weete [to let her know] when I am there."

There are frequent entries in Dee's diary of summons to the Queen in her privy garden at Greenwich or at Hampton Court. He seems to have been Court Astrologer without a place or title, for he wrote to Lord Burghley, Elizabeth's Lord Treasurer, that after twenty years' hard study he had not gained the rewards to which he was entitled. He said that "in zeal to the best lerning and knowledg, and in incredible toyle of body and mynde, very many yeares, therefore onely endured, I know most assuredly that this land never bred any man whose account therein can evidently be proved greater than myne." In the same letter he offers to discover a mine of gold and silver in the Queen's dominions which is to belong to her Majesty on condition that he shall have a right to all the treasure-trove found in the country—a suggestion that was scarcely calculated to appeal to a practical business man like Robert Cecil, Lord Burghley.

Dee records another visit of the Queen, shortly after he had drawn up a document showing her Majesty's right to the lands and islands discovered by Frobisher during his voyages in search of the North-West Passage. Burghley reported favourably upon "the twelve vellum skins fair written for her Majestie's use," wherein the Queen's title was proved by Dee. Hearing that his mother was dead, Elizabeth paid him a personal visit of condolence to show her pleasure with "the twelve vellum skins." "The Quene's Majestie to my great comfort (hora quinta) cam with her trayn from the Court, and at my dore graciously calling me to her, on horseback, exhorted me briefly to take my mother's death patiently, and withall told me that the Lord Treasurer had greatly commended my doings for her title."

Whether it was owing to his failure to obtain Court preferment or any settled income from Elizabeth, or whether his astrological studies has given him a bias in that direction, neither his diary nor his many writings give any sign; but it was shortly after drawing up this profoundly learned geographical chart that Dee turned his attention to alchemy, and to intercourse with the spirit world. To the end of his life Dee stoutly maintained that he dealt only with good spirits; popular opinion, however, judged otherwise.

Dee possessed a crystal globe which he declared had been brought to him by angels. This he believed possessed the power of showing apparitions and even of giving forth sounds. But only one person, called a seer—or as Dee puts it a "skryer"—could see the spirits in the globe or hear sounds: what in these days would be called a medium. Dee himself was never able to see anything in his "angelicall" globe. After much search he discovered a man named Barnabas Saul, a licensed preacher, who gave himself out as an adept in occult sciences. The first *séance* took place on December 21, 1581, when Dee took down in writing all that the "skryer" declared

he saw and heard in the "great crystalline globe." Saul summoned the Angel Annael, who said that many things would be declared to Dee not by that angel "but by him that is assigned to the stone." He was also told that after New Year's Day, or any day save the Sabbath, the stone was to be set in the sun, the brighter the day the better, and then "sight would be given." Saul never got beyond generalities, and a month or two later was tried on some charge at Westminster Hall, and being acquitted "he confessed he neyther herd or saw any spirituall creature any more."

The first excursion of John Dee into the occult world paved the way for a man whose friendship cast a sinister reflection upon his reputation for the rest of his life. This man was Edward Kelly, who preyed for years upon the credulity and ignorance common alike to princes and people in that age, when the physical presence of Satan, of good and bad spirits upon the earth, were firmly believed in, and when it was also believed there existed a magical stone by which all metals could be changed into gold—the Philosopher's Stone.

Kelly had been a lawyer in London, but being convicted of forgery at Lancaster had had his ears cut off in punishment. In order to disguise the loss he always wore a peculiarly shaped black cap, completely covering his head and his neck. Kelly introduced himself to Dee under the name of Talbot, and afterwards confessed that he had been sent to see him in order to entrap him into an admission that he had dealings with the Devil—an offence punishable by a hideous death; but perceiving that it would be more advantageous to himself to work upon Dee's credulity he became his "skryer" at a salary of fifty pounds a year. Dee was led to make this offer by the ready response made to Kelly's appeals to the globe. The first time, Uriel, the Spirit of Light, appeared; the second time, it was the Angel Michael, who gave Dee a ring with a magical seal engraved upon it. He believed implicitly all that Kelly told him, writing it down with the greatest care.

At the fourth *séance*, the Angel Michael bade Kelly go to Lancaster to get some books of Lord Monteagle's, which would be destroyed unless they were brought away. Dee was a great collector of books, and seeing in this message angelical assistance in his hobby, he sent Kelly post haste to Lancaster. Upon his return he was installed "skryer." The records of these *séances* during many years were published after Dee's death in a great volume called *A True and Faithful Relation of what passed for Many Years between Dr. John Dee and Some Spirits.*

The further story of John Dee and Edward Kelly is so amazing, so strange, that were it not vouched for and attested by the prosaic entries in State papers and independent testimony of the time, it could only be regarded as one of the "magicall and romantic" tales so eagerly read by our Elizabethan forefathers.

Kelly drew up an elaborate system of communicating with the spirits, part of the paraphernalia being "the table of practice," made of sweet wood, with four legs. In its centre was a seal made of purified wax, an inch and a quarter in thickness, twenty-seven inches in circumference, and nine inches in diameter. Each leg of the table stood upon a waxen seal precisely like the larger one. The upper side of these seals had forty-nine squares filled with the seven names of God, "names not known to the angels, neither can they be spoken or read by man." Their magical property lay in this : "These names bring forth seven

angels, the governors of the heavens next unto us. Every letter of the angel's name bringeth forth seven daughters. Every daughter bringeth forth her daughter, every daughter (of) her daughter bringeth forth a son. Every son hath his son." Thus Dee was duped into believing that, by virtue of the seal, Kelly could call the heavenly host by speaking the letters of the first seven angels' names. Upon the under-side of these seals, called *Sigilla Dei*, or The Seals of God, was this mystical sign, which was used by the soothsayers in the East and greatly favoured by Elizabethan astrologers.

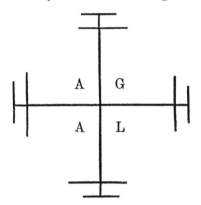

The letters in the centre stand for the initials of the Hebrew words, "Thou art great for ever, O Lord." They were looked upon as a charm against evil in the Middle Ages.

Two of the large seals, and one of the smaller seals upon which the legs of the "table of practice" rested, as well as the crystal globe belonging to John Dee, are now in the British Museum.

At the end of the first year of the companionship of Dee and Kelly another stone or crystal was miraculously produced, being believed by Dee to be a gift of one of the seven angels. It was supposed to possess even more marvellous qualities than the other.

EDWARD KELLY EVOKING THE SPIRIT OF A DEAD PERSON AT
WALTON-LE-DALE

Amongst his many gifts of wizardry Kelly was believed to have the power of evoking spirits of the dead; and in an old book called *Illustration of the Occult Sciences* a plate is given (from which our drawing has been made), showing Kelly and a companion standing within a magic circle before the spirit of a dead person Kelly has summoned from its grave. The scene was said to have taken place in the churchyard of Walton-le-Dale, near Preston.

This was the formula laid down by the soothsayers and magicians: "But if instead of infernal or familiar spirits, the ghost or apparition of a departed person is to be exorcised, the magician with his assistant must repair to the churchyard or tomb where the deceased was buried, exactly at midnight, as the ceremony can only be performed in the night between the hours of twelve and one. The grave is first to be opened, or an aperture made by which access may be had to the naked body. The magician having described the circle and holding a magic wand in his right hand, while his companion or assistant beareth a consecrated torch, he turns himself to all the four winds, and touching the dead body three times with the magical wand, repeats as follows: "By the virtue of the Holy Resurrection and the torments of the damned, I conjure and exorcise the Spirit of N. deceased, to answer my liege demands, being obedient unto these sacred ceremonies, on pain of everlasting torment and distress.

"BERALD, BEROALD, BAL-BIN, GAB, GABOR, AGABA. Arise, arise, I charge and command thee."

These words being said, the ghost of the dead person would appear and answer any questions put to it by the magician.

To evoke the spirits of those who had committed suicide there was a different ceremony which had to be performed upon the spot where the body was lying, and before it had been touched. It was this: "The exorcist binds upon the top of his wand a bundle of St. John's Wort or *Millies Perforatum*, with the head of an owl; and having repaired to the spot where the corpse lies, at twelve o'clock at night, he draws the circle solemnly and repeats these words: 'By the mysteries of the deep, by the flames of Banal, by the power of the East and the silence of the night, by the Holy Rites of Hecate, I conjure and exorcise thee, thou distressed Spirit, to present thyself here and reveal unto me the cause of thy calamity, why thou didst offer violence to thy own liege life, where thou art now in being, and where thou wilt hereafter to be.'" After the corpse had been smitten gently three times with the rod, the magician added: "I conjure thee, thou Spirit of this N. deceased, to answer my demands that I propound unto thee, as thou ever hopest for the rest of the holy ones, and ease of all thy misery; by the Blood of Jesus which He shed for thy soul, I conjure and bind thee to utter unto me what I shall ask thee."

The body was then laid with the head to the East, with a chafing-dish of fire at its right hand, into which wine, mastic, gum-aromatic, and a vial of the sweetest oil had been poured. They were also to have a pair of bellows and some unkindled charcoal, "to make the fire burn bright when the carcase rises." Then came this conjuration—

"I conjure thee, thou Spirit of N., that thou do immediately enter into thy ancient body again and answer my demands; by the posture of the body of the Saviour of the world I charge thee, I command thee, on pain of the torments and wanderings of thrice seven years, which I, by the force of sacred magic rites have power to inflict upon thee to utter thy voice. So help thee God and the prayer of the Holy Church. Amen."

This ceremony being repeated three times, whilst the fire of mastic and gum-aromatic is burning in the chafing-dish, we are gravely told, "the body will begin to rise, and at last will stand upright before the exorcist, answering with a faint and hollow voice the questions propounded unto it : why it destroyed itself, where its dwelling is, what its food and life are, how long it will be ere it enter into rest, and by what means the magician may assist it to come to rest ; also of the treasures of this world, and where they are hid. Moreover, it can answer very punctually concerning the places where ghosts reside, and of the manner of communicating with them, teaching the nature of the astral spirits and hellish beings so far as its capacity alloweth. All this when the ghost hath fully answered, the magician ought out of commiseration and reverence for the deceased to use what means possibly can be used for procuring rest unto the spirit, to which effect he must dig a grave, and filling the same half-full of quicklime, with a little salt and common sulphur, must put the carcase naked into it. Next to the burning of the body into ashes, this is of great force to quiet and end the disturbances of the Astral Spirit."

The magicians were solemnly warned to keep within the magic circle during the raising up and consulting of the spirits, for ghosts could bring sudden death to those born under a particular constellation of the planets if they were not protected by the circle.

In his *True and Faithful Relation* Dr. Dee frequently refers to the use of Talismans, but to what precise order they belonged he gives no indication. Amongst magicians and sorcerers talismans were greatly resorted to, more perhaps to impress a credulous and ignorant public than from any belief in them on the part of the sorcerers themselves. Thus, under the talismans of the Sage of the Pyramids there are two, here illustrated, which give a sufficient indication of the powers these talismans were supposed to possess.

Talisman V, embroidered on gold-coloured satin with the figures embroidered in gold, would make the most taciturn man unbosom himself to its possessor ; its possessor likewise would have this happy fortune—his enemies would be forced to confess to him all their machinations. In conjunction with these talismans there were rings engraved with mystical characters, the magic of the talisman being brought into play by placing this ring on the little finger of the left hand and the talisman itself against the right ear, and by saying the words "Noctar Raiban" out loud.

Talisman VIII had even more wonderful properties. It gave invisibility to its possessor even to the eyes of genii, and in addition he had the power of passing through brick walls and going wherever he wished. This talisman was of yellow satin embroidered with black silk, and the magic words which set it in operation with the turning of its ring were: "Benatis Carakan Dedos Etinarmi."

After undergoing his punishment at Lancaster, and standing in the pillory there, shorn of his ears, Kelly is supposed to have gone into Wales, where for some time he lived at an obscure inn. During this sojourn the innkeeper showed him an old manuscript which neither he nor his neighbours could read. Kelly, who was an expert in all kinds of writing, discovered the paper to be a treatise on the transmutation of metals. His interest and his cupidity both being aroused he inquired as to its history, and was told that it had recently been discovered in a neighbouring church, in the tomb of a Roman Catholic bishop, which had

TALISMAN V

been rifled during the fanatical outburst against that faith, known as the Elizabethan Persecution. According to popular tradition immense riches were concealed in the tomb of this bishop, and its desecrators only seized upon the religious question as an excuse for gain. They were rewarded however with nothing but this manuscript and two small ivory bottles, one containing a red and the other a white powder. One of the bottles was broken on the spot, and a portion of its contents with the other bottle and the manuscript, were given to the innkeeper in exchange for a skinful of wine. The innkeeper gave the unbroken bottle to his children for a plaything. Having deciphered the document Kelly offered a pound sterling for it and the remaining bottle. The report is that Kelly disclosed the secret to Dee, and proved to him, by ocular demonstration, that this marvellous powder, used according to the directions on the crabbed manuscript, changed ordinary metals into gold. So, besides

the communications with spirits, Kelly and Dee gave themselves up to the old alchemists' dream of making gold. Little wonder that the good folk of Mortlake believed Dee and Kelly to be wizards. Night after night strange fires glowed in the windows of Dee's laboratory, as the two men heated the crucibles and watched the mercury bubbling that the magical powder was to turn to gold. Shuddering neighbours saw strange shadows flickering in the room after nightfall, and, despite Dee's favour at Court, the rumours spread and spread that he and Kelly were communing with the evil one.

The belief that Dee had the power of making gold reached the Court, and when Albert Laski—Viadode, or Prince, of Saradz in Bohemia—visited England in 1583, some word of Dee's powers seems to have reached him. He was almost

TALISMAN VIII

ruined, and, like so many princes and nobles of his time, hoped to restore his fortunes by the discovery of the Philosopher's Stone, or of some alchemist who could turn metal to gold. The famous Earl of Leicester seems to have been the means of introducing Dee to the Bohemian Prince, and Elizabeth herself was certainly a party to the introduction. In July 1583 Dee says in his diary : " Her Majestie being informed by the Right Honourable Earl of Leicester that, whereas in the same day in the morning he had told me that his Honour and Lord Laski would dine with me within two daes after, I confessed sincerely unto him that I was not able to prepare them a sufficient dinner unless I presently sell some of my plate, or some of my pewter for it. Whereupon her Majestie sent unto me very royally within one hour after, forty angels of gold from Sion, where her Majestie was now come by water from Greenwich." The dinner was, therefore, given in all pomp and circumstance befitting the exalted rank of the Prince and the Queen's favourite.

Laski's curiosity was greatly excited by all that he heard and saw at the house at Mortlake, and, after a great show of reluctance had been made, he was allowed to join Dee and Kelly in their researches. But a considerable amount of money was required for the purchase of the mysterious drugs and chemicals used in these magical experiments, and the Prince being short of cash suggested that it would be easier to provide these materials in his own country. Three months later Dee with his wife and children, Kelly and his wife and children, departed secretly from Mortlake ; and, joining the prince's train, proceeded with him to his castle of Laskoe, near Cracow.

Then followed a series of amazing episodes, in which it is impossible to believe that Dee could have been so entirely the dupe of Kelly as he has been represented. The day after Dee's departure from his house, a mob, which regarded him as a wizard and a necromancer, broke into it and destroyed a great part of his furniture and books, but wreaked their execration chiefly upon his laboratory, where they destroyed all his chemical apparatus, his stone and crucibles, and a fine quadrant for which he had given thirty pounds.

Prince Laski speedily discovered the imposture to which he had been subjected, and, anxious to get rid of his alchemists, persuaded them to visit the Emperor Rodolph II. of Germany at Prague, which was at that time the headquarters of alchemists, soothsayers, crystal-gazers, and all the charlatans who battened upon the ignorance and superstition of the age. There are the most conflicting stories as to their reception by the Emperor. One has it that, disgusted by Dee's extravagant stories at the first interview, he refused to see him or Kelly again, and ordered them to quit his dominions within six days ; also that after many wanderings it was only upon the earnest plea of Count Rosenberg, who seems to have believed in them, that the magicians were permitted by the Emperor to remain in any of the count's towns, cities or castles. They took up their quarters at Tribau, in Bohemia, which was Count Rosenberg's principal residence.

Another story runs that Kelly, with a single drop of red oil, transmuted a pound of mercury into excellent gold, " the superabundant virtue of the agent leaving in addition at the bottom of the crucible a small ruby." This marvel is carefully reported to have taken place in the house of the Emperor before his own face. In honour of this great feat the Emperor made Kelly a Marshal of Bohemia. If the experiment ever took place—the " transmuting " of the mercury into gold was probably a clever trick on the part of Kelly, for shortly afterwards the Emperor was persuaded " to practically imprison this living philosophical treasure and to extract his alchemical secret." Kelly was ordered to make a considerable quantity of his marvellous powder or " stone philosophical." This he was unable to do, and his inability being taken as a contumacious refusal he was thrown into a dungeon. He then represented that he would comply with the Emperor's demand if he were allowed to seek assistance, and being set at liberty he rejoined Dr. Dee. But, unhappily, the ancient manuscript from the bishop's tomb gave no directions for the manufacture of the magical powder, it merely indicated its use; consequently their experiment failed.

They had been closely watched in order to prevent Kelly's escape, and in his desperation at the failure he murdered one of his guards. Kelly was at once thrown into prison, where he remained until 1597, the Emperor, it is said, firmly believing in his gold-producing powers and detaining him with the hope of eventually extracting his secret. Some of his friends endeavoured to help him to escape from his prison by means of a rope, but he fell from the window and died from the injuries he received. So much for romance !

History tells us that during their stay at Tribau, Kelly, by placing one small grain of the magical powder upon an ounce and a quarter of mercury in a crucible, produced nearly an ounce of gold. He likewise transmuted into gold a piece of brass cut out of the bottom of a warming pan, and sent it to Queen Elizabeth together with the warming pan with the hole in it, into which the piece of gold fitted exactly. It was also related that Arthur Dee, Dee's eldest boy, who was about eight years old at the time of their residence in Tribau, used to play at quoits with pieces of gold made by the magical powder.

Count Rosenberg was entirely duped by the two men ; Dee's European reputation as a mathematician and scholar doubtless favouring the imposture. So universal, indeed, was his fame that it had penetrated even to Russia,[1] and it was whilst he was at Tribau, in 1586, that the old chronicler Aubrey reports that the Emperor of Russia, " upon report of the great learning the mathematician (possessed) invited him to Mosceo with an offer of two thousand pounds a yeare, and from Prince Boris one thousand markes, to have his provisions from the Emperor's table, to be honourably received, and to be accounted as one of the chief men in the land. All these offers Dee accepted not."

There are two circumstances in the year 1587 which show one of two things, either the depth to which Dee had sunk, or the ascendency which Kelly exercised over him. Kelly frequently declined to take part in the *séances* with the spirits, and as Dee was never able to see anything himself in the magical globe, he therefore resolved to initiate his son Arthur. After much prayer and preparation the boy made the experiment but was unable to see anything, whereupon Kelly returned to his old post as " skryer," and the angelical visitants immediately made their reappearance. Three days later Kelly made the astonishing announcement that the angels had said to him it was the divine pleasure that he and Dee for the future should have their wives in common, and in his own handwriting Dee has recorded that " on Sunday the 3rd May anno 1587, I, John Dee, Edward Kelly, and our two wives covenanted with God, and superscribed the same, for indissoluble and unfailable unities, all charity and friendship keeping between us four ; and all things between us to be in common, as God by sundry means willed us to do." As a result of this arrangement

---

[1] Then practically an unknown land to the rest of Europe.

bitter and frequent quarrels broke out, and finally they separated. Kelly left Tribau for Prague, and Dee set out for England. The two men never met again, but they still maintained a regular correspondence.

Elizabeth had not forgotten her astrologer. She had indeed written asking him to return some time previously, and within a fortnight of his arrival received him very graciously at Richmond. But Dee returned to find his reputation as a mathematician and a geographer entirely swamped by the general belief that he was a sorcerer. He was shunned by all classes of society, and for three years was only saved from starvation by pawning his plate and jewellery, and by borrowing money. Frequent appeals were made to the Queen by the few friends who still remained to him at Court, and finally, in 1595, after endless disappointments, he was given the wardenship of Manchester College. But here again Elizabeth hesitated, ever loath to let her astrologer go far away. "January 8th," says Dee in his diary, " the wardenship of Manchester spoken of by the Lord Archbishop of Canterbury." "February 5th. My bill for Manchester offered to the Quene before dinner by Sir John Wolly (the Queen's Lord Chamberlain) to signe, but she deferred it, and it was only on the 18th of the following April my bill for Manchester wardenship signed by the Quene, Mr. Herbert offeringe it to her."

Some idea of the leisurely method of those days may be gathered from the entry in Dee's diary of July 31st: " The Cowntess of Warwicke did this evening thank her Majestie in my name and for me for her gift to the Wardenship of Manchester. She tooke it gratiously and was sorry that it was so far from hence, but that some better thing near hand shall be found for him; and if opportunity of time should serve her Majestie would speak with me herself." It was only on the 8th November that his library and furniture were despatched " toward Manchester," and on the 26th " my wife and children all by water toward Coventry." Dee himself arrived in Manchester on the 15th February 1596, having joined his family on the way, and on the 20th was installed in his new office with great pomp.

The Manchester College, or College Church, now the Cathedral, had been founded by Thomas de la Warre, lord of the manor of Manchester in 1420; he built houses for a warden, priest and choristers, thus creating what was practically a monastic foundation, which in the reign of Henry VIII. met the fate of similar institutions and was dissolved. It was refounded in the same reign, but by the time Dee was appointed warden the lands which produced its income had been either stolen, sold or leased, the Queen herself profiting largely by the spoliation. In 1578 John Nowell of St. Paul's, a Lancashire man, despite Queen Elizabeth's dislike to him,[1] had succeeded in bringing about an inquiry into the state of the college, and as a result a new charter was granted by the Queen. Under this charter the college was called Christ's College, and was to consist of a warden, four fellows, two chaplains and choristers. Its Warden under the new organization, Dr. Chadderton, Bishop of Chester, persecuted the Roman Catholics with brutal and relentless severity, filling the Manchester prisons with followers of that faith. It was under his rule that the famous Marprelate Press was discovered, as will be recorded in a later portion of these Lancashire Stories. Chadderton's transference to the see of Lincoln

[1] See " Queen Elizabeth and the Lancashire Divine."

gave Queen Elizabeth the tardy opportunity of rewarding Dee, who, whatever his follies or faults, had served her faithfully for nearly forty years with no other reward than fine promises and golden angels, thrown to him from time to time, as one throws bones to a dog to keep it quiet.

Dee only held the wardenship of Manchester College for nine years. During that time he was engaged in endless disputes and difficulties over the tithes and lands belonging to it. He became on very bad terms with the Fellows of the College, either owing to his own haughty bearing and mismanagement, or to their turbulent behaviour. There seems to have been faults on both sides, but Dee looked upon his wardenship solely as a means of income, which apparently the College found it difficult to supply, owing to the spoliation of the lands. We read of Dee being compelled to pawn his plate of "double gilt potts with a cover and handells, bowles and cupps with handbells" with Edmund Chetham, the High Master of the Grammar School; and when, in 1603, Chetham's father and executor made his will, he records in it that Dee had delivered to his son "6 severall parcels of Plate to be kept as a payne or pledge for the same (loan) which by reason of my said executorshippe are now come into my possession." The ten pounds which had been lent upon it by Edmund Chetham the father left to his other sons: Humphrey (the founder of the Hospital) and Ralph. As the value of silver at that time was five and twopence an ounce, the six "parcells" of Dee's plate would be worth twelve pounds eight shillings.

But one of the most noteworthy happenings of Dee's career as warden was his refusal to exorcise a woman and some children who were said to be possessed of devils. His reputation as a magician followed him to Manchester, and he was likewise firmly believed to be a conjurer, that is, one who had the power to cast out evil spirits. The women and the children were believed to have become demoniacally possessed through the influence of a man called Hartley, who, doubtless by the use of hypnotism, threw people into the most extraordinary condition, and then prayed over them to exorcise the demon of which he declared they were possessed. But Dee resolutely refused to have anything to do in the matter, and sending for Hartley "so sharply rebuked him that the children had more ease for three weeks after." Dee's reputation as a caster out of evil spirits rested on no foundation of gossip or slander, for in his diary, August 2, 1590, he writes: "Anne my nurse a long time tempted of a wicked spirit, but this day it was evident how she was possessed of him. God is, and hath bin and shall be her protector. Amen." Three days later he writes: "Anne Frank was sorrowful, well comforted and stayed in God's mercyes." "August 16. At night I anoynted (in the name of Jesus) Anne Frank her breast with the holy oyle." "August 30. In the morning she required to be anoynted, and I did very devoutly prepare myself and prayed for vertue and power, and Christ his blessing by the oyle, to the expulsion of the wicked one, and then afterwards anointed; the wicked one did recessed awhile." On the 8th September the "wicked one" would seem to have returned: "Nurse Anne Frank would have drowned herself in my well, but by divine providence I came to take her up before she was overcome of the water." On the 29th September: "Nurse Anne Frank most miserably did cut her own throat, after noon about 4 of the clock, pretending to be in prayer before her keeper, and suddenly and very quickly rising from prayer and going toward her chamber, as the maiden her keeper thought, but indeed straightway down the stairs into the hall, of the other house behind the door, did that horrible act; and the maiden who waited on her at the stair-of the astrologer's and the alchemist's art. A few months after his installation, the Earl of Derby with a large party, including Lady Gerard, wife of the Master of the Rolls, Sir Richard and Lady Molyneux, the Earl of Sefton and his son-in-law, Mr. Richard de Hoghton of Hoghton

THE CIRCLE FOR RAISING THE SPIRITS OF THE DEAD BY BLACK MAGIC

foot followed her, and missed to find her in three or four places, till at length she heard her rattle in her own blood."

Although Dee was feared as a magician, he was greatly respected as a scholar by the neighbouring Lancashire gentry, who paid him frequent visits at College to see his library and his wonderful instruments Tower, paid him a surprise visit: "They came suddenly upon me after 3 of the clock," he says. "I made them a scholar's collation and it was taken in good part I brought his honour and the ladyes to Ardwick Green and Lime to Mr. Leigh, his house 12 miles off." Lady Molyneux and Mrs. Leigh were both Lady Gerard's daughters, so it was a family party that rode over to Manchester that summer's day to see the old warden, about whom such curious stories were rife.

Such evocation of the dead as that said to have been used by Kelly came under the heading of White Magic. But it was also claimed that the spirits of the dead could be raised by Black Magic—one of the most revolting superstitions into which mankind has ever fallen. There is no evidence to show that either Dee or Kelly dabbled in this horror. The details of spirit-raising by the Black Magic need no description, it being sufficient to say that the circle, shown in the illustration on the preceding page, in which the magician and his assistants stood, was formed from the skin of the dead person, and fastened to the ground by four nails taken from the coffin of an executed criminal. The skull and thigh-bones on the right-hand side are those of a parricide, the bat on the other side must have been drowned in blood; the black cat, whose head comes next, must have been fed on human flesh; the horns must be those of a goat. The two candles, burning on either side of the triangle were "Hand of Glory" candles, the horrible making of which is described below. The three rings in the centre of the triangle indicate the position of the magician and his assistants.

The last years of Dee's life were spent in misery and in poverty. After the death of Elizabeth he besought James I. to give him a trial that he might be cleared of the horrible slanders that he was or had been a "conjurer or caller or invocator of divils, therefore offering himself willingly to the punishment of death, yea, either to be stoned to death or to be buried quick, or to be burned unmercifully, if by any true and just means the name

of conjurer or caller or invocator of divils or damned sprites can be proved to be duly or justly reported of me." King James dismissed the petition.

In 1605 that terrible scourge, the plague, came to Manchester, and among its many victims was Dee's devoted wife Jane, who for twenty-seven years had been his prop and mainstay in all his troubles and difficulties. Forthwith he gave up his wardenship and retired to Mortlake, where, three years later, he died in the midst of preparations for leaving England. Stricken with poverty and forced to sell his books and instruments in order to live; broken in spirit by the charges of necromancy persistently brought against him, he had decided to end his days in Germany. He died at the age of eighty.

The chronicler Aubrey visiting Mortlake fifty years after Dee's death, had much talk with Goodwife Faldo who, "did know Dr. Dee, and told him he died at his house in Mortlake next to the house where the tapestry hangings were made." She also told him that Dee "did recover a basket of clothes" which she and one of his daughters had carelessly lost; that he used to distil egg-shells; and warned Queen Elizabeth of an attempt upon her life. Dee had also "laid a storm for Sir Everard Digby." The old woman's gossip showed that Dee was resorted to by both gentle and simple when his "magical" aid was needed. She told Aubrey of his finding a basket of plate which a butler lost "coming from London by water mistaking another basket that was like his. Mr. John Dee bid him go by water such a day and look about, and he should see the man that had the basket, and he did so." She added that Dee would not get some lost horses although he was offered several angels, from which it may be gathered that Dee received payment for his "magical" advice. "He was a great

164

peace-maker," said Goody Faldo ; " if any of the neighbours fell out he would never let them alone till he had made them friends." But in the same breath she added that " he told one of his neighbours, a woman, that she laboured under the evil tongue of an ill neighbour which came to her house and who he said was a witch"—a statement which would scarcely tend to peace-making. She described him as tall and slender, and wearing a gown like " an artist's gown with hanging sleeves and a slit."

The " Hand of Glory " was one of the most dreadful objects amongst the paraphernalia of the wizards and necromancers of the sixteenth century, and no horrors were spared in its preparation. According to an old book of necromancy the "Hand of Glory " could be either the right or the left hand of a criminal who had been hanged, wrapped in a piece of winding sheet. The hand was to be well squeezed, in order to remove any blood that might remain in it. Then it was to be placed

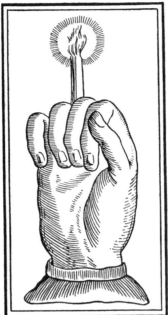

HAND OF GLORY

in an earthen vessel with some saltpetre, common salt, peppercorns and zimost (whatever that might be), all finely pounded. In this vessel it was to remain for fifteen days, and when taken out was to be exposed to the heat of the sun during the time of the dog-star, until it was completely dried up. If the heat of the sun was not sufficient it could be placed in a furnace which was to be heated with bracken and vervain. The object was to extract all the grease from the hand. This horrible grease, mixed with virgin wax, and sesame from Lapland, was made into a candle which, when it was lighted, deprived spectators of all power or motion, so that the sorcerer could do what he wished. Brother sorcerers could destroy the influence of this appalling candle by anointing any place through which entrance could be gained to a house, with an ointment composed of grease from a white fowl, the blood of a screech owl, and the gall of a black cat.

SIR GUALTER

At Northen, near Manchester, there was in ancient times a ferry across the Mersey from Lancashire to Cheshire, which was called the "Northern Boat." The following ballad appeared in a Manchester literary paper called the *Phœnix* in 1828, purporting to be original and having been preserved by one "Maister Lovelle," but in reality it was written by a young Manchester poet called William Rowlinson, who, with this, and other poems of the same kind, perpetrated a literary fraud not uncommon at that time. Like Chatterton, who had fabricated a whole story, *Rowley's Romance*, supposed to be written by a monk of the fifteenth century, so ingeniously that even Horace Walpole was for a time deceived, Rawlinson wrote his ballad in the old spelling, and then declared that he had discovered it. Rawlinson was drowned whilst bathing in the Thames in 1829.

"NOW ferry me o'er, thou good
        boatman !
        I prithee ferry me o'er !
That I may see my lady to-night,
    Or I never may see her more."

"The wind blows high, and the stream runs
        strong,
    And I dare not ferry thee o'er ;
Thou canst not see thy lady to-night,
    If thou never dost see her more."

"I shall see her to-night if my life be
        spared,
    For I've heard the death-owl's scream ;
Who has heard it once may not hear it twice,
    She must hear my awful dream."

"My boat is moor'd, and I will not cross :
    Sir knight, thou may'st away ;
Or rest thee to-night till the morning's
        light,—
    We will o'er at break of day."

"Here's gold in store, and thou shalt have
        more,
    To venture across with me ;
If we die ere we reach the other bank,
    A mass shall be said for thee."

The boat is unmoor'd, and they both leap
        in,
    And steer for the other side ;
Now swim thou swiftly, thou fearless boat,
    Against the rushing tide.

Now, now for thy life, thou boatman, push,
    For the stream runs swifter on ;
Another boat's length, with all thy strength,
    And the bank ye have safely won.

'Tis past, 'tis past, they have reached the
        side,
    And they both leap on the bank :
'Tis well ! 'tis well ! with an eddying
        whirl
    That boat hath swiftly sank.

Sir Gualter hath given the boatman gold,
    Thence hastes to the trysting-tree ;
What a woful sight for a gallant knight
    Was there for him to see.

The Lady Isabel blacken'd and scorched,
    By the lightning blast of heaven ;
And that stately tree where they oft had
        met,
    Was leafless, and blasted, and riven !

He kneeled him down o'er that lifeless
        form ;
    And the death-owl o'er him flew,
And it screamed as it pass'd on the rushing
        blast ;
    Then his fate Sir Gualter knew.

Then he gather'd that form within his
        arms,
    And rush'd to the river's side ;
Then plung'd from the bank, and both of
        them sank
    In the darkly rolling tide.

HARTSHEAD PIKE

TOWARDS the end of the eighteenth century the view from Hartshead Hill, near Staly-bridge, upon the top of which stood the Pike, was described by Dr. Aikin as being "most delightful." A hundred years ago Butterworth said that on a clear day Haslingden and Horwich Moor, Stockport, Manchester and the Welsh hills could be clearly seen. To-day the view consists entirely of tall chimneys, factories and the refuse heaps of coal-pits.

OLD HARTSHEAD PIKE

bridge, upon the top of which stood the Pike, was described by Dr. Aikin as being "most delightful." A hundred years ago Butterworth said that on a clear day consists entirely of tall chimneys, factories and the refuse heaps of coal-pits.

Dr. Aikin also says it was generally supposed that the Pike was a "sea mark," but it was actually a beacon, such as were scattered over the whole country to be used as signals in time of war. How all England was warned of the coming of the Spanish Armada by these beacon fires is told in Macaulay's *The Armada*—

" From Eddystone to Berwick bounds, from
    Lynn to Milford Bay,
That time of slumber was as bright and busy
    as the day ;
For swift to east and swift to west the
    ghastly war-flame spread,
High on St. Michael's Mount it shone : it
    shone on Beachy Head.
Far on the deep the Spaniard saw, along
    each southern shire,
Cape beyond cape, in endless range, those
    twinkling points of fire."

From London the fires sent the signals to the north—

"And on and on, without a pause, untired
    they bounded still :
All night from tower to tower they sprang ;
    they sprang from hill to hill."

The fiery message doubtless came to Hartshead and was sent on towards Lancaster, whence

" . . . Skiddaw saw the fire that burned on
    Gaunt's embattled pile,
And the red glare on Skiddaw roused the
    burghers of Carlisle."

The tower shown in the illustration was built in 1758 upon the site of the old beacon. It was used for heliographing. Upon its western side was this inscription—

Look me well before you go,
And see you nothing at me throw.

This Pike was erected by public subscription in 1758.

Some forty years later the building split from top to bottom, " near half a yard in width," and speedily fell into ruins. There was a general desire that the Pike should be rebuilt, but nothing was done—although a few pounds would have sufficed for its repair when the split first appeared—until 1863. In that year the foundations of a new tower were laid with much ceremony and circumstance.

An inscription on the present Pike states that it was " Re-erected by Public Subscription to commemorate the marriage of H.R.H. Albert Edward, Prince of Wales, to H.R.H. Princess Alexandra of Denmark and to restore the Ancient Land Mark of Hartshead Pike." In 1912 the Pike, together with nearly two acres of ground around it, was given to the Hartshead Parish Council by the Trustees of the Earl of Stamford and Warrington for the use of the public.

A TRAFFORD AND A BYRON FEUD

BY

THOMAS BARRITT

IN our Fourth Edward's fickle days
    A serious quarrel, story says,
    Took place near Rochdale, we are told,
    'Twixt Trafford and a Byron bold.
The cause was this, we understand,
About some privilege of land.
Oliver Chadwick from Chadwick Hall,
On Byron's part that day did fall ;
But afterwards it came to pass,
Lord Stanley arbitrator was,

Who fixed it upon this ground,
Trafford should pay full sixty pound,
In holy church at Manchester ;
And from this contract not to err,
To Chadwick's heirs, to keep them quiet,
And never more to move a riot :
Ten marks at birth-day of St. John,
And ten at Martin's day upon
Each year until the whole was paid ;
And to be friends again, he said.

A View of Manchester 1800

LOOK OUT FOR...

THERE WAS A TIME
(Ken Loran)
Childhood during World War Two.
ISBN 1 872226 10 8   £4.95

FOR THE CHILDREN
Poems and Stories by well-known childrens' authors and personalities. Produced for the Tay
Sachs Society.
ISBN 1 872226 14 0   £4.95

A HISTORY OF LANCASHIRE COOKERY
Tom Bridge takes us deep into Lancashire's culinary past to reveal the classic dishes of the
region.
ISBN 1 872226 25 6   £4.95

CAMMELL LAIRD — The Golden Years
(Dave Roberts)
Well illustrated. A full history of this great shipyard.
ISBN 1 872226 48 5   £4.95

COMPLETELY LANKY
(Dave Dutton)
Two best sellers collected in one volume.
ISBN 1 872226 61 2   £4.95

NORTHERN CLASSIC REPRINTS

The Manchester Man

(Mrs. G. Linnaeus Banks)

Re-printed from an 1896 illustrated edition — undoubtedly the finest
limp-bound edition ever. Fascinating reading, includes Peterloo. Over
400 pages, wonderfully illustrated.

ISBN 1 872226 16 7   £4.95

The Manchester Rebels

(W Harrison Ainsworth)

A heady mixture of fact and fiction combined in a compelling story
of the Jacobean fight for the throne of England. Manchester's
involvement and the formation of the Manchester Regiment.
Authentic illustrations.

ISBN 1 872226 29 9   £4.95

Hobson's Choice (the Novel)

(Harold Brighouse)

The humorous and classic moving story of Salford's favourite tale.
Well worth re-discovering this enjoyable story. Illustrated edition.
Not been available since 1917, never before in paperback.

ISBN 1 872226 36 1   £4.95

Stories & Tales Of Old Lancashire

(Frank Hird)

Over 70 fascinating tales told in a wonderful light-hearted fashion.
Witches, seiges and superstitions, battles and characters all here.

ISBN 1 872226 21 3   £4.95

Poems & Songs Of Lancashire

(Edwin Waugh)

A wonderful quality reprint of a classic book by undoubtedly one of Lancashire's finest poets. First published 1859 faithfully reproduced. Easy and pleasant reading, a piece of history.

ISBN 1 872226 27 2   £4.95

The Best of Old Lancashire — Poetry & Verse

Published in 1866 as the very best of contemporary Lancashire writing, this book now offers a wonderful insight into the cream of Lancashire literature in the middle of the last century. Nearly 150 years later, edited and republished, the book now presents a unique opportunity to read again the masters of our past.

ISBN 1 872226 50 7   £4.95

The Dock Road

(J. Francis Hall RN)

A seafaring tale of old Liverpool. Set in the 1860s, with the American Civil War raging and the cotton famine gripping Lancashire. Period illustrations.

ISBN 1 872226 37 X   £4.95

The Lancashire Witches

(W. Harrison Ainsworth)

A beautifully illustrated edition of the most famous romance of the supernatural.

ISBN 1 872226 55 8   £4.95

Stories Of Great Lancastrians

(written Frank Hird)

The lives of 24 great men of the county, told in easy reading style. Complete with sketches and drawings, a good introduction to the famous of Lancashire and Manchester. John Byrom, Arkwright, Tim Bobbins, Duke of Bridgewater.

ISBN 1 872226 23 X   £4.95

THE STORIES
AND TALES SERIES

Stories and Tales Of Old Merseyside
(Frank Hird, edited Cliff Hayes)

Over 50 stories of Liverpool's characters and incidents PLUS a booklet from 1890 telling of the city's history, well illustrated.
ISBN 1 872226 20 5 £4.95

Stories & Tales Of Old Lancashire
(Frank Hird)

Over 70 fascinating tales told in a wonderful light-hearted fashion. Witches, seiges and superstitions, battles and characters all here.
ISBN 1 872226 21 3 £4.95

Stories Of Great Lancastrians
(written Frank Hird)

The lives of 24 great men of the county, told in easy reading style. Complete with sketches and drawings, a good introduction to the famous of Lancashire and Manchester. John Byrom, Arkwright, Tim Bobbins, Duke of Bridgewater.
ISBN 1 872226 23 X £4.95

More Stories Of Old Lancashire
(Frank Hird)

We present another 80 stories in the same easy, readable style, very enjoyable, great. With special section for Preston Guild 1992.
ISBN 1 872226 26 4 £4.95

OLD
ESHIRE

erine Rothwell
Cliff Hayes

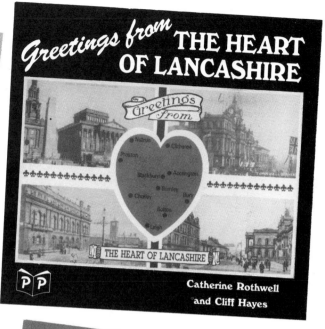

Greetings from THE HEART
OF LANCASHIRE

Catherine Rothwell
and Cliff Hayes

LD
FORD

Greetings from THE
LANCASHIRE COAST

Catherine Rothwell
and Cliff Hayes

look out for...

price £4.95

A MUST FOR EVERY KITCHEN

The History of Lancashire Cookery
by
Tom Bridge

price £4.95